Shaping the Scriptural Imagination

Cover Design by Nita Ybarra, Nita Ybarra Design

The Library of Congress has cataloged the hardcover edition as follows:

Library of Congress Cataloging-in-Publication Data

Juel, Donald.
  Shaping the scriptural imagination : truth, meaning, and the theological interpretation of the Bible / by Donald H. Juel ; edited by Shane Berg and Matthew L. Skinner
      228 p. cm.
  Includes bibliographical references.
  ISBN 978-1-60258-381-8 (hardcover : alk. paper)
  1. Bible--Theology. 2. Bible--Sermons. 3. Sermons, American. I. Berg, Shane, 1971- II. Skinner, Matthew L., 1968- III. Title.
  BS543.J84 2011
  230'.041--dc22
                    2010052528

The paperback ISBN for this title is 978-1-60258-383-2.

Printed in the United States of America on acid-free paper.

Shaping the Scriptural Imagination

Truth, Meaning, and the Theological Interpretation of the Bible

By Donald H. Juel (1942–2003)

SHANE BERG & MATTHEW L. SKINNER

EDITORS

BAYLOR UNIVERSITY PRESS

Contents

Credits

" 'Your Word Is Truth': Some Reflections on a Hard Saying" was originally published in *Princeton Seminary Bulletin* 17 (1996): 9–28.

"The Strange Silence of the Bible" was originally published in *Interpretation* 51 (1997): 5–19.

"A Disquieting Silence: The Matter of Mark's Ending" was originally
published as chapter 8 ("A Disquieting Silence: The Matter of the Ending")
in Donald Juel, *A Master of Surprise: Mark Interpreted* (Minneapolis:
Fortress, 1994), 107–21.

"Interpretation for Christian Ministry" (coauthored with Richard
Nysse) was originally published in *Word & World* 13 (1993): 345–55.

"Hearing Peter's Speech in Acts 3: Meaning and Truth in Interpretation"
was originally published in *Word & World* 12 (1992): 43–50.

"Interpreting Israel's Scriptures in the New Testament" was origi-
nally published in *A History of Biblical Interpretation*. Vol. 1, *The Ancient
Period*, edited by Alan J. Hauser and Duane F. Watson (Grand Rapids:
Eerdmans, 2003), 283–303.

"The Trinity and the New Testament" was originally published in
Theology Today 54 (1997): 312–24.

"Interpreting Mark's Gospel" was originally published as the introduction in Donald Juel, *The Gospel of Mark*, Interpreting Biblical Texts
(Nashville: Abingdon, 1999), 15–51.

All previously published material is reproduced here with the permission
of the respective publishers.

Preface

Donald Harrisville Juel was born on March 4, 1942, in Alton, Illinois. After receiving his B.A. at St. Olaf College in 1964 and a B.D. from Luther Seminary in 1968, Juel entered the doctoral program at Yale University. He was awarded the Ph.D. in 1973 (M.Phil. 1971) after writing a dissertation on the trial of Jesus in the Gospel of Mark with Nils Dahl.

Juel's first academic appointments were as visiting assistant professor at Indiana University (1972–1974) and as assistant professor of New Testament at Princeton Theological Seminary (1974–1978). In 1978 Juel took a post at Luther Seminary, where he was eventually promoted to professor of New Testament. He spent many fruitful years at Luther Seminary, establishing himself as a masterful teacher and a productive scholar. In 1995 Juel returned to Princeton Theological Seminary as the Richard J. Dearborn Professor of New Testament Theology, a chair he held until his death in 2003.

Juel's scholarly contributions to the study of the New Testament are considerable. In addition to important translating and editing work and a steady stream of articles and essays, he wrote an introduction to the New Testament, several popular commentaries, and a study of history in Luke–Acts. Some of his most significant works explore the literary and theological dimensions of the Gospel of Mark. These include *A Master of Surprise: Mark Interpreted* (Minneapolis: Fortress, 1994) and *The Gospel of Mark* (Nashville: Abingdon, 1999). Juel also penned a well-received and oft-cited volume on the early church's interpretation of Israel's Scriptures:

Messianic Exegesis: Christological Interpretation of the Old Testament in Early Christianity (Minneapolis: Fortress, 1988).

The excellence of Juel's publishing record is easily matched by his teaching and speaking legacy. Juel's classes at both Luther Seminary and Princeton Theological Seminary regularly saw large enrollments, and he was much in demand for church conferences, continuing-education events, alumni gatherings, and the like. He was a provocative, insightful lecturer with a wonderful sense of humor. His rhetorical skills made him renowned for turning phrases and bringing home key points with power and effectiveness.

But Juel was revered as a teacher not merely for his abilities as a communicator but because of the substance of what he communicated. He was a penetrating exegete, and his grasp of the complexity of interpreting the Bible in contemporary communities of faith was truly impressive. One always came away from his lectures seeing the interpretive task in an entirely new and exciting (and sometimes unsettling) light. This volume brings together essays, articles, and sermons that capture Juel's brilliance as a reader and interpreter of the Bible.

We, the editors, have many people to thank for making this volume possible. Beverly Roberts Gaventa and Patrick D. Miller, Juel's longtime colleagues and friends at Princeton Theological Seminary, offered invaluable feedback as we conceived of this book. Richard W. Nysse, a friend and colleague at Luther Seminary, graciously agreed to let us reprint an essay he coauthored with Juel. We are grateful to all the publishers who granted permission to reproduce the writings contained herein.

Mary Schmitt, a doctoral student in New Testament at Princeton Theological Seminary, provided crucial editorial support in the production of the manuscript for the volume. She proofread everything diligently and offered several pieces of helpful advice about the structure and order of the included pieces. Her sharp eye has played a key role in bringing the book to its final form. Victoria Smith, faculty secretary at Luther Seminary, was also utterly essential. She carefully transcribed all of Juel's writings and sermon recordings. Paul Daniels, archivist/curator of the Luther Seminary library, and his staff tracked down those recordings amid a mass of old cassette tapes. Melanie Howard, a first-year doctoral student in New Testament at Princeton Theological Seminary, worked efficiently and carefully to prepare the indices.

We have had a great experience working with the staff at Baylor University Press. Carey Newman, director of the press, has skillfully guided the book. We are deeply grateful for his sage advice and good humor. Jenny Hunt, assistant production manager, was responsible for shepherding the volume from rough manuscript to finished product. Her competence made our responsibilities in the production process a light and easy task.

We also want to thank our families. Cathy Skinner and the Skinner children (Alexandra, Miranda, and Samuel), and Corrie Berg and the boys (Anders, Mathias, and Soren) were patient and gracious (as always) as we took extra time in the evenings and on weekends to complete our work on the manuscript. They knew and understood that this book is a labor of love for a beloved teacher and mentor.

Finally we offer our deepest gratitude and appreciation to Don's wife, Lynda, and their children, Kristin and Mark, and we dedicate this book to them. Everyone who knew Don was aware that his family was the great joy and pride of his life. Lynda has been a great help in making this book possible. In addition to giving us her blessing and encouragement to proceed with the project, she made available to us both the physical and the computer files from which some of the included pieces are taken and which provided the inspiration for the concluding essay. It is our sincere hope that she, Kristin, and Mark will find this book a fitting tribute to Don's enduring power and grace as a reader of Scripture.

Donald Juel's Scriptural Imagination

Matthew L. Skinner

This book aspires to make the ideas of Donald H. Juel available to readers who are unfamiliar with his life's work, as well as to readers who have known this work but may remain less than fully aware of how influential it has been to their ways of thinking about God and the Bible.

Even more than that, however, this book is about God and the Bible. It aspires to help those who pick it up understand that reading and interpreting the Bible is a theological endeavor—that is, an opportunity for encountering God through the words of Scripture.

Don Juel (1942–2003) spent his professional career as a professor of New Testament at Luther Seminary and Princeton Theological Seminary. He devoted most of his energy as a teacher and writer toward understanding what it means to read the New Testament as Scripture. This description might sound obvious to those who assume that most New Testament scholars do the same thing. But Juel's work went beyond the historical, linguistic, and literary scholarship that is foundational to the academic training that all biblical scholars receive. As devoted as he was to illuminating the Bible's past, its origins and environments, he was even more interested in the Bible's present and future. What happens when people read the Bible? How is God present or made known in the act of reading? What is the Bible supposed to *do* when a community of faith hears its promises and wrestles with its often disconcerting stories about a God who draws near to humanity only to have humanity do all it can to shield itself? Juel raised and pursued answers to questions like these, whether he was studying how ancient people wrote, studied, and referred to Scripture, or was thinking about how a parable describing a man sowing seed or a story of an empty tomb might affect people of faith today. Weaving its way through his writings and sermons is an interest in highlighting biblical texts' capacity to bring us face to face with God (or to show us something about God), as well as an interest in considering the character of this God. Juel emphasized to Christian audiences that reading the Bible is always a theological act. It is theological because it calls to the fore our understandings of who God is. It is also theological because it makes possible an encounter with God—an encounter that can reaffirm or totally unsettle our previously held understandings of God's nature.

The eight chapters collected in this book represent some of Don Juel's most accessible writing; they were written for churchgoers, pastors, and seminary students. The eight sermons that follow were originally preached in chapel services on seminary campuses; therefore the sermons taught the Bible to people who were preparing for ministry, even as they proclaimed the word of God to a congregation. In all of these writings Juel was trying to articulate a particular view of God and model a particular way of engaging Scripture faithfully, intelligently, and imaginatively. Juel advocated *faithful* reading, in that he was interested in how the Bible nourishes faith—or, rather, how the Bible makes faith necessary by leaving its readers with more promises than proof. By reading *intelligently* we reject simple naiveté about the Bible and seek to be instructed by what we can know about a biblical text's history, language, and original setting. Finally, *imagination* is required. Imagination amounts to neither escapism nor credulity; it is a willingness to perceive a text and reality differently. It is a creative appropriation of a biblical text, allowing ourselves to consider what consequences a curious biblical image (like the tearing of the heavens at Jesus' baptism in Mark 1:10) might have for our understandings of God and the world. It is allowing ourselves to consider what it really means for us if God is really like what a biblical text suggests. Indeed, what if God will not remain passive in response to all of our attempts to isolate ourselves from divine influence? What if not even death itself can stop this God?

Together, the eight chapters and eight sermons show Juel working in the ways he was most influential: not on the level of dry theory and abstract speculation, but in conversation with the Bible itself. While other scholars might spend most of their time discussing *the idea* of biblical interpretation and proscribing how it should be done, as a writer Juel tended to *do* interpretation. In the process of working with individual texts he often reflected more broadly on the possibilities and challenges that biblical interpretation presents, but he never set forth a complete summary or a how-to manual about Bible reading. The remainder of this introduction, therefore, will identify some overarching commitments and movements that shaped his work, thereby connecting the contents of this book. First we will review themes and tendencies that arise frequently in his analysis of biblical texts. Then we will explore how his work with Scripture is truly *theological* interpretation, meant to nourish Christians' expectations and imaginations about what it means to encounter God through the Bible.

Donald Juel as a Bible Reader

Sometimes, probably most of the time, just a few big or central ideas shape the whole span of a person's ways of thinking. One helpful way into Don Juel's writings and influence is to survey the ideas that recur throughout his work. These determinative themes and emphases by no means exhaust the depth of Juel's contributions to our thinking about the Bible, but they do offer an avenue into what this book is about.

God Seeks; We Defend

Like the master of the house in Jesus' parable in Luke 14:15-24, God spares no effort to seek out more and more guests to share in a great banquet. Juel's sermon on this passage depicts God as sending out Sunday-school buses to snatch up unsuspecting people. God is on the move, "on the loose," in Juel's parlance. But Juel also focused attention on what this relentless divine initiative means for us who encounter it as readers of the Bible. As he put it in "'Your Word Is Truth,'" when dealing with a God who refuses to remain sequestered at a safe distance from humanity, "I find myself dangerously vulnerable to the presence of God." Such a reaction was not Juel's alone; his writings amplified other occasions of human self-defense against God throughout the pages of Scripture. As he said in a sermon on Psalm 139, "The Bible's story is far more about people seeking to escape God than to search God out." Humanity's discomfort in the face of God's presence extends even into our interpretive efforts. As we interpret, we often do all we can to domesticate and control God by putting faith in theological systems instead of in God's own self (see "A Disquieting Silence" and "Interpretation for Christian Ministry," as well as sermons on Luke 23:34 and Gal 4:9-11). Bible reading, Juel claimed, brings all our theological anxiety to the surface. Yet it also becomes an occasion for God to break through our defenses.

Irony

If Juel was writing or teaching about a biblical passage, odds were good that it came from the Gospel according to Mark. Among the many aspects of this Gospel that provoked his interest is the book's powerful use of irony. Particularly in the story of Jesus' arrest, trial, and crucifixion, Mark exploits irony to name who Jesus is and what is happening to him. As Juel discussed in "The Strange Silence of the Bible" and in his sermon on Mark 14:53-65, Jesus' enemies identify him accurately through their spiteful mockery and derision. Juel saw deep theological significance to this irony. It indicates much more than God's ability to remain hidden; irony points to God's power to reshape our world and how we perceive it, even to use our own defenses against us. When God comes near, things are not what they once seemed. Our religious words and convictions can no longer protect us; they may come to mean more than we ever thought possible.

The Power of Imagination

Words matter, because through them God can become apprehended. As Juel contended in "'Your Word Is Truth'" and in his sermon on 2 Corinthians 10:1-6, God encounters us through the witness and promises of Scripture. When the Bible confronts us with images and stories of God that show our conceptions of the world and the divine to be too small or too self-centered, we can resist those words or allow them to expand our imaginations. Juel did not read Scripture so he could "get everything right" or construct a secure, foolproof theology capable of answering all the questions that Scripture raises; he read so he and those he taught could develop richer imaginations about God—greater hopes about and greater commitments to what God can make possible. The words of Scripture cannot establish facts about God and the gospel. If they could, they would render faith unnecessary. But these words can mediate promises that confront us now, driving us toward God, even as they have with people over the centuries.

Scripture as a Living Word

The Bible's ability to shape readers' theological imaginations is not a newly acquired ability. As a collection of writings meant to be read and interpreted corporately (see "The Strange Silence of the Bible"), the Bible has always made its home among communities of faith and guided them. Juel's sermon on John 14:25-27 and 16:13 asserts that God continues to speak and confront us through our reading of the Bible. Moreover, the *truth* of a biblical text is not something that can be verified by historical analysis or the text's ability to reinforce a theological conviction. This truth has a present-tense aspect; it stakes a claim on the life of readers if it is to be discovered. As Juel explained in "Hearing Peter's Speech in Acts 3," the truth of a passage's claims depends upon the "activity it engenders" among its readers. The biblical narrative can neither define nor confirm any of the promises it makes. That work belongs to God and is discovered by God's people through their reading of Scripture and their lives of faith. It is participatory.

Donald Juel as a Theological Interpreter

What makes interpreting the Bible a theological endeavor? How does it involve God or result in an expanded imagination about God? At one level, most Christians can agree with the premise that the Bible occupies an important place in our understanding of who God is and how we come to know God. The Bible speaks about God and the world, and it plays key roles in our self-understanding and worship as people of God. Once we move beyond those basic affirmations, however, people of good faith start to disagree about exactly *how* we come to know God through the Bible and about exactly *what* the Bible is. These disagreements and the questions they generate are not limited to recent history. Yet over the last decade or two some Christian scholars have poured energy into new conversations about theological interpretation, by which they mean (among other things) the matter of how people of faith come to encounter God through Scripture. These conversations are diverse, including a variety of voices. It seems Don Juel never used the expression "theological interpretation of Scripture" and related jargon, but his writings show a keen interest in exploring, like these other scholars, how Bible readers might encounter God and how words, the words of Scripture, can be a vehicle by which God becomes present to us. Our introduction to this book therefore concludes with a brief overview of what Juel's works reveal about his understanding of the relationship between God and the reading of Scripture.

God as the Beginning and Goal of Our Reading

Scripture talks not only about God, of course, but its writings shape how we understand who God is. Likewise, our expectations about God shape our experience of reading Scripture. The goal of reading Scripture, according to Juel, is to have an encounter with God that hones the perceptions of

God that we bring to our reading. Through this process, our engagement with Scripture equips us to live a life of faith.

Simply stated, our previously held beliefs about God and the world influence what we see in the Bible's pages. Juel embraced this idea (for example, much of his biblical interpretation reflects theological convictions he inherited from his Lutheran tradition) even as he expressed suspicion of the ways in which we try to box God in with our theological constructs and assumptions. As seen in his sermons on Galatians 4:9-11 and Mark 16:9-20 and in his essay "'Your Word Is Truth,'" Juel was wary of human beings' propensity to use anything—even theology itself—to protect us from God or provide us with a false sense of assurance before God.

Many theological interpreters devote much energy to discussing "the doctrine of revelation," the nature of the biblical "canon," and "the doctrine of providence" as they approach the question of how we apprehend God by reading the Bible. Not Juel; he began with God and texts, not theology (even as his own theological commitments surely penetrate his work). The issue of delineating exactly *how* God relates to Scripture was not his concern. This is probably because he thought that God is more likely to transform readers than is theology, doctrine, or an assured definition of the church and its potential ("ecclesiology").

Juel was therefore not interested in making arguments to establish God as Scripture's author or authenticator. At the same time, for him God is more than a historical memory relegated to Scripture's pages. God is a character in the Bible's narrated dramas but also a still-active participant on our side of the Bible's pages, in the drama of reading the Bible. Scripture attests to God, just as it still does when people read and interpret it.

It is worth noting again that Juel did not pretend he was coming to Scripture with a tabula rasa, a blank slate with no theological presuppositions. Just as many theological interpreters stress the value of reading the Bible in full embrace of an inherited theological tradition, Juel declared (in "The Trinity and the New Testament," for example) that the church's creeds prepare us for reading the Bible. Over and over in his writings Juel also demonstrated what this experience looks like, especially in his comments about God's promises and our tendencies to supplement those promises through our own cleverness and effort. This will be discussed in more detail shortly, but for now it suffices to note that Juel's interpretation of biblical texts often reflects Lutheran theological precepts, even though he rarely indentified these in such a way in his writings.

A Dynamic Understanding of Scripture's Identity and Functions

Scripture did not sit still for Juel. It is not a static thing. Things happen when people read it. The essay "Interpretation for Christian Ministry" best reflects his views on this. The question "What is the Bible?" became completely uninteresting for Juel in comparison to the question "What does the Bible do?" Such a question does not sprout from convictions about the Bible's essence or its supposed unique nature. Juel did not consider the Bible a talisman. The question of the Bible's functions springs from a conviction that the Bible's testimony about God is captivating—at once enticing and disturbing to our human needs and selfishness. The Bible has no ability to change people on its own, but insofar as it brings us into an encounter with God, it participates in God's actions of confronting us and nourishing our faith.

But before we succumb to temptations to move from those convictions about Scripture's functions to a blithe confidence in our ability to understand *how* God works through Scripture, Juel reminds us that the idea of *Scripture* itself is not easily nailed down. To those who would say, "God uses the canon of Scripture to accomplish x, y, and z," Juel's writings would reply, "Which Scripture are we talking about? Whose Scripture? Who decides what constitutes 'the canon'?" As an astute interpreter of Mark's Gospel—which begins with mixed evidence from manuscripts over how rightly to read 1:1, and ends with the great text-critical (and theological) issue of figuring out exactly where and how the Gospel originally ended—Juel knew that any definition of "Scripture" rests on the decisions of countless manuscript copyists, translators, editors, and committees of scholars assembled in conference rooms. Such decisions are rightly revised in the face of new evidence, as with the decision to end Mark's Gospel at 16:8. His sermon on Mark 16:9-20 and his essay "A Disquieting Silence" reflect his fascination with the parameters of Scripture. His disdain for the later-added endings of Mark's Gospel (such as the so-called longer ending in 16:9-20), no matter how long they have been read by the church as "Scripture," did not arise from his fidelity to the methodological tenets of textual criticism but from his theological interpretation of the whole Gospel. He regarded Mark 16:9-20 as a cop-out, a banal attempt to make Mark's God and Mark's disciples more palatable and encouraging. Juel saw simplistic attempts to consider "Scripture" as a settled canon to be attempts to exert authority over our reading of the Bible, and perhaps over God. Be careful of what gets handed down to us as authoritative, Juel warned; we will probably use it to make Bible reading more comfortable than it should be.

The Diversity of the Scriptural Witness

Juel's writings and sermons demonstrate his fluency across the breadth of the Bible's pages. He understood how the various writings in both Testaments cohere and complement one another. At the same time, he kept readers' eyes on the diverse perspectives that the biblical books present. His writings on the Gospel according to Mark, for example, emphasize the need for grappling specifically with Mark's account of the story and message about Jesus Christ. Juel made much of Mark's unique perspective, including the account of heavens tearing (not "opening") in 1:10 and the irony woven through the question that the high priest puts to Jesus during his trial: "Are you the Messiah, the Son of the Blessed One?" (14:61; phrased this way in no other Gospel). Likewise, the sermons reproduced in this volume (especially the one on Luke 23:34) show us his commitment to consider each biblical writing on its own terms.

Biblical Interpretation as a Public, Communal Act

Juel was hardly alone in emphasizing this, but for him the reading and interpretation of Scripture are first and foremost public activities. They reside within Christian community and are a staple of this community's life together. This principle derives from the corporate nature of Christian existence, for one thing. Juel also rooted it in the history of the New Testament writings, which were originally composed to be read aloud in contexts of fellowship, instruction, and perhaps worship. In "The Strange Silence of the Bible," Juel made a case for churches to recover the oral and aural nature of Bible reading. His appeal was not for reenactment, nor did he advocate reading aloud to recreate a certain historical and aesthetic authenticity. Rather, he insisted that public reading puts before us the need to interpret the Scriptures for our lives of faith. To read them communally requires communal interpretation, which calls into service all of our diverse traditions, preunderstandings, and perspectives.

Suspicion Aroused by Interpreters' Defensive Instincts

Biblical interpretation made Don Juel suspicious, not so much suspicious of texts themselves but suspicious of their confident interpreters and the methods they wield. Yes, he advocated interpreting the Bible in communal settings, and he made room for theological traditions to inform interpretation, but he knew that these things in no way guarantee that we will encounter God through Scripture. They cannot assure that we will, even over time, get our interpretations right. Juel's writings join his voice to those of many others who have recognized that all of our interpretive methods, no matter how theologically informed or academically rigorous, can actually become means by which we obstruct ourselves from genuine engagement with God. Interpreters often do whatever it takes to make a text or a canon say something they find palatable. Our yearning for closure and security exercises a firm hold on us. We resist certain biblical images (see, for example, the sermon on 2 Cor 10:1-6) as too disturbing, especially if they make God appear too unwilling to play according to our rules and expectations.

Probably again exhibiting some of his Lutheran commitments, Juel often found the Bible portraying God as elusive, impossible to pin down with complete accuracy. Ultimately, truth and sheer confidence remain out of our reach, leaving us only with promises. These promises are God's promises, or promises about God, and so they strip away the pretensions we construct to buttress faith. Promises made by a God we cannot control drive us back to this God; we have no other footing, apart from a hope in God's mercy. Our inclinations to build an edifice stronger than faith alone make Bible reading precarious work, leaving us exposed as much as comforted.

According to Juel, this state of affairs derives in part from the nature of God and God's ways of being in and for the world. Yet it derives, too, from the nature of the Bible itself. The form of testimony we discover within the Bible does not allow us to get too far inside—at least, not close enough where we can control the action. This is especially true with the Gospels and the Acts of the Apostles, because they are narratives. Juel held, following the late literary critic Frank Kermode (with whom he contends in, among other places, "A Disquieting Silence"), that narratives simultaneously attract and repel their readers. On one hand, we instinctively try to make sense of narratives—both fictional and nonfictional—and all their details. Narratives draw us in by making implicit promises that they will hold together, that their parts will create a coherent whole. But many of their details resist our efforts to interpret them. For example, biblical interpreters have done all they can to explain the young man in Mark's Gospel who runs away naked as Jesus is arrested (14:51-52), but at the end of the day these interpretive hypotheses bring us no closer to understanding the true significance of this scene. We cannot shake the sense of our distance from the narrative and our uncertainty about its significance.

For Juel, the elusive character of narrative results in an important theological consequence. It leaves us who interpret the Bible left to choose between two options. We might pretend we can make every detail fall into line, bending jigsaw puzzle pieces until they all submit to our makeshift portraits. (Following Kermode, Juel lamented the "cunning and violence" that interpreters inflict upon biblical texts to make them behave in a more orderly fashion.) Or we might acknowledge that part of doing theology and living a life of faith is to live in light of promises that are never fully explained—only made.

Conclusion

Relaying his impressions of the Gospel according to Mark, musician and author Nick Cave described the crucified Jesus Christ as "the victim of humanity's lack of imagination."[1] A lack of imagination expresses closure and resistance. If the crucifixion of Jesus was indeed perpetrated by a sinful absence of theological imagination, as humanity's last-ditch response to the threat posed by a God who comes too close, what hope remains for Bible readers to do any better? Is imagination even within our reach?

Don Juel maintained that God would have to be a part of the interpretive equation, lest all our efforts to make sense of the Bible turn out to be attempts to play it safe. This goes beyond saying that God was once active, nostalgically recalled in the stories preserved in Scripture. God must continue to break in. In the lead chapter in this collection, "'Your Word Is Truth,'" Juel recounted a story he was fond of telling about a Bible study on the baptism of Jesus in Mark's Gospel. An exchange with a teenager who saw something different at work in the story became nothing less than a moment for God to reorient readers' imaginations. Juel described the consequences like this: "The actual reading of the story of Jesus' baptism *did something* within the world on this side of the biblical page. . . . Through ordinary words, God intruded into the intimate realm of our imagination and began *reshaping our world*" (emphasis added). Juel's ways of reading Scripture neither force nor guarantee God to stimulate our imaginations, but they do bear witness to his experiences of God's having done so time and again.

Writings

1

"Your Word Is Truth"
Some Reflections on a Hard Saying

In this, his inaugural lecture at Princeton Theological Seminary, Juel asserts that the question of the Bible's "truth" is a question about whether God will do what the Bible promises. Interpreting the Bible is not an attempt to establish foundations of certitude; it is to encounter a God who meets us in words, stories, and promises. The Bible cannot guarantee our future; only God can.

———

> If you continue in my word, you are truly my disciples, and you will know the truth, and the truth will make you free.
>
> —*John 8:31-32*

> When the Spirit of truth comes, he will guide you into all the truth.
>
> —*John 16:13*

> What is truth?
>
> —*John 18:38*

For the last decade, a colleague and I have taught a course with the modest title "Truth and Meaning: Interpreting the Gospel of Mark." The first assignment is to write a brief essay on the question "When we say the Bible is true, what do we mean, and what methods of interpretation appreciate its truthfulness?" The exercise—the prospect of which is as unnerving to colleagues as to students—reveals a great deal about students and the culture from which they come and has been enormously fruitful as a way of surfacing questions central to the theological enterprise. As proud as we are of our pedagogical daring, however, there are moments when even such an exercise is shown to be academic and distant. A few years ago, a letter found its way to my post office box. Written in a shaky hand, it was addressed only to "A Professor." It reads as follows:

Dear Professor,

I'm writing only to a professor not a student or someone in the office. This is very important. I want someone I can contact again if I want to get to the bottom of things. I consider this an important letter. I want the truth. I want to know what Luther Seminary is teaching these days. Please answer short and sweet.

1. Does the (Lutheran) church believe all the Bible is true or has it gone through so many hands you got to take it with a grain of salt?
2a. Do you believe in profecy? b. Do you believe in Revelations? or is that book been thrown out.
3. Do you believe in Heaven and Hell? Is heaven real? Is Hell and Fire real? What do we believe?
4. Is Christ coming again to take us home?

I'm 69 years old and I been a Christian and a Lutheran many years and I hear different voices blowing in the wind. I want the truth. Please answer soon.

Sincerely, a Disturbed Christian

I am still overwhelmed by the letter. Someone actually cares what goes on in theological seminaries and trusts professors to answer questions about life and death matters. There is a sweet naiveté about the letter. Imagine asking an academic to "answer short and sweet," not to mention the nature of the questions to which concise answers are expected. And imagine anyone wanting to "get to the bottom of things." I suspect the prospect of being contacted by the letter writer—of being held accountable for answers—would make it tempting to ignore the letter or to put off the old saint with simple assertions: "Yes, we believe the whole Bible; yes, we believe in prophecy and Revelation; yes, we believe in heaven and hell; and yes, Christ is coming. Faithfully yours, Professor Donald Juel."

I cannot imagine the "disturbed Christian" being satisfied with such answers. In fact, there are some of "us" who believe the Bible has gone through so many hands you got to take it with a grain of salt. There are some of "us" who do not believe in prophecy as the letter writer understands. Some of us are uneasy about traditional notions of heaven, hell, and Christ's return and will never offer a course on Revelation. And even if "we" all believed such things firmly, that would not make them true. Getting to the bottom of things will involve more than assertions. It will require reflection and arguments. Luke wrote two whole volumes for Theophilus, who, if we may trust the translation in the NRSV, had already "been instructed." He needed, as our letter writer, someone to help him "know the truth concerning the things about which you have been instructed."

When we say the Bible is true, what do we mean? Some version of that noun *asphaleia* in Luke 1:4 isn't a bad place to begin. "True," as the NRSV renders the word, means something like "certain," "reliable," or "trust-worthy." Some Christians are prepared to move quickly to aggressive and fulsome statements about the Bible's trustworthiness, with strong adjectives and a series of metaphysical compliments. Most of us to whom the church looks for answers, however, would probably prefer some breathing space before writing our few pages. The matter is complex, and complexity is what keeps us employed.

"Which Bible?" one might ask. There is a remarkable variety in English alone. In addition to the Authorized Version of 1611, there is the Revised Standard Version and the *New* Revised Standard Version; there is the Jerusalem Bible and the *New* Jerusalem Bible; there is a New International Version and a New American Bible, the Good News Bible and the Living Bible, not to mention versions by *Reader's Digest* and Robert Schuller. The Jesus Seminar has published its own four-color edition of the Gospels. Which Bible is the one worthy of our trust?

This is an enlightened audience, and some will surely make the reasonable suggestion that our Bible should be the original Hebrew and Greek on which the translations are based. Such statements send shivers down the spine of the textual critics among us. We have no originals. We have thousands of Bible manuscripts, many with strong claims to respectability. There is a multitude of differences among those manuscripts, some minor, some major, which someone must sort out simply to decide what Bible will be printed. Whole careers have been dedicated to the task of producing a "standard" Greek New Testament. It takes work, and decisions come down to votes. Our "standard" Greek Bible is the result of committee votes that will be taken again every generation as old evidence is sifted, new evidence considered, and arguments reevaluated.

The information is not new, but it seems scholars have preferred to keep such matters largely to themselves. One of my students told me of a conversation she had with her Korean pastor. She wondered what to make

of her English Bible that indicated choices about what to read as the ending of Mark's Gospel ("The Longer Ending" or "The Shorter Ending"). The
pastor, who described himself as conservative, could see no problem. We
simply read the Bible, he insisted, and what is written is what we believe.
His Korean Bible had twenty verses in Mark 16; Mark thus ended with
16:20. He was never struck by the irony that his Bible was a translation
from the Chinese, which was in turn a translation of the King James
English of 1611, itself a translation of inferior tenth-century Greek manuscripts that included verses 9-20. Since 1611 we have discovered older
manuscripts with far greater claim to priority. No one had made that clear
to the pastor.

So which Bible do we read? The truth is, when it comes to the text of
"the Bible," we will never "get to the bottom of things," as our letter writer
hoped. There is no "bottom" we can reach. Textual criticism is not like
excavating for foundation stones. Beneath every apparent foundation may
be another layer. Some young person may find a whole new cave full of
manuscripts, one of which may be an ancient copy of the New Testament.
When it comes to the text of the Bible, there is only a past, a present, and a
future of a process on which we shall continue to depend. Someone must
continue to sort out alternatives and offer reasons for a decision; committees must vote. One might well ask, in the face of such facts, what it means
to speak of the Bible as "true." Trusting the Bible has to do with trusting
scholars and committees and processes. Is a Bible that has gone through so
many hands reliable? Confidence that it is reliable will include confidence
that the Spirit of truth continues to work through scholarly conversation
and committee votes.

Different Voices Blowing in the Wind

Agreeing on a Hebrew or Greek text to translate as "the Bible" is only the
tip of the iceberg. Biblical works must be translated. New decisions must
be made. In whose idiom shall we render the Bible? Do we wish to make
it sound old-fashioned—like a classic? Or should it speak in the everyday
language of the street? If street language, whose? What clues do we get
from the style of biblical language itself? Is it high class or low class, classic
or slang? We must make such decisions—or someone will make them for
us. If there are rules for making a case, we will have to formulate and agree
on them. We will even determine who gets to participate in the conversation and who needs to be convinced by our arguments.

Translations multiply, and so do interpretations of agreed-upon
renderings. The extraordinary diversity of interpretations is one of the

most striking features of contemporary biblical studies. Bible readers do not agree about what they read. There is good precedent for disagreement, of course. Most of us are children of the Reformation, a movement that began by calling into question traditional readings of the Bible and the sovereign rights of authorized interpreters. The Reformers disagreed with their predecessors, however, with great confidence that reading the Scriptures would finally unite the church. What made their exalted statements about scriptural authority significant was their deep conviction that the Bible was clear to everyone who read it, so clear that no one devoted to the Scriptures could really get the message wrong.[1]

Hardly anyone believes that anymore—and even if you believe it, whom can you convince? Our reality is that people do not agree when they read the Bible. Interpretation leads not to unity but to extraordinary diversity. For those raised within authoritarian traditions, the possibility of new readings still comes like a breath of fresh air. Having loosed the bands that riveted the Bible to the stony rocks of ecclesiastical doctrine,[2] scholarship has flourished. The Society of Biblical Literature is an embodiment of incredible productivity over the last half century. The diversity that seems to increase geometrically is not an unmixed blessing, however. The more we read, the more we disagree—and I need hardly point out how significant and painful some of those disagreements are.

Nor is it accidental that scholarship has flourished at the expense of church tradition. Modern biblical scholarship is heir to a project begun by the great philosopher Baruch Spinoza, whose conceiving of historical reading of the Bible arose from suspicion of the church and synagogue and his concern to free society of the harmful effects of theological controversy.[3] One of the significant features to emerge from the whole Enlightenment project is confidence in suspicion. Heirs of Descartes have been led to believe that when tradition and institutions and common opinion are subjected to the acids of critical suspicion, the dross will be burned away and the truth remain.[4]

Suspicion has not led to the brave new world Enlightenment philosophers had imagined. It appears, rather, to have undermined the trust and goodwill necessary for conversation about truth, leading to what Wayne Booth calls the "modern dogma": people take for granted there are no good reasons for believing one thing or another when it comes to matters of value like religion and politics. There are only personal opinions.[5]

In a context where difference of opinion and suspicion are the norm, does it make sense to speak of the Bible as "true," if "true" has to do with actual interpretations that claim public assent? To do so may only make matters worse. It raises the stakes, unwisely so if we have no way to converse in such a way as to change anyone's mind. Some, in fact, like the literary scholar Frank Kermode, insist there are no sound ways to convince anyone of a particular reading of the Bible—or of any other literary work, for that matter. Distinguishing meaning and truth is not simply a strategic move designed to allow room for reason to operate, but an absolute one. The conditions do not exist for measuring interpretations against absolute standards. We live in a realm where only meaning is possible. To move beyond differences of opinion, he argues, we are forced to resort to cunning or violence. Talk of the Bible's truth, in this view, is either a harmless abstraction or a thinly veiled power play designed to offer support for private interpretations when persuasion fails—as it must.[6]

However inadequate the philosophical underpinnings of his argument, Kermode's thesis sounds chillingly familiar in a culture where persuasion is understood as manipulation of public opinion. Cunning and violence are the only means open to us if interpretation aims at truth. Best to settle for what is meaningful.

The Way, the Truth, and the Life

Most students are quite aware of the problem but are likewise convinced that the Christian church cannot afford to abandon truth questions. They recognize the church is invested in a God who is known in the particular—in the history of a specific people and in the career of one individual who claims to be "the way, the truth, and the life." They are unsure how to proceed beyond the boundaries of the private opinion, however. Their papers quickly move from "truth" to what has been meaningful to them; talk of revelation or faith or the working of the Spirit takes the place of arguments as a kind of last resort. Such traditional imagery seems to suggest there is a safety zone where their private beliefs are untouchable and their assertions about the Bible's truthfulness are beyond contesting.

The result is a divide between public and private, fact and value, a division not unfamiliar to our society. To speak of the Bible's "truth" as a private matter may offer some satisfaction, but "truth" implies a public claim. We may choose to speak only to our own kind, to those who will agree with us; or, if we choose to speak with strangers, our witness may take the form of assertions. But assertions will help no one; arguments are required. If we are possessed by something we believe to be true, we shall have no choice but to work at changing minds in a public forum where we have no privileged position, where rules of argument are themselves open to debate. Paul speaks of it as taking every thought captive in obedience to Christ.

The Christian enterprise is utterly invested in changing minds. The gospel truth, for which the church has regarded the Bible as a reliable source and norm, matters only when it enters bound imaginations and frees people who have no hope and dare not dream of living abundantly. But if people are to hear a strange new word, someone will have to learn their language and speak with them. Genuine conversation is required, and conversation is risky. God talk may touch sensitive nerves. Strangers to our culture and religious traditions may ask embarrassing questions—about the Bible, for example—that the church has trained the faithful not to ask. In the process of conversation, everyone may be changed. A real question is whether there is a Spirit of truth who may be trusted with the future of those conversations.

Appealing to the Spirit is not an excuse for evading our responsibilities as interpreters. The Spirit of God works through means. We may well ask, therefore, what means are most promising. When we say the Bible is true, what do we mean, and what methods of interpretation appreciate its truthfulness?

Just the Facts

One way scholars have paid their respects to questions of truth is to attend to "hard facts." Interpretations should be constructed on something substantial, the sorts of things to which historians attend. The enterprise is not unique to Bible scholars or to the Christian church; nor is it inappropriate. The creeds make particular claims about a first-century Jew named Jesus who was "born of the virgin Mary, suffered under Pontius Pilate, was crucified, died and was buried." Affirmations about Jesus' resurrection, enthronement, and return are bound to the particularity of his person and career. Discussion of the second person of the Trinity requires focus on a very specific historical setting. Jesus is not a typical figure who can appear in a variety of guises. He was crucified under Pontius Pilate. Whatever is known of God's graciousness was played out on that stage.

Is that true? The question is entirely appropriate. Given the kinds of answers historical investigation yields, I would suggest a modest formulation: can a reasonable person look at the facts and take them seriously? That remains to be seen. Christians occupy no privileged position here. Historical arguments are required; rules of evidence pertain. A strong case can be made that the story of Jesus is too outrageous to be invented.

I believe people can be persuaded by sound reasons that the climax of Jesus' career was much as it is described in the Gospels.[7] Such belief, of course, requires testing. We must actually make the arguments in the face of current opinion among some members of the Jesus Seminar who are convinced the passion narratives have been so thoroughly worked over by the church that historical investigation cannot penetrate the theological and ideological curtain.

A question, of course, is what such persuasion accomplishes. The issue is not the appropriateness or even necessity of historical study but its utility. Some might say that historical investigation can provide a solid foundation on which theology can build—more solid, certainly, than books and creeds. Some students of the Bible have devoted their lives to studying the history behind the biblical texts, convinced they will unearth those unmovable foundation stones. The most elementary knowledge of the state of professional societies should sober anyone seeking foundations, however. History is less like giant rocks and more like that hypothetical river that is different every time you step into it. The most interesting thing about the past is its future. Yesterday may look very different the day after tomorrow than it looks tomorrow.

I recall my family's visit to the battlefield at the Little Bighorn. Growing up during the hopeful years between the end of the Second World War and the Korean War, I had been raised on the story of Custer's Last Stand. The story of his courage in the face of insurmountable odds was as much a part of the mythology that shaped my world as the story of the little train that could (a story, I suspect, that most of you have never heard). Our guide at the battlefield was a Lakota woman with a doctorate in history. She told the story I knew very differently. The site of the battle hadn't changed; the positioning of Custer and his troops was the same. The story, however, was utterly new. Someone could speak of Sitting Bull and the chiefs as "our" leaders, about the arrogant and headstrong Custer, and of the provocations and broken promises that led to such battles. "The facts" about the battle at the Little Bighorn—facts that had shaped my view of the world—now gave me an entirely different sense of my neighbors and the world we inhabited together.[8]

Biblical history is not essentially different. It is told from perspectives. There are some solid realities—like the Red Sea and Solomon's temple and Pontius Pilate and Golgotha. People are always finding new shards and bones, however—new solid realities that demand attention. Archaeologists may well have stumbled onto the bones of Caiaphas—the first certain

bones of someone mentioned in the Bible. Like other solid realities, however, bones are silent. Someone must give them voice; we must give them
voice. And our knowledge and our experience of the world are essential
to the way "the facts" are arranged. Shards and bones and city walls are
constraints on our imagination—but they do not speak without someone
to tell a story.

Evaluation of "the facts" may be fundamentally altered when strangers
are allowed into the conversation. Our past looks rather different now that
women and minorities have offered their versions of the story. Christian
tradition sounds different when narrated by Jews who have been its victims. And because it is only within the context of those evaluative structures that the facts exist at all, we can hardly say that "the facts" provide
any solid, stable foundation. There are constraints on our imagining; the
particularity of the biblical story must be attended to. But if we imagine
that building things is what we are about as interpreters, we will find no
solid foundation in the past. "The facts" are not irrelevant to those who
believe the Bible is true, but they do not establish the Bible's truthfulness.

Getting to Know You

Interpreters have sought another kind of stability that will sound familiar. A colleague speaks of this branch of scholarship as the search for a
"mind" and scholars as "mind readers."[9] You'll recognize it in sentences
like, "Mark is using the parable in this context to instruct his community
that . . .", "As an advocate of the poor, Luke used his sources to portray a
Jesus who was likewise an advocate of the poor and enemy of the rich."
Interpretation is conceived as conversation with another person who has
something important to say.[10]

Such a view suits well a culture preoccupied with personalities. The
Romantic movement has succeeded at a level that would make its nineteenth-century proponents blush. The culture of the U.S.—at least that
aspect of the culture dominated by the media—seems convinced that the
only thing of importance is individual feelings. When someone writes a
great book, people want to know intimate details of the author's personal
life, as though such knowledge were a necessary condition for evaluating
the book. Audiences may be more interested in such personal gossip, in
fact, than in the book.

There are still professional interpreters who are persuaded that the
most stable features of the text—and those most worthy of our attention—
reside in the "intention of the author." Narratives and letters, according to

this view, provide an avenue into the mind of someone worth knowing. Interpretation is truthful to the degree it represents what Matthew, Mark, or Paul intended to say to their audiences.

Seeking to locate a stable personality behind the Gospels and Paul's letters has proven difficult. No one can agree about the authors of the Gospels. Precisely who were they? When did they write? For whom did they write? What did they "intend"? Solid answers would require more than we could possibly know about past figures. And even if we could know what the biblical authors intended, what would we have achieved? Those who have written anything will acknowledge that you don't really know what you intend until someone reads your piece and tells you. What you may intend that people hear is no guarantee that's what they will hear. Meaning is something that happens when texts are read or sermons heard—and people may hear differently and see things in ways no one could fully anticipate. Written works come to life among readers.

Intention is a shaky foundation on which to construct anything. While appropriately acknowledging that the Word becomes concrete through the pen or the mouth of real people, single-minded fascination with authors and their intentions can inhibit the liveliness of conversation with the actual work produced by Luke or John or Paul.

It may be that in ten years such an approach will have been so thoroughly discredited among Bible readers that it need not appear in a survey of options. "Intentionality" is under attack everywhere. Nevertheless, the option continues to live on in some circles where the "truthfulness" of the Bible resides in the mind of inspired individuals whose identities and personalities we seek to reconstruct.

The Linguistic Paradigm and the Ascendancy of Narrative Worlds

The last decades within biblical studies have witnessed a dramatic move to literary methods of interpretation. There has been a shift in paradigms from historical to linguistic.[11] Literary methods are not incompatible with historical, but their focus is different. Of interest is how words form semantic units: sentences, paragraphs, and, finally, whole narratives or letters. Significant is how words and images within a Gospel narrative refer to one another to form a world.

Interpretation that focuses on the literary appreciates another feature of language. Words are not only containers of meaning. They do things. They wound and heal, kill and make alive. The prophets and the psalmists knew that. So did Paul and the Gospel writers. They wrote to make some impact on an audience. They were as aware as Peter Berger and Thomas Luckmann that language not only reflects experience and culture, it creates them.[12] Language determines the way we will experience the world and ourselves; it creates the conditions necessary to have an experience. While we must read Paul's letters and Mark's Gospel and attempt to make sense of them (which includes translation and all the historical work that entails), we ought not imagine that the works themselves are simply objects. They have the power to change us. They make arguments that intend to persuade. Their language may indeed infect everything we think and do.

For this reason, as an interpreter I have found Ricoeur's image of "the world in front of the text" far more useful than images that suggest the task of readers is to get "into" stories. Analogies with the arts are helpful here. In drama it is the "world in front of the text" in which actors and audiences are interested. The play comes to life on the stage. There must be interpretation prior to the performance, sometimes requiring extensive study when the drama comes from another language and culture. Actors and directors consider various ways of making sense of the script. Finally, however, there must be a performance. The "truthfulness" of the drama cannot be determined prior to performance. The same is true of music and dance. The goal is an encounter with an audience when the symphony comes to life here and now. This ought to be the case with the Bible as well.

It is interesting how such insight is resisted within biblical circles. Habits of the Enlightenment persist. While recognizing that narratives and letters require an audience and that they were written to reshape the symbolic universe of the reader, scholarship has continued to ask principally about other audiences at other times and places. The performances in which scholarship invests itself are those that allegedly occurred in first-century Rome or Asia Minor. It is no wonder that preachers and teachers whose task is to bring the Bible to life in the present, on this side of the printed page, should find much biblical scholarship frustrating. We study only completed performances—or, to use an image from another colleague, we make do with the spent voice of the text. Dredging a sermon out of the leftovers of a hypothetical performance of a passage from Matthew in its "original" setting is a dreary task.

Word Alive: Conversation and Truth

Having suggested that questions about the Bible's truthfulness cannot be divorced from performance and that literary methods will prove most fruitful, let me suggest what interpretation might look like by giving three brief accounts of engagements with the Bible that have helped me clarify the goals and limits of interpretation as well as my role as teacher.

Rending the Veil: Mark 1:9-11

A Bible passage that has fascinated me since seminary days is the account of Jesus' baptism in Mark. Of particular interest is verse 10: "And as he was coming up out of the water, he saw the heavens being torn apart and the Spirit, like a dove, coming down into him." I like the verse, perhaps, because I learned something new about it. I discovered that the old RSV rendering, "Jesus saw the heavens opened," was inadequate on several grounds. The verb in Mark is *schizō*, not *anoigō*, as in Matthew and Luke. *Schizō* means "tear, rip." Further, the participle here is not aorist but present. Jesus sees the heavens not "torn" but "being torn." Translation dramatically alters the way the story feels to readers. I have also wondered, since being a student, what the image means. Did Mark really imagine that the heavens can be torn apart? If so, what do we make of such imagery, since this is hardly our view of the cosmos? With a little information, we can at least make sense of the image by noting the connection with another tearing, this one at the moment of Jesus' death: "The curtain of the temple was torn in two from top to bottom." The curtain, in front of the holy of holies, provided a barrier separating God's real presence from worshipers in the temple—necessary, of course, because standing face to face with God would mean death.

We can at least understand what the imagery means. The heavens are pictured here not as a firmament—a great dome holding back the waters—but as a curtain. God spread out the heavens like a curtain, says the psalmist—perhaps as protection for the whole creation from the blinding brilliance of God's presence and the searing holiness that would consume us all. The structure of the temple in Jerusalem suggests such a picture of the cosmos.

In the story Mark tells, with Jesus' baptism God begins to tear through that barrier; at Jesus' death the temple curtain is torn and the barrier destroyed. Interpreters may seek to capture the "message" in a sentence or two. "The tearing means that in Jesus God has removed the barrier, affording us access." I encouraged such a view. It's close to the argument of the author of Hebrews: Jesus our high priest has entered the holy of holies once for all, so that we may with confidence approach the throne of grace.

At a sleepy Sunday afternoon Bible study, a young high school student, who had come with his mother and had not said a word throughout the class, suddenly challenged me. "That's not what the passage means," he said. "It isn't that we have access to God; it's that God has access to us. The protection is gone. God is here among us, on the loose."

The moment the words were out of his mouth, I knew he was right—and something invaded my imagination that has reshaped my experience of Mark's Gospel, the Christian message, God, and the world. A curtain has been torn, never to be repaired. I find myself dangerously vulnerable to the presence of God whose medium is familiar language that has suddenly come to life.

The class could have focused all its energies on what the words in that passage might have meant to a hypothetical audience at another time and place. We could have gathered information about the passage. I could have convinced them to leave interpreting to experts, since they will never know as much as I do. What happened in that class session, however, did not require that people understand everything. It helped to know some things about the meaning of the Greek and the place of the imagery within some coherent framework—but the actual reading of the story of Jesus' baptism did something within the world on this side of the biblical page. Words were let loose in the imaginations of a small class (and their teacher) that tore gaping holes in their imaginations. Through ordinary words, God intruded into the intimate realm of our imagination and began reshaping our world.

Our question about the Bible's truthfulness must deal with the life of the narrative in our midst. This story claims to be the beginning of the good news—*the* good news—about Jesus Christ. The claim is true only if the Bible is good news to someone—to us. Is it? Is it true that in Jesus God comes dangerously close, so close that people—so that we—are driven to take defensive action? In the telling of this story, does God who "watches from a distance" tear away the curtains drawn over our imaginations, intruding into our private space? Is it the case that Jesus, out of the tomb and on our side of Easter, is still on the loose, coming unbidden to free people who do not even know of their bondage? To put the matter in a form close to the heart of the American pragmatic tradition: does the Bible work?

Such questions are best asked in the context of performance. Interpretation cannot give a theoretical answer. The question is whether or not the gospel story does what it promises. The critical issue is whether repentance and forgiveness are actually preached to all the nations—and that people repent and are forgiven.

The question of truthfulness in this sense does not evade attention to the way we invest the story with meaning. I have suggested a particular way of reading the story that shapes my performance—and, I trust, that of my students. I will do my best to prepare an audience to hear that story, highlighting what I regard as the critical features. I have not always told the same story, with the same highlights. A young man reshaped my appreciation of the gospel story. Fortunately, he felt free to speak. What other such enlightening and disquieting experiences await all of us? What stranger, whether an ancient commentator or a sainted woman or a salty pagan or a naive young student, will change the way you read and hear the Bible? That remains to be seen—and the question of "truth" and truthfulness cannot be separated from the experience of the Bible by particular audiences at particular times and places. Interpretation will not—ought not—provide the kind of stability that closes off new experiences of the story. To do so would be effectively to silence the Word of God.

Adrift? Irony and Mark 15:39

New experiences of familiar texts can be unsettling. During a discussion of Mark's passion story and its ironic tone, a student suggested we read the "confession" of the centurion at the moment of Jesus' death ironically. I tried it: "And when the centurion who stood opposite him saw how he thus breathed his last, he said, 'Sure this was the Son of God.'" (On my printed text there are no performance rules. This is one place where you must hear someone read the text to get the point.) I was immediately convinced and now cannot hear the "confession" in any other way.

When I read the passage with my advisees, one of the older members of the group became terribly upset. The younger people could not understand why he was so irritated. They liked irony (actually, sarcasm). Besides, even if the statement of the centurion is ironic, they pointed out, it still functions as a testimony to the truth for readers—just like the soldiers' mockery of Jesus as King of the Jews and Pilate's inscription of the charge. Readers know the statements are true. That they are spoken by enemies does not change that. My troubled advisee finally put his finger on what bothered him. "If you can read this verse ironically and change an entire tradition of interpretation by your tone of voice, what is to say you cannot do that elsewhere? What is to protect the Bible from your fondness for irony?"[13]

A fine question—and one that explains a principle for public reading I was taught in worship class: pastors should never inflect their voices when reading the Scriptures in church, lest they interpret them. Apparently, that is the work of the Spirit who must function in a disembodied way. The result, of course, has been that people think the Bible is as boring as the readings to which they are subjected!

To protect the Bible is to silence it. It must be read, heard, and interpreted—which will lead to different readings and hearings. "Creative" readings must be justified. There are rules. How to play the role of the centurion in Mark requires attention to the rest of the passion narrative, to how characters play their roles, and to the whole notion of irony. Rules and arguments and methods do not get us to the truth, however. For that we must rely on creative imagination—or, to use a nice word, divination. If the Spirit is at work among us, we may trust there will be such moments of illumination.

Determining what is a valid reading and where minds need changing are community tasks. Conversation is not only a means of testing, however; it is the way communities are formed and grow. Disagreements are not a sign of community breakdown, but of life. The possibility of edifying conversation in the face of differing opinions, however, requires a measure of trust and goodwill—the result, the church claims, of the presence and work of the Spirit.[14] Here is why interpretation should not be divorced from the life of a worshiping community that engenders goodwill and trust.

The Limits of Interpretation: Hosea as a Test Case

Interpretation does not always engender trust and goodwill. It easily becomes a means by which we protect ourselves from one another, from God, and from the truth. There are, of course, reasons why we may need protection. A female colleague, a professor of Old Testament and a convert from Judaism, spoke at a conference dealing with the authority of the Scriptures. Hosea was the focus of our study. Her presentation dealt with the way the ancient prophet's words worked for her. She said two things: First, Hosea's prophecy is one reason she is a Christian. She explained briefly how the book had been important in her life. Second, as a woman, she found the language in chapter 2, comparing God's humiliation of Israel to stripping a woman naked and parading her in public, increasingly offensive and utterly unpalatable theologically. What kind of a God would speak such words through a prophet?

The moment she sat down, a male colleague stood up, as he said, half in jest, to "fix her problem." He offered an ingenious interpretation of the chapter according to which the prophet was offering males an opportunity to experience the shame and humiliation usually reserved for women. That would presumably change the way women felt about the text. When women in the group indicated that didn't do it for them—that the words of the prophet still frightened and angered them—other hands went up from the male contingent. The point seemed to be that if people were offended by words it was only because of a misunderstanding. Interpreters, like Moses, stepped boldly into the breach, interposing themselves between God and the women so as to blunt any offense.

What if they had succeeded? A campus pastor spoke to me about such interpretation. "I read the Bible from beginning to end when I was fifteen," he said. "It frightened the daylights out of me. I thought, 'What if God is really like this?' Since that time, my pastors and seminary teachers have helped me to see there is nothing to be frightened about. They taught me sophisticated ways to domesticate the Bible. I am no longer frightened— but I also have difficulty finding the Bible interesting."

Fortunately, the interpreters at this conference were not successful. Women in the group sensed that creative renderings of the prophet's terrible words held no promise. The words can be silenced for a while, but then suddenly they come roaring off the page into the imagination of those who have no protection, and they are capable of doing real damage. As the group polarized around this issue, speeches began to take on an edge. Those who sought to help became frustrated and irritated. When cunning proved unsuccessful in convincing women that the God whose prophet spoke the words in Hosea 2 could still be trusted, violence seemed near at hand. Even within this group of reasonably like-minded Christians, the goodwill and trust necessary to work on seemed imperiled.

The problem is that people trust interpretation to do more than it is able. Those who seek to assure troubled readers that everything will work out sound like Hosea's audience:

> Come, let us return to the Lord;
> for it is he who has torn, and he will heal us;
> he has struck down, and he will bind us up.
> After two days he will revive us;
> on the third day he will raise us up. (Hos 6:1-2)

One may well ask, however: is that true, or is the invitation simply pious prattle—or worse, a power move designed to silence the cries of the hurting? Interpreters cannot answer. The words of the prophet must do what they promise, or assertions about the truthfulness of the biblical text will fall on deaf ears.[15] The problem here is God, whose will seems hidden in words enmeshed in a culture for whom women are expendable. If the hurtful words of Hosea 2 are to serve some positive function for women as well as men, God must somehow redeem them.

One way of dealing with a wrathful God is to seek protection in any way we can—from reducing the capacity of language to frighten and judge to locating meaning at another time and place. The problem is that by so doing, we undermine the power of speech to heal and to give life. If we refuse to allow the parallel drawn between God's sense of betrayal and the experience of Hosea as husband, God's speech in 11:8-9 lacks all poignancy:

> How can I give you up, Ephraim?
>   How can I hand you over, O Israel?
> How can I make you like Admah?
>   How can I treat you like Zeboiim?
> My heart recoils within me;
>   my compassion grows warm and tender.
> I will not execute my fierce anger;
>   I will not again destroy Ephraim;
> For I am God and not a man,
>   the Holy One in your midst,
>   and I will not come in wrath.[16]

The relevant question for interpreters is whether or not God's words in chapter 11—and beyond—redeem the language in chapter 2 for actual hearers and reconcile those who have been alienated. Only then can we expect from one another the trust and goodwill necessary to proceed with our joint reading. The answer, however, depends upon what God does with actual readers and hearers.

If the principal feature of language in which we are invested is its ability to heal and liberate and make whole, our scholarly enterprise must focus on performance of some sort. That means acknowledging the limits of interpretation. Our scholarly work cannot solve the real problems we bring to an encounter with the Scriptures. Interpretation will not liberate us from sin, death, and the devil and in fact may serve to protect us from liberating encounters. Only God can deliver. The question is whether God does such things. The Bible makes promises. Will they be kept?

The testimony of the church is that God will finally gather together the scattered human family and wipe the tear from every eye. The creation that groans in travail will be made new. We can trust God to keep those promises if in Jesus God intrudes into our private worlds to lay claim to us, if the barrier between God and the creation has been breached and continues to be breached through the medium of words that accomplish reconciliation and forgiveness and liberation.

This will occur only if words are spoken by someone, only if they address particular people in their own language and setting. If the words of the Bible are true, they must do what they promise. That is another reason why interpretation is best done within a context where the word is preached and the sacraments celebrated. Does the God who speaks such terrible words in Hosea make them right? Will the God who spoke at Jesus' baptism breach our defenses, tearing the curtain that separates us, so as to come alive in our imaginations and actually set us free? Will our capacity to change the Bible merely by inflecting our voices be used for good or ill? That remains to be seen.

Locating scriptural interpretation within the worship and tradition of the church does not mean to domesticate or play safe. On the contrary, it is to insist to colleagues that reading the Bible cannot exclude potentially dangerous questions about God—the sorts of questions Spinoza's historical criticism was designed to rule out. Nor does reading within the context of church practice preclude surprises. The most interesting thing about the Bible is what it is yet to become within the vast company of strangers among whom we are called to preach the good news about Jesus. And the crucial question is, does it work? Does the Bible provide language and norms for ways of speaking that do what God promises? Does it generate hope that will not disappoint? If not, our enormous investment in the Scriptures will yield little.

That we do not and will not ever possess the whole truth should be clear to those who live by faith in God's promises. "For who hopes for what is seen?" The way we conceive our task as interpreters ought to reflect what is the case. I am suspicious of foundational language, as though our reading of the Bible will yield solid, immovable rocks on which to locate our edifices. Living with the Scriptures is more like sailing than like building cathedrals. We don't have control over the elements—just enough to navigate in the face of surprising shifts of wind and changed water conditions. Some would perhaps hope for more stability, but for sailors bedrock is where sunken ships lie.

Is the Bible true? That remains to be seen. And whose interpretations will be most deserving of attention? Will suspicion give rise to more faithful and fruitful readings, or will suspicion lead only to further alienation? These matters, likewise, remain to be seen. Such questions cannot be settled apart from actual conversation among interpreters that must include not only those of like mind but strangers to whom God extends hospitality. There is no method that promises a way through the labyrinth. No ecclesiastical regulations or structures can guarantee anything. We have only our wits, some suggestions offered by the host of witnesses that surround us, and the promise that the Spirit of truth will lead us into the truth.

Will our letter writer be satisfied with such an answer? That remains to be seen. She would undoubtedly prefer something shorter. My guess, however, is that she and others like her will find sailing out into the deeps far more interesting than remaining anchored in some protected harbor. The one whose Spirit brooded over the face of the deeps has promised that same Spirit will lead us into the truth. However bleak the present state of our conversation around the Scriptures, we do our work in hope that the breath of God will fill our sails and carry us into the promised future where we will one day know the whole truth.

The Strange Silence of the Bible

Reflecting on passages that occupied much of his attention throughout his career, Juel emphasizes the importance of reading the Scriptures publically, aloud. Such reading practices place the Bible within a community setting and within the conversations a community undertakes to understand itself, its purpose, and its God. Corporately hearing the Bible read leads us to recognize that it beckons us to interpret it, and that in our interpretations it speaks.

————

In 1970 James Smart, already professor emeritus at Union Seminary in New York, wrote an influential little book entitled *The Strange Silence of the Bible in the Church.*[1] In the book he puzzled about the relationship between biblical scholarship, which seemed to him a thriving enterprise, and what he perceived to be a growing lack of interest in the Bible within the church. Reflecting many of the same concerns more than a quarter century later in the fiftieth anniversary issue of *Interpretation*, Leander Keck considers as well the relationship between scholarship and the use of the Bible in his article "The Premodern Bible in a Postmodern World." His essay is a plea for reading the Bible:

> By no means does living with the Bible imply that we should ignore or disdain whatever information about it we can acquire, usually through some form of criticism. Such information can help understand with whom we are living, even if not everything produced by biblical scholarship is reliable. Still, nothing can replace reading the text again and again, questioning and being questioned, objecting and being objected

to, discovering and being discovered. Without this, the Bible remains an extrinsic authority imposed on the church by the past; by living with it, it becomes an internalized authority because it authorizes a way of living before God and among our fellows.[2]

In the essay Keck employs the image of human relationship—the Bible as "companion"—as a metaphor helpful for conceiving engagement with the Scriptures. He employs an image developed by Wayne Booth in his masterful *The Company We Keep*.[3] As one whose vocation over the last two decades has been interpreting the Bible within the context of theological seminaries, I am likewise concerned about the state of Bible reading in the church. I have become aware how important and problematic are those basic metaphors that shape our engagement with the Bible.[4] In this essay I want to explore what is meant by "reading the Bible" and to suggest that while the image of "companion" may be helpful, it may not take sufficient account of public, oral/aural engagement with the Bible that has always been an important feature of church tradition.

I teach at a school with a long tradition of preparing preachers. It is not surprising that the tradition includes strong emphasis on speech. While most college and university liberal arts faculties seem to stress preparing students to write, there are still some who know the power of the spoken word and are prepared to train students in the tradition of classical rhetoric. Students at Princeton Seminary, for example, must take a year-long required course in speech.

One facet of the course is devoted to public reading of the Scriptures. Students begin with a passage like the account of Belshazzar's feast in Daniel 5 and are asked to "play" with different ways of reading the story. Resistance is great among most students who may not know the Bible but have a fixed notion of how it should be read—usually with great reverence and solemnity, but with very little inflection. The course aims to give them a greater sense of the possibility of the spoken word and of their options as readers. Their exercises include attention to the wide variety of literary genres from narratives to psalms to letters, while exploring oral means appropriate to the public performance of such material. In view of my own experience as a member of congregations where Bible reading is a regular feature of worship and yet is almost never interesting or engaging, I can only applaud such efforts.[5]

At the same time, as a professional interpreter of the New Testament, I am increasingly struck that much biblical interpretation occurs without the Bible ever having been read. I am not referring to the tendency among many of us to bury the biblical text beneath layers of historical data and methodological considerations, though that is a serious problem. I mean exegesis is carried on without ever reading aloud, especially in a public setting where one reads and others listen. Actual engagement with the biblical text is an essentially private encounter, done best in a library or study. Commentaries are consulted and papers written without ever voicing words that were written to be heard. It is not only that pastors are given little training in public reading. The whole interpretive enterprise suggests that public reading is unimportant to understanding the Scriptures. The Bible is a mute companion whose access to the imagination is dramatically limited to the sense of sight. The Bible is strangely silent among its most devoted students.

This is remarkable. Biblical works were written to be heard. Even personal reading in the ancient world involved making sounds. And while reading a passage from the Fourth Gospel is very different from reading the opening chapters of Romans, something quite different happens in both cases when ink on paper is translated into sound. The debate about the oral and the written word initiated by Werner Kelber is probably less a comment on the Bible than on the culture within which the Bible functions.[6] For most people in the church, the Bible is part of an oral/aural culture. For scholars, the Bible is studied largely in a silent world.

One reason may be an almost single-minded concentration on "meaning." The language of the Bible is understood as referential, whether the referent be historical events, community dispositions, or the "mind" of an author. The task of the interpreter is to help readers clarify to what the words and sentences of a biblical work point. Debates revolve around related questions, like the range of possible referents or the confidence we can have that Jesus actually spoke a parable attributed to him or that it was included in Q. Some argue that no stability is possible for interpreters—and that we can never know what lies outside the realm of language.[7]

Jane Tompkins chronicles the shift from what she terms a more rhetorical view of language to a preoccupation "not with action but with signification." Language, she argues, was previously understood first as a means of moving people:

> The concept of language as a force acting on the world, rather than as a series of signs to be deciphered, accounts for the absence of specificity in ancient descriptions of literary response. Aristotle, although he speaks of pity and fear as the emotions proper to tragedy, judges the merit of poetic production in general on "vividness of impression," and

"concentrated effort," and says that the end of the art is to be "striking." In other words, it is not the nature of the impact that concerns him, but the degree. The concept of poetry as an instrument of power whose value is to be measured by the force of the impression it produces takes a more extreme form in Longinus. Longinus's notion of the sublime is equivalent to a conception of poetry as pure power. His descriptions of the sublime center on the effect sublime poetry produces in its hearers, but instead of specifying this or that emotion, Longinus speaks only in terms of intensity or strength of feeling. The sublime is impact, effect, raised to the highest power.[8]

Such notions of language are familiar to the writers of the Scriptures. Speech is the medium by which God created the heavens and the earth (Ps 33:6). Jeremiah compares God's word to "fire" and to a "hammer that breaks the rock in pieces" (Jer 23:29). Isaiah speaks of God's word as rain that waters the earth, "making it sprout and bring forth" (Isa 55:10); "it shall accomplish that which I purpose, and succeed in the thing for which I sent it" (Isa 55:11). Words can wound as well as heal, kill as well as make alive. The biblical writers were well aware of the power of words—a power not unrelated to their meaning but not equivalent to it.

Such knowledge is not confined to ancient societies. Many in our culture are also aware of the power of words, perhaps especially those who have been victims of slander and abuse or who have never had a place in the world created for us by our language. It is not accidental that those who have been most impressed with the power of language in recent times are those opponents of racism, classism, and sexism who have observed its destructive capacity.

The reasons for the shift from understanding language as power to a concentration on signification are a topic worthy of careful study. It is sufficient here to suggest that interpretation interested only in what the Bible "means" is overly narrow and does not take seriously the oral/aural setting within which the Bible functions and ought to function within congregations and society. The appreciation of language as power opens possibilities for those whose vocation is interpreting the Scriptures. A worthy challenge is to bring our extraordinary interpretive projects to bear on the experience of reading and hearing the Bible—still the primary setting within which the Bible is engaged for many people. Whether concentration on the actual performance of biblical texts for real audiences requires only a refocusing of the task of interpretation or a more ambitious reconceiving remains to be seen.

The Experience of Hearing

I still recall the first time I saw the Gospel of Mark "performed" in public. I had regularly begun my lectures on the Synoptic Gospels by pointing to the episodic nature of the prose, which many have taken to be the mark of oral sources. Looking at the printed page, it was not difficult to make the case that the narratives were in major ways deficient. The strategy of the course was to demonstrate that despite such deficiencies, the stories contained treasures for those willing to dig. The person who "performed" Mark, however, recited in such a way that the breaks in the story were not a problem. The sense of coherence was accomplished in several ways, like changing positions and looking at different sections of the audience. It worked. The audience had little sense that the Gospel was deficient as a narrative. There were gaps and jumps, but the way they were handled by the performer made them enticing rather than irritating and distracting.

I also noted there were times during the performance when people laughed. I did not recall ever laughing to myself when reading through Mark. The most obvious case is in recounting Jesus' feeding of the four thousand. To Jesus' suggestion that the people need to be fed, the disciples reply, "How can one feed these people with bread here in the desert?" (8:4). The look of weariness on the face of the performer and the gentlest sarcasm as he recited Jesus' line, "How many loaves do you have?" (8:5), set the audience off. How could the disciples forget how Jesus had fed more people with fewer loaves in a similar setting only a few minutes earlier? The story elicited laughter because it was read in the larger narrative setting—and because the storyteller played on the effects of the repetition. Stories that source critics term "doublets" function differently when played against one another in a single performance.

It has occurred to me more than once that all these features of the performance were due to the performer as much as to the text. I have been impressed in subsequent performances, for example, by the ease with which the "reader" can play the disciples as buffoons or as sympathetic characters. The debates among commentators about the role of the disciples take on flesh and blood in a performance, and the results are unnerving.[9] I can understand the anxiety that such insight awakens. It explains why, for example, my liturgics professor would urge us to read the Bible without inflection, lest we interpret it for someone. The reader has considerable power, including, as it turns out, the power to make the Bible so uninteresting that people do not bother to read it.

All this makes the issue of oral performance more interesting. Biblical scholarship has focused largely on "critical distance," choosing to deal with "implied" or "ideal" authors and readers as a way of broadening the horizons of actual readers bound by their own culture, experience, and language world. Biblical works are written in ancient languages and were composed for people who were different from us in many ways. Historical-critical study is one way of respecting the strangeness of the texts. Such work is only preparatory, however; it is not the same as performing a narrative in a particular setting. How are interpreters to factor in the particularity of communication? How can they know what will happen when a story is read—what people will hear when the words are given voice—apart from the actual experience of reading and listening?

Being present at a performance of Mark's Gospel and dealing with the reactions of the audience have convinced me that without the actual experience of reading and hearing, biblical interpretation is deficient. An interpretation that fails to take into account what happens when written words are spoken seems adequate neither to the "original" setting in which they were spoken nor to the contemporary settings in which they continue to function.

What follows are three examples of biblical passages where interpretation and oral performance are intimately related. My own fascination with these passages arises from the discussions generated by reading and hearing.

A Family Story

Readers with some daring may shape an audience's experience of a particular story. Those who object to daring readings in church simply ignore how thoroughly interpretive traditions have shaped what people read and hear. The so-called parable of the Prodigal Son (Luke 15:11-32) is one of the most familiar among Jesus' stories. If asked how they intend to "play" the story, most readers would probably follow a long-standing tradition of interpretation: their reading would portray a younger brother, the "prodigal," who acts foolishly, repents, and is welcomed home by his forgiving father. Such a reading would play the parts of the younger son and the father warmly. Helmut Thielicke's alternative, "the Waiting Father," still tends toward a reading in which the father and younger son appear in a favorable light.[10] In both cases, the older son is largely unnecessary to the main plot.[11] He regularly appears as a resentful presence who elicits a steady stream of moralisms from preachers. In the history of Christian art, this is the almost universal interpretation. The focus is the reconciliation of father and son, with the resentful presence hovering outside. Most congregations have been "helped" to think of themselves as younger, irresponsible children who have strayed from home but who can repent and find a waiting parent.

In reading the story of the prodigal son, I choose to play the younger son as a classic manipulator. That interpretation had occurred to me when I read a letter a parishioner sent to his pastor after hearing the parable read in church. As an older, responsible child in a family of irresponsible siblings, the letter writer objected strenuously to the usual reading according to which the older brother is the villain. He had himself kept the family farm afloat despite the best efforts of his siblings to sink it, largely without any expressions of appreciation from his parents. They were endlessly preoccupied with his siblings and the crises they precipitated. He argued that the older brother was really taken for granted, was not appreciated, and that the father had no right to "forgive" the younger son and bring him back into the family. "If there is anything in the story that approximates the love of God," he wrote, "it would be the love of the older son if he could find it in his heart to forgive his brother and his father."

There seems ample justification for reading the story from the perspective of the older brother. We know nothing about the prodigal except that he is irresponsible, wasteful, and keeps bad company. When he is reduced to feeding pigs, he "[comes] to himself." It is difficult to imagine how the phrase can be interpreted as repentance. "[Comes] to himself" is absolutely neutral, and the words introduce a rehearsed speech. The prodigal's first response to his desperate plight is the preparation of a speech by which to secure himself a place back at the family farm. The phrases he rehearses to move his father can as easily be insincere as sincere. It takes only a little practice to read the story in such a way as to introduce suspicion within the listeners about the sincerity of the younger brother—and once that is done, the story is utterly changed.

What of the father, who, though utterly uninterested in the speech, is so moved at the sight of his son that he welcomes him into his home like a prince? The father has traditionally been viewed as a noble parent whose love is without bounds. Perhaps he should rather be viewed as a parent unable to say no to a manipulating child—a classic "enabler." His willingness to welcome the prodigal back home without taking care to determine the sincerity of his repentance and to insure more responsible living is genuinely dangerous.[12]

The older brother suddenly becomes a more sympathetic character. We meet him at work in the field. No one apparently thinks to inform him that the calf is being killed and a party prepared to celebrate his brother's return. He must find out by asking a servant after he has finished his chores. The party is already in full swing, presuming a considerable lapse of time. Little wonder that he is angry and refuses to join the celebration. His "lament" to his father is worthy of more interest than it has received. "I have slaved for you all these years . . . have never disobeyed a command . . . you have never given me a goat." It is true, of course. The father has not acted justly, and justice is not a trivial matter. The story is about a lack of fairness that proves incendiary in many families. The older brother is not exemplary; his resentment makes it impossible for him to celebrate the deliverance of his brother. But it is his plight—one whose passion for justice is turned against him and creates a resentment that holds him in bondage—that should be the focus of the story.

The disposition of the audience will also determine the way the story is heard. If given some interpretive elbow room, the responsible members of an audience will suddenly hear someone championing their cause. Virtually everyone has been part of a family system in which fairness has not been the normal experience. There are many responsible people who know that society, like parents, takes them for granted and treats them unfairly. They end up paying the bills for the actions of the scoundrels. And as the older siblings begin to express their resentments, the prodigals will suddenly be put on the defensive, as will parents who know that children who need more get more. When the story is told from the perspective of the older brother—relatively easy to accomplish—the interpretive drama that follows within a group will be quite different from the usual response. The audience will, of course, be reacting to a different story.

Which is the "correct" reading? Can we say that the lament of the older brother should be the focus? Formulating an argument for one reading or another would seem to be an appropriate task for biblical scholarship. One might argue this way. The notable absence in the story of any vocabulary relating to repentance, with which Luke-Acts is replete, makes the usual moralizing interpretation less plausible. The use of passive verbs to describe the reaction of the father and the older brother ("was moved with compassion," "was moved to anger") suggests that we are dealing with more than simple moral choices. And the target of the story—the scribes and Pharisees who grumble that Jesus eats with sinners and tax collectors (15:1-2)—suggests that the elder brother is an essential character.

This is a place where historical and cross-cultural research can play a significant role. From his years of experience among peasants in the Middle East, Kenneth Bailey offers comment on the social realities of rural life that highlight the riskiness of a father's lack of decorum and the threat to a fragile society posed by the lack of respect and justice.[13] Studies of "Pharisees" that have appeared over the last decades have provided a necessary critique of stereotypes that have dominated Christian exegesis for centuries.[14] Pharisaic concern for the law is not "legalism"; it is part of a concern for the social structure of a religious community, difficult for members of our own antinomian culture to appreciate. Scholarship can help make clear that the protest of the pious is taken far more seriously in Luke's story than in most of Christian interpretive tradition.

Any who have actually tried out alternative readings of the parable of the Prodigal Son and have dealt with the reaction of actual audiences know that the old story can still elicit strong emotions. That experience of reading and hearing the story is something different from looking at the words on a page and asking what they "mean." Biblical interpretation that is helpful will consider how the story will be played and what relation that performance will have to particular audiences. It will also allow for the possibility that "my" experience of the story requires critique and supplement from others.[15] There is a difference if the Bible is "our" companion or "mine."

The Case of the Sarcastic Centurion

Now when the centurion, who stood facing him, saw that in this way
he breathed his last, he said, "Truly this man was God's Son!"

—Mark 15:39

While discussing how to read the account of Jesus' death in Mark's Gospel in an exegetical course, a student offered a suggestion: why not read the "confession" of the centurion in 15:39 sarcastically? The student intended the suggestion as a joke, as I recall. The suggestion was in large measure a response to my shaping of their reading experience. I had managed to convince them—through reading the story and discussing their reaction—that Pilate's lines ("What do you want me to do with the one you call the King of the Jews?") can be read as taunting the Jewish leaders and mob, and that the formulation of the charge "King of the Jews" is likewise intended as an insult. I had gone further in arguing that irony should be the most significant feature in an experience of hearing the passion story. "Why not the statement of the centurion?" suggested a student who had found my reading intriguing. "Why not read, 'Sure this was the Son of God' (dripping with sarcasm)?"

I tried it and the effect was remarkable. The student was stunned to discover that it worked. Some liked it; others did not. That line came to dominate the class's experience of and discussion of the whole passion story. It still does when I read the story in classes or congregations. It completely changes how the story is heard, even though the words are the same. The line traditionally understood as a genuine confession, a glimmer of hope in the darkness that envelops the story, suddenly becomes a last indication that no one understood. Jesus dies abandoned by everyone, mocked even by those executed with him, forsaken by God, his last words misunderstood by the crowd (who think he is calling Elijah). Now with his death comes a final statement from those who know power: the claim is a joke! Jesus is a dead pretender, a would-be king and Son of God.

With so much at stake, the class had to decide how to adjudicate the alternative readings. Grammar is indecisive. The phrase from the centurion's statement can be translated "the Son of God" ("God's Son," NRSV) or "a son of God." Whether it is ironic or genuine is as unclear as whether the words are to be taken as reference to a divine figure ("Son of God") or a religious person ("a son of God"—or even "a son of a god"). "Surely" is no guarantee that the statement that follows is to be read at face value; it is used on only one other occasion in the Gospel (Mark 14:70). And in any case, the past tense ("this man *was . . .*") makes the statement less than a full-blown Christian confession.

The real issue is how one knows irony when one sees it. A good argument can be made that the statement of the centurion should be read with the statements of the other Romans in the story.[16] The soldiers mock Jesus as "king"; Pilate interrogates him as "King of the Jews"—an appropriate Roman version of the Jewish "Christ, the King of Israel"—and employs the designation as the charge against him. All the characters in the story use the titles—"Christ," "King of Israel," "Son of the Blessed," "Son (son) of God"—in derision. The usage indicates the distance between Jesus' apparent identity and what the titles stand for. There is nothing royal about Jesus, nothing to suggest he is Israel's expected deliverer and possible rival to Caesar's dominion. The so-called confession of the centurion, in this reading, is simply the last in the series of such statements, highlighting the impossibility of the claim, slamming the door of plausibility.

It is likewise clear that the truth of these epithets does not depend on the ability of the characters in the story to understand them. Readers are privileged. We are told from the outset that Jesus is the Son of God. We hear, with Jesus, God's declaration at his baptism and transfiguration that he is "my Son." We are privy to the exclamations of the demons who recognize Jesus as "the Holy One of God," "the Son of God," "the Son of the Most High God." The author makes available to us knowledge of biblical passages like Psalm 2 that link "Son" and "Anointed One." We know long before Jesus' trial that he is the Christ, the Son of the Blessed, the King of the Jews, God's Son. The tearing of the temple curtain, paralleling the tearing of the heavens at Jesus' baptism, is one of the events that seem accessible only to readers.

That the truth about Jesus is expressed through the titles used by his enemies makes possible the experience of irony: hearers understand the words differently from the way the characters in the story understand them.[17] The words are experienced differently from the way they are heard and intended at the story level.

The truth of the centurion's "confession" is thus not dependent upon his sincerity. What is at stake is an experience of reality. Is the world rendered by the story a place where words mean what they say, where people understand what they do, where God's will is accessible, clear, and distinct? Is the world after Jesus' death any more transparent to the reality and will of God than before? Answering such questions depends upon a reading of the whole narrative and in particular upon the ending. Given the ambiguity of the concluding verses in Mark 16, it would be difficult to sustain an interpretation that claims any sort of resolution of the tension occasioned by the mystery surrounding Jesus.

One of my students understood the issue well. "It isn't that I doubt your interpretation," he said. "What bothers me is that you have the ability to determine the meaning of the story by your tone of voice. By reading something ironically, you change everything. Pious people in my congregation will not be happy to learn that their interpretation of the story all these years has been wrong. They won't want to give up the idea that there was a convert there at the foot of the cross. You have the ability as reader to throw their world into confusion. I don't want to grant you that power, and I certainly don't want it for myself."

If the ability to undermine traditional interpretations is available through vocal inflections, the character of speakers and readers is suddenly thrust into the center of the whole interpretive enterprise, and one must ask who can be trusted. It is too simple to say God can be trusted. In the story there are many appointed to speak for God, and all of them are blind. Who speaks for God now? Who can be trusted to read the Bible in church? The experience of irony gives birth to a recognition that such questions cannot be answered with absolute confidence. A hermeneutic of suspicion is generated from an encounter with the Bible itself.

Contemporary church practice has apparently agreed with my student that people are not to be trusted with interpretation. Lay readers in congregations would never dare offer a striking reading of a passage from the Bible. Even pastors hesitate. Verses are omitted by lectionary committees from the appointed readings because they might raise anxieties or elicit anger when read aloud. The result, however, has been a tradition of bland, uninteresting, unengaging oral treatment of the Scriptures that undermines their ability to move and to shape imaginations. It also means traditional interpretations go unchallenged.

Theological Engagement

My colleague Patrick Keifert and I hosted a gathering of colleagues, Bible teachers, and theologians to consider the teaching of the Scriptures within theological seminaries. We chose to begin our weekend conversation with a Bible study. The passage was Mark 4:1-20. The ground rules were simply that we would spend an hour interpreting the passage, in this case a parable. The group listened as the passage was read and began a lively discussion that was just warming up as the hour ended.

The discussion was unlike those familiar from professional society meetings. The discussion began not with a particular feature of the parable or a specific methodological approach but with reactions to hearing the parable. "What I heard this time . . ." was the common refrain of initial comments. "I didn't hear Jesus' 'reprimand' of the disciples in 4:13 as harsh. I have always interpreted it as rebuking, but the reader offered a different interpretation, and now I'm not sure what I think." The first observation immediately raised questions about the actual process of reading and hearing, with some brief reflection on the sorts of rules that might govern the "performance." The notion that interpretation has to do with performance seldom arises in most academic discussions. A whole agenda for further discussion was generated: What is the role of the reader? What does the reader intend? What does a reading do to or for an audience? What is the relationship of "implied" to "real" audiences?

There was an interesting discussion of allegory as a legitimate method of interpretation. One, in fact, suggested that for his students who are "stuck" on the literal level, the use of the parable and its allegorical "explanation" in verses 13-20 is useful as an exercise in imaginative interpretation. The discussion was far from the historical preoccupation of the last half century in parable scholarship, for which allegory has been the enemy of interpretation.

Substantial issues surfaced early. It was perhaps not surprising that one of the theologians raised the issue of free will and election, albeit indirectly. "What strikes me is the freedom God gives to humans, allowing us to choose what kind of soil we will be." Most in the group had not experienced the same sense of possibility in the parable. The discussion, in fact, moved in the other direction, focusing on the passive character of the metaphor "soil." It makes little sense to say that soil is free to choose anything. Most in the group, in fact, were arrested by Jesus' statement about insiders and outsiders in verses 10-12, verses that are omitted from the lectionary and dismissed by most commentators in one way or another. One's place in the kingdom seems to depend upon Jesus, who reveals and conceals. The allusion to the famous verses from Isaiah 6 suggests that revelation and concealment are ultimately God's work.

What is significant is the way in which a theological agenda surfaced. It was not imposed but arose within a conversation initiated by a reading and hearing of the parable. The issue of seeing and not seeing raised the question of divine agency—and not only in the abstract. Before long, some who spoke earlier of free will noted, with sadness, the apparent obduracy of some relatives who simply could not (would not?) believe. Another spoke pointedly about a God who would leave some on the outside and suggested an insider might be tempted to join those outside. A few gave examples of students whose reading of the words actually "hardened their hearts."

Though issues about the history of the parable tradition were raised, the group seemed committed to a "canonical" reading of the parable, though we never discussed the matter. Questions about the place of the parable within the larger narrative setting were far more prominent than questions about the compositional history of the chapter. Perhaps one reason is that we began with a reading of the whole section, 4:1-20, and the group assumed what they heard was to be the focus of interpretation.

The discussion among the assembled "experts" followed the course of virtually every class discussion when the theological issue is voiced: the group did everything possible to rein in the passage. The "problem" to which our interpretive energies were directed was explicitly theological: the problem is a God who seems to have determined that some will succeed and some will not. This group was far more sophisticated than assemblies of students. We were able to appeal to the history of parable tradition and to theories of metaphor. We were aware of a range of interpretive strategies. Such sophistication, however, did not solve the "problem" of the passage. And when, like students, my colleagues spoke of their own experience of the parable or their experience of God, the same questions, uneasiness, and resentments surfaced.

Time ran out before we were able to ask what it would mean to say the parable is "true," but in a way it was implicit throughout much of the conversation. What if God is like this? What if this is how it is with the kingdom of God? The one who seemed most comfortable with the implications was a visitor raised in the Dutch Reformed Church for whom the doctrine of election is a central tenet of the faith.

The conversation took the course it did largely because we began with the experience of reading and hearing the narrative. Without the obvious prejudice of a study focusing on one topic or another, and without the insulation of academic and historical distance, interpretation became a grappling with the biblical material. Scholarly matters were not irrelevant, but they did not establish the agenda for the group. And in this particular instance, God questions did not need to be artificially imposed.

Reading, Interpretation, and Control

What is to control oral performance? Perhaps this is one way to think about interpretive method. It can help develop rules for oral performance. It is not enough to ask what a passage means; we must ask what it intends to do—or perhaps even more accurately, what we intend to do with it. While it may enlarge our horizons to ask about another speaker and another audience at a distant time and place, we are the ones who must give voice to the Scriptures; it is to our contemporaries that we must read. If we do not read critically, we will be moved and shaped by whatever traditions of interpretation have become fixed within the communities to which we belong; we will be captives to our own experience. If we must finally read in the company of others, however, we will be forced to make decisions (while scholarship may be more interested in multiplying options) and then determine what it will mean to be accountable for our reading. The task requires no less imagination and intellectual effort than more traditional historical conceptions of the interpretive task, but the focus is different.

I propose—and I am certainly not the first or the only one to make such a proposal—that images drawn from the realm of rhetoric will prove fruitful in orienting and focusing the discipline of interpretation.[18] Our vast scholarly apparatus with its accumulated wisdom should be enlisted in the task of assisting contemporary readers of the Bible in the actual oral/aural communities in which they must perform. Public reading is the beginning, not the end, of our engagement with the Bible. Conversation generated by reading the Scriptures will be the forum in which the Bible actually shapes a community, exercising its authority. The conversation will benefit from knowledge of the environment within which the biblical works were composed and the history of biblical interpretation. For the Scriptures to have a place in that conversation, however, they must be read in ways that take imaginations captive. It will make a difference if the Scriptures are read well in worship and if readers take seriously alternative ways of performing a text. Classes and small group Bible studies will proceed differently if interpretation works from and returns to oral reading of texts.

Teachers and preachers may find their lives more complicated if people actually begin to listen. Children may be frightened by the story of how Elisha cursed small boys who mocked him for being bald and two she-bears mauled forty-two of them (2 Kings 2:23-24). Enlightened readers will discover that Hosea's words which announce God's judgment of Israel in terms of humiliating a woman (Hosea 2) have a capacity to harm. And there will be disagreement if people are given the chance to respond to the "word event" when the Bible is read. For one thing, those who have traditionally been excluded from the critical community will have an opportunity to shape the group's experience of a Bible story as they speak about their own. Pastors and teachers not preoccupied with arriving immediately at the right answer may gain as many new insights into a passage from their contemporaries as from learned commentators.

Rhetorical models and strategies take seriously the power of language to move people. Such interest does not exclude meaning, referentiality, and particularity, but it recognizes that the goal of biblical language is to shape ways of living with God and with our fellows, to use Keck's words.

If we must use an image by which to understand our work, something that includes persuasion and conversation seems more suitable to the appropriate place of the Scriptures in the life of the church, a model that focuses attention on real "performers" and real hearers in the present. Oral/aural engagement will not dismiss concerns proper to the academy. If ancient words are to be heard in the present, they must be translated from critically constructed texts. Translation involves knowing something about a foreign language and the culture to which it belonged, as well as about a contemporary language and its culture into which the material is to be translated. Audiences must be prepared. There are words they need to know, Old Testament passages they must learn so that they will pick up allusions and echoes. Faulty prejudices must be exposed and fruitful ones suggested. Habits of reading and listening must be formed. The purpose of such study is not to obviate the need to read the Bible, but to make possible a richer and more productive engagement with it.

Reading the Bible is not the sum of pastoral activities. It is not the same as preaching, which must take a word and make it absolutely particular "for you." Biblical material must be brought to bear on the particular aspects of our lives. But for the Bible to exercise any power, it must be read and heard. We will have to live with the biblical works as companions, as Keck suggests. The shape of that engagement, however, ought to give pride of place to reading—public reading in which the Bible comes to life within a community. The strange silence of the Bible is due in large measure to the privatization of engagement, against which Smart wrote a remarkably fierce polemic:

> [I]n spite of what it may have meant as inspiration to countless individuals, it may have to be reckoned as a hindrance to the understanding of the Bible in the church. It has tended to make the Bible primarily a book for use in private devotions. But the Bible was not written to be used in that way and certainly not to be read in snippets of five or six verses each. No part of it . . . in its origin was intended for private consumption. It is a distinctively public book. The prophets brought their nation before God. . . . The psalms are the prayers and praises of the whole *community* of Israel. The Gospels are the *church's* remembrance of the words and events that called them into existence as a new people of God. . . . The Bible is marching orders for an army, not bedtime reading to help one sleep more soundly.[19]

His polemic could as well be directed against scholarly traditions for which a silent Bible has become the norm. It is at least possible that focusing scholarship on the performance of biblical works in public settings may breathe new life into our academic disciplines and engender conversations in which the Bible, no longer silent, can do what it promises.

3

A Disquieting Silence
The Matter of Mark's Ending

In this chapter from a book on the Gospel according to Mark, Juel argues forcefully for reckoning with the earliest known ending of Mark, where the women at Jesus' tomb flee in terror. That scene, which captivated Juel's imagination, becomes for him emblematic of our encounters with God through Mark and indeed through all of Scripture. Our interpretive efforts cannot conjure tidy closure out of the Bible's stories, for the message of the gospel is about a God who eludes humanity's attempts to make God predictable or controllable. If Bible reading brings us into an encounter with God, the tools of biblical interpretation cannot keep us safe in the process.

————

No point in a story is as significant for appreciation and interpretation as its ending. That is surely the case in Mark's Gospel. The abrupt and unsatisfying conclusion has not surprisingly spawned a massive secondary literature—most of recent vintage, however. Interest in the ending became possible only with the publication of editions that relegated verses 9-20 to the footnotes. Until the great Alexandrian Codices were known, few paid attention to the scattered references to a Gospel of Mark that lacked a proper conclusion. Further, only after a scholarly consensus had determined that Mark could no longer be read as Matthew's epitomizer could readers become fascinated—and troubled—by the mysterious anticlimax that forms the end of our Gospel: "So they went out and fled from the tomb, for terror and amazement had seized them; and they said nothing to anyone, for they were afraid" (Mark 16:8).

There are perhaps additional factors in the current fascination with the Markan ending. One is the willingness to read Mark as a narrative. When the text is broken down into component parts that are the focus of investigation, as among form critics, the strange conclusion can be explained more easily. The episode at the empty tomb may be read as an effort to explain why the story appeared so late in the tradition (the women never told anyone) or as an effort to put distance between the apostolic testimony and the resurrection from the empty tomb. Such explanations require detaching the verses from their narrative setting and proposing another, hypothetical *Sitz im Leben* in the context of which the snippet is to be understood. The verses sound rather different as the conclusion of a narrative. Any who have been present at one of David Rhoads' "presentations" of Mark can testify to the uneasiness in the audience when the last words are spoken—even in an audience of sophisticates who know in advance how the narrative will end.[1]

There is much ground to cover in any study of Mark's ending. Fortunately the whole field need not be replowed. Andrew Lincoln's fine piece in the *Journal of Biblical Literature* has made it unnecessary to review all of the research.[2] His analysis of current studies, his examination of words for "terror" and "amazement" in Mark, his brief review of evidence for ending a sentence with *gar*—such matters require little additional comment. I prefer to confine my study to the experience of the ending and to ask if criticism has any role at all to play in commending a particular experience of the Gospel's ending—and thus of the narrative as a whole.

While we might speak of a scholarly consensus regarding the ending of Mark, there is surely no consensus regarding its interpretation. In fact, there is still reluctance among interpreters to settle with 16:8 as the conclusion of the Gospel. That reluctance gives evidence of a feature of public imagination well analyzed by Frank Kermode in his *The Sense of an Ending:*[3] people do not tolerate unfinished stories easily. Consider the comment in the *Oxford Study Bible* (RSV):

> Nothing is certainly known either about how this Gospel originally ended or about the origin of vv. 9-20, which cannot have been part of the original text of Mark. . . . Though it is possible that the compiler(!) of the Gospel intended this abrupt ending, one can find hints that he intended to describe events after the resurrection.[4]

Such speculation is a clear refusal to read the work as it appears in the best-attested readings; it is very much of the same order as the endings tacked on by ancient copyists who could not tolerate a Gospel that ended with frightened women. Interpretation of the ending will necessarily involve scrutiny of our own needs as readers—in this case, suspicion about interpretations that cannot reckon with "for they were afraid" as a conclusion of a Gospel.

Perhaps it should be stated explicitly that the Gospel according to Mark that we are interpreting ends with 16:8. That is not the Gospel read by most generations of Christians. Modern text critics and editors believe there are good reasons to omit the "spurious" endings that for centuries constituted the conclusion of the church's Gospel. While it would be satisfying to describe our printed text as the original version of Mark's Gospel, greater modesty is advisable. The task of text critics is to establish the "best" text that can then be printed. Through judicious selections among the alternatives available in the manuscript tradition, scholars can establish a version of the Gospel for which the best arguments can be advanced.[5] The plausibility of text-critical arguments can be tested through a variety of means, both historical and literary. Interpretations that demonstrate coherence in a version of Mark ending with 16:8 add probability to arguments that deal with manuscripts of the Gospel. The reconstruction of an implied audience for whom such a narrative would be appropriate likewise adds plausibility. For example, the abrupt ending makes more sense if the Gospel is addressed to believers than if it were intended as missionary propaganda. Such an implied audience would have to be tested by interpretation of the remainder of the Gospel as well as by historical arguments: Could such an audience have existed in early Christianity as we know it? What setting and function for a narrative might we suggest within such a religious community? The point is that even decisions about what will be printed as the Bible will require arguments that proceed according to agreed-upon ground rules. For our purposes, it is enough to note that the majority of experts in the field of Gospel criticism believe there are good reasons to print as the Gospel according to Mark a version that ends with 16:8. Because that is the case, the format chosen for printing the Gospel ought to make it crystal clear to readers that Mark ends at 16:8. The use of paragraph headings like "longer ending" and "shorter ending," and the use of double brackets in both the Greek New Testament and in the NRSV, is an unfortunate compromise that is more confusing than helpful. One suspects that the use of critical symbols rather than using different size print for alternative versions of the Markan ending represents equivocation on the part of translation committees. The stubborn refusal of commentators to accept sound text-critical arguments in their interpretation of Mark and the continuing creation of hypothetical conclusions say more about commentators than about Mark.

Comments by Brevard Childs in his singular *The New Testament as Canon* bear at least some passing comment in this regard.[6] Childs argues that the alternative ending ought to be read as part of the canonical Mark. His concern arises in part from acknowledgment that the Mark known to most generations of Christians included verses after 16:8. Childs seeks a compromise interpretation. He argues that verses 9-20 should be read as the canonical reading of Mark because the verses employ bits and pieces from the remaining three Gospels. The verses, he believes, seek to prevent aberrant readings of Mark that might suggest undue differences from the other Gospels. There is no real problem with reading the verses as part of the canonical Mark because "the same theological point made by the original ending has been retained, but extended," namely the disciples' unbelief in the face of the resurrection.

Such an argument is interesting, but it largely misses the point. Endings are important more for what they do than for the ideas they include. Verse 8 does something radically different as an ending than does verse 20, something that shapes the whole experience of reading the Gospel. It is the whole impact of the canonical Mark that ought to be of interest to readers, not simply the ideas extracted from it. If we agree that the version of the Gospel in the manuscript tradition with the strongest claim to logical priority deserves to be printed in Bibles, it is this version—ending with verse 8—that will function as canon. It is the function of this ending that I wish to explore, with the help of Kermode.

The Experience of the Ending

An ending does things. It can achieve closure, pulling together loose threads from a story, or it can resist closure, refusing to answer burning questions posed in the course of the narrative. Kermode's analysis both in *The Sense of an Ending* and *The Genesis of Secrecy*[7] explores that experience of closure in narrative. His analysis of the wide range of interplay between reader and story necessarily involves attention to the expectations and needs of readers. We write and read stories, he insists, because we must. Stories, and the interpretation of stories, represent a way of dealing with a confusing and "unfollowable" world. His analysis does not seek to replace the reading of stories with something else but to prepare readers to be a more responsive and critical audience. As is the case with other art forms, the Gospel must be experienced; study prepares hearers to listen for themes, for invention, for irony and surprise.

Study is necessary because we are not obviously good readers. In a culture suspicious of words, students need to be coaxed to give them a try. Further, readers must develop a sense of expectancy, learning what to look for and where to find clues. Preparing readers for engaging a narrative with an image or a suggestion makes them susceptible to ideological and institutional biases, of course. Yet without such biases, communication would be impossible. There must be some rules of communication, some sense of what to expect. Kermode has no illusions about objective readings of narratives, but he does seek to prepare critical readers by alerting them to institutional biases. Given the importance of the Bible to the life of the church as well as to the academic community, it is hardly surprising that representatives of such institutions carefully protect their investments by regulating interpretation. We study to see more deeply and to overcome confusion and bewilderment in our reading. Study can, however, protect vested interests and permit personal satisfaction at the expense of what is read.

The ending of Mark's Gospel provides a particular challenge to interpreters. The reason is its failure to resolve the tensions in the story and to provide some sense of closure that seems appropriate to "good news about Jesus Christ." Taken at face value, the concluding verse constitutes a disappointing end: nothing comes of the whole enterprise because the women do not speak. Few interpreters will accept such a reading of the Gospel, of course. For the less sophisticated readers who are familiar with Matthew, Luke, and John, it is difficult even to hear Mark. Endings are automatically supplied, probably much like the familiar "longer ending" printed in the NRSV. Imagination does not even attend to the discord. The same is true of commentators—sensible Bible readers who insist that disappointment in the performance of the women is the result of misunderstanding. One senses a kind of desperation in the otherwise fine study of Schüssler Fiorenza who must at all costs find heroism in the women at the tomb.[8] A similar defensiveness seems to dominate those who argue that the *tromos* and *ekstasis* that take hold of the women at the conclusion of the story, and the fear that drives them to flee, are positive emotions.[9] At least at first reading, the failure of the women to spread the good news is hardly commendable, and the fear with which they are possessed is little different from the fear that plagues the disciples throughout the story. Our need to overcome this experience of disappointment is the primary motor that drives interpretation.

There may well be good reasons to read the ending as hopeful, but that hopeful reading cannot be purchased at the expense of Mark's narrative. I do not wish to belabor the point, but the history of the Markan ending in manuscript and commentary betrays an unwillingness or inability to take the disappointment seriously. It is as if there is an emotional barrier that must be broken through if the Gospel is to be heard.

In the midst of a discussion of Mark 16 in class, in which young interpreters were finding one reason after another for regarding the Gospel's ending as upbeat, one student raised her hand and said, "I read the ending over several times last evening in preparation for class. I thought about it—and I cried." There was something about that experience—an honesty, an ability to read with defenses down, a willingness to acknowledge disappointment—that changed the course of the class discussion.

One of Kermode's great contributions is a willingness to entertain the possibility that there are no satisfying endings—in Mark or in life. Intrigued by the tension between literary form and the formlessness of the world explored by such writers as Kafka, aware of the power of language and story to satisfy and to console, and of the deep human need for satisfaction and consolation, he is well suited as a critic to examine the experience of reading Mark's Gospel. He is particularly adept at unmasking fraudulent readings that refuse to take Mark's narrative seriously—readings that, more often than not, are proposed by representatives of institutions with considerable investment in interpretation (for example, the church or the learned community); his distaste for Jeremias' approach to the parables is particularly striking, and his critique effective.[10] His critical reflections suggest certain questions are central, and I would like to deal with them. Does the Gospel make sense in light of the ending, or is it nonsense? Are there ways to offer good reasons for one reading or another? And finally, do the troubling verses give reason to look forward to an ending that is inviting and hopeful?

As with many other students of Mark, I wish to focus on the last two verses. In his study, Lincoln characterizes the experience of verses 7 and 8 in terms of promise and failure.[11] Focusing on the response of the reader, I would speak rather of hope and disappointment. Much is invested in a reading of these two verses and their bearing on the argument that the Gospel seeks to make.

"As He Told You": The Argument for a Satisfying Ending

The astonished women do not find Jesus in the tomb, as they had expected. Instead, they encounter a young man dressed in a white robe. While several interpretations of this figure are possible, we are probably to think of a heavenly messenger. That is surely the way Matthew and Luke heard the term, and both eliminate any possible ambiguity with their embellishments.

The women are appropriately terrified. The herald offers customary assurance that they need not be alarmed. He points to the obvious: Jesus is no longer in the tomb. Hoping to achieve some sort of closure to Jesus' unpredictable career by anointing his body for burial, the women are stunned by one more surprise: Jesus cannot be confined by the tomb any more than by the hopes of his followers or the designs of his enemies. The grave clothes have been shed; Jesus is out of the tomb, on the loose.

Perhaps the most important feature of the herald's announcement is the closing: "Go, tell his disciples and Peter, that he is going ahead of you to Galilee; there you will see him, just as he told you" (Mark 16:7). "As he told you." The reminder takes on considerable significance when the verse is read within the context of the whole story. Jesus has, in fact, made such a promise. The little collection of prophecies recounted just prior to Jesus' arrest (14:28-30) include a scriptural reference to Zechariah ("I will strike the shepherd, and the sheep will be scattered;" cf. Zech 13:7), a detailed forecast of Peter's denial, and the promise that he will precede his disciples to Galilee after his resurrection.

The prophecy of Peter's denial is quite precise. The rhyming couplet (nicely captured in the KJV's "Before the cock crows twice, you will deny me thrice") is repeated by the narrator at the conclusion of Peter's trial: "Then Peter remembered that Jesus had said to him, 'Before the cock crows twice, you will deny me three times.' And he broke down and wept" (14:72). Jesus' prophecy is fulfilled to the letter. Even the detail about the second crowing of the cock is noted carefully (14:72). And while this unlikely scenario of Peter's collapse is being played out in the courtyard of the high priest's house, inside Jesus is being taunted to prophesy by the servants of those who have condemned him to death. Jesus' prophecies, we are reminded, do indeed come to pass, a detail that offers a glimpse into the deeper dimensions of the narrative Mark recounts.

"As he told you." The specific forecast of Jesus' resurrection in 14:28 is only one of many statements Jesus makes about what will happen. Three times Jesus formally predicts his death—and his resurrection (8:31; 9:31;

10:33)—predictions that are given the added force of necessity (*dei*, 8:31; 9:11). That "necessity" has to do with the will of God recorded in the Scriptures: "The stone that the builders rejected has become the cornerstone" (12:10, quoting Ps 118:22); "The Son of Man goes as it has been written of him" (14:21); "But let the scriptures be fulfilled" (14:49).

The collection of parables in chapter 4 offers figurative predictions of what lies beyond the boundaries of the narrative: planting, despite obstacles, will result in harvests; a tiny seed will produce a full-grown bush. "There is nothing hidden, except to be disclosed," Jesus promises (4:21-24). Jesus speaks to his disciples of the inevitable onset of birth pangs that precede the coming of the Son of Man with the clouds of heaven (13:8). He promises that the Gospel must be preached to all nations (13:10). James and John are told that they will indeed share in his cup and baptism (10:39). His numerous promises have important functions in the narrative. They foreshadow; they give to the story a sense of direction and purpose; they point to what lies beyond the story. Promises that are fulfilled provide a basis for confidence that others will be. His glimpses of what lies ahead create a momentum that drives readers beyond the ending into the period beyond the story. "There you will see him, just as he told you" (16:7). The narrative offers reason to believe that what Jesus promises will take place.

The announcement from the empty tomb that Jesus has been raised—as he said he would be—thus opens a gateway to the future. The disciples will surely see him. Whatever the obstacles, the harvest will come; the tiny seed will grow into a shrub large enough to provide nesting places for the birds; at the end of the birth pangs one can expect new life. There is reason to recount Jesus' story as good news because the reader can believe what Jesus "told you." That, at least, is one argument the narrative offers. There is someone to tell the story, itself an indication that it did not end with fearful women.

"They Said Nothing to Anyone": The Argument for an Unsatisfying Ending

Were Mark's Gospel to end with 16:7, there would be far less interest in chapter 16, and in Mark's Gospel. It does not. As readers, we have been led to expect something other than verse 8. When Jesus enjoins his bewildered disciples to say nothing about the events on the Mount of Transfiguration, he suggests a limit to their silence: "until after the Son of Man had risen from the dead" (9:9). That Peter, James, and John understand nothing of what Jesus is saying to them only heightens interest in what is to come. Expectations are planted in readers. There will be a time of openness, a time for disclosing and speaking (4:21-22). There is good reason to believe that Jesus' resurrection will mark the transition from one time to another. Yet, in the narrative world at least, that is not to be.

Neither the stirring words of the divine messenger nor the empty tomb succeed in making evangelists of the women who have come to do their duty to a corpse. Like the disciples (14:50) and the young man seized in the garden (14:52), they flee (the word *pheugo* appears also in 5:14 to describe the actions of the swineherds in the land of the Gerasenes, and in Jesus' warnings in 13:14). The reason, we are told, is that "trembling and ecstasy held them fast." They say nothing to anyone—they were afraid, you see (Kermode's paraphrase). The terrible irony is that now is the time to speak. The tomb is empty; the crucified King is alive, vindicated by God, as he said he would be. What is hidden may now come to light (4:21-22); the disciples can tell secret things they were commanded to withhold now that Jesus has risen from the dead (9:9). The faithful women have the opportunity to do what the men could not. And they fail. They flee, just as the men—because they are afraid.

Arguments that the trembling, ecstasy, and fear are positive terms, appropriate to the presence of the divine, seem akin to Matthew's reading of Mark: "So they left the tomb quickly with fear and great joy, and ran to tell his disciples" (Matt 28:8). Slight changes in wording yield a very different sense; "They left quickly with fear and great joy" is worlds away from "They fled . . . for they were afraid." Their flight and their inability to do as they were commanded remains.

Insisting that the women told no one "for the present" has little support in the narrative. The story has offered no reason to place confidence in any insiders. While the women at least do their duty, like the disciples of John the Baptist did when they claimed his body and laid it in a tomb (6:29), they do not anticipate a miracle. They come fully expecting to find a corpse. Auerbach's analysis of Peter's performance seems an appropriate reading of the women's performance as well: they come closer to genuine greatness than the other disciples, only to fall further.[12] Even in the face of an empty tomb and testimony to Jesus' resurrection, the women cannot believe in such a way as to perform the most basic task of disciples: testimony. They tell no one the good news. They flee, and we are left to imagine what became of them, as we are left to imagine the fate of Judas, and the naked young man, and Peter, and the Twelve.

If Mark argues that there is reason to believe the gospel will be preached to the nations, the narrative simultaneously undercuts any confidence in the performance of characters without whom the whole enterprise seems lost.

Mark's Gospel ends with both hope and disappointment. The relationship between the last two verses embodies the critical tension in the story between blindness and insight, concealment and openness, silence and proclamation. The tension is not resolved. Why is this so? To what end does the tension lead? It is to that question we now turn, with the help of Kermode.

Doors

Kermode's study of endings is driven by a conviction that stories are essential to life as a way of making sense of an unfollowable world. His fascination with Kafka and other existentialist writers arises from the perceived tension between reality and form. Human beings create order and form, so the argument goes, as a necessary response to the formlessness and meaninglessness of the world. To make that argument, to be sure, writers like Kafka must employ traditional forms that purport to represent reality—narrative forms that feature genuine endings—but they do so in such fashion as to create doubts about our ability to make contact with some fundamental order. Kermode senses that there is something hollow, even untruthful, about imitations of a coherent and purposeful reality, however noble the motivations of artists and however necessary their fictions to our sense of well-being. Art imposes order on what is beyond our ordering; it attempts to grasp what is beyond our reach. While one can imagine some ultimate plan or design, it remains out there, unfollowable. Art can achieve meaning, therefore, only at the expense of truth.

Art is most interesting, therefore, for what it tells us about ourselves. It arises from our need for order, a need that seems basic to the species. In analyzing stories, Kermode entertains, with structuralists, the possibility that basic paradigms underlie all narrative:

> Now presumably it is true, in spite of all possible cultural and historical variations, that the paradigm will correspond, the more fully as one approaches a condition of absolute simplicity, to some basic human "set," biological or psychological. Right down at the root, they must correspond to a basic human need, they must make sense, give comfort.[13]

If that is so, the closing verses of the Gospel are all the more intriguing, for the initial experience of the ending suggests that it does not fit the paradigm. The conclusion does little to offer a sense of an ending without which the story makes no sense.

> Mark's book began with a trumpet call: "This is the beginning of the gospel of Jesus Christ, the Son of God" (1:1). It ends with this faint whisper of timid women. There are, as I say, ways of ending narratives that are not manifest and simple devices of closure, not the distribution of rewards, punishments, hands in marriage, of whatever satisfies our simpler intuitions of completeness. But this one seems at first sight wholly counterintuitive, as it must have to the man who added the twelve verses we now have at the end.[14]

Part of the difficulty in conversing with Kermode is that he offers no sustained interpretation of Mark, because that is not his purpose. He offers only hints. He seems willing to entertain the possibility that the ending does "make sense," although such an interpretation is not obvious. He seems most disposed to the imaginative work of people like Austin Farrer, whose creative exploration of literary patterns places him outside the usual guild of Markan scholars.[15] Offering his interpretation of the Markan ending would accomplish little, however, because his major concern is to bring naive readers face to face with the genuinely enigmatic character of Mark: the Gospel generates secrecy, not just secrets. While it holds out the prospect that readers can become insiders, the possibility turns out to be illusory. Placed in this hermeneutical bind, interpreters with institutional allegiances and an investment in coherence and meaning are forced to employ cunning and violence to extract what they need from the text. The experience of disappointment must at all costs be overcome.[16]

Kermode is by no means exempt from such institutional allegiances, of course, and he is capable of employing cunning and violence to achieve his own ends, as he would readily admit. Few would accuse him of violence, but we should not fail to appreciate the single most remarkable act of cunning in his approach to Mark: the selection of Kafka's parable as a controlling image. Here is Kermode's version of the parable:

> A man comes and begs for admittance to the Law, but is kept out by a doorkeeper, the first of a long succession of doorkeepers, of aspect even more terrible, who will keep the man out should the first one fail to do so. The man, who had assumed that the Law was open to all, is surprised to discover the existence of this arrangement. But he waits outside the door, sitting year after year on his stool, and conversing with the doorkeeper, whom he bribes, though without success.

Eventually, when he is old and near death, the man observes an immortal radiance streaming from the door. As he dies, he asks the doorkeeper how it is that he alone has come to this entrance to seek admittance to the Law. The answer is, "This door was intended only for you. Now I am going to shut it." The outsider, though someone had "intended" to let him in, or anyway provided a door for him, remained outside.[17]

The parable, introduced in chapter 2, moves in and out of the study and provides Kermode with the dramatic conclusion to his book:

This is the way we satisfy ourselves with explanations of the unfollowable world—as if it were a structured narrative, of which more might always be said by trained readers of it, by insiders. World and book, it may be, are hopelessly plural, endlessly disappointing; we stand alone before them, aware of their arbitrariness and impenetrability, knowing that they may be narratives only because of our impudent intervention, and susceptible of interpretation only by our hermetic tricks. Hot for secrets, our only conversation may be with guardians who know less and see less than we can; and our sole hope and pleasure is in the perception of a momentary radiance, before the door of disappointment is finally shut on us.[18]

The image gives to Kermode's work a genuine ending; it makes sense of his study and his passion to explore the whole matter of secrecy. Mark, Kermode argues, has no ending in the sense that it can be grasped by any particular reading. The enigmatic conclusion becomes symptomatic of a deeper hermeneutical problem: there can be no ending. Mark will continue to generate new readings. Readings will always be particular—and limited. If ultimate reality is inaccessible to us, as Kafka's parable argues, if the most we can hope for is a glimpse at best, if we are and always will be outsiders, then the lesson for scriptural interpreters seems to be that they would do best to remain satisfied with questions of meaning, never to claim too much for an interpretation, and to bracket out questions of truth from interpretation.

In an important sense, this is quite different from the argument made by Mark's narrative. Consider the differences between Mark's Gospel and Kafka's parable. As in Kafka's work, Mark's narrative generates expectancy. Jesus' parables speak of seed time and harvest, of small seeds and large shrubs. Apparently insignificant beginnings drive toward magnificent conclusions, despite obstacles that stand in the way. Jesus daringly labels the tribulations that lie ahead birth pangs; creation groans in anticipation of what will come. He promises his resurrection and his return with the clouds, when he will gather his elect from the four winds. As in Kafka's parable, there is also disappointment. The world into which the reader is invited is one in which people fail. Longed-for resolutions do not occur. Loose ends are not tied up. It is as Jesus says: "the end is still to come" (13:7).

The difference between Mark's story and Kafka's has to do with closure. There is genuine closure in Kafka's parable. The door is shut as the old man dies, and with it the possibility of insight. There is no more waiting. The message is clear: we have been permanently shut out. Meaningfulness, such as it exists, is accessible to us only as we are able to supply it. We remain outside the door, forever.

Mark's Gospel forbids precisely that closure. There is no stone at the mouth of the tomb. Jesus is out, on the loose, on the same side of the door as the women and the readers. The story cannot contain the promises. Its massive investment in the reliability of Jesus' words becomes a down payment on a genuine future. Caught up in the narrative's momentum, the last words of the messenger at the tomb impel the reader beyond the confines of the narrative: "There you will see him, as he told you" (16:7). There will be enlightenment and speaking; the disciples will somehow play the role for which they have been chosen.

The door is a powerful image. It can open to possibilities or it can bar entrance. It is precisely the possibility of opening that makes the conclusion of Kafka's parable—the shutting door—so devastating. Kermode has not attended to such imagery in Mark. The doors in Mark's Gospel are emphatically open: the curtain of the temple is rent asunder (as is the curtain of the heavens at Jesus' baptism) and the stone is rolled back from the tomb. There is surely disappointment as the women flee, dashing hopes that at least one group of followers will prove faithful. But Jesus is out of the tomb; God is no longer safely behind the curtain. To hear in Mark's elusive ending the strains of Handel's "Hallelujah Chorus" would require drowning out the music being performed. But to insist that the discordant ending offers no promise of resolution whatever is to do equal violence to the story. Jesus has promised an end. That end is not yet, but the story gives good reasons to remain hopeful even in the face of disappointment. The possibilities of eventual enlightenment for the reader remain in the hands of the divine actor who will not be shut in—or out.

Kermode's analysis clearly exposes the human need for closure, structure, and control. One can argue theologically from the same premises that interpretation can become a way of defending ourselves against truths that make a claim on us. The argument of Kafka's parables is that whatever truth exists is inaccessible to us—except the truth that we are alone in the face of the impenetrable. Mark's Gospel—and, we might add, the whole Christian tradition—argues that our lack of enlightenment and bondage arise from attempts to box God in or out of experience. All such attempts come to grief in the resurrection of Jesus. He cannot be confined by the tomb or limited by death. In Jesus' ministry, God tears away barriers that afforded protection in the past. God cannot be kept at arm's length. Such a possibility that light dawns even on those who inhabit the realm of darkness is disquieting; it means there is no refuge for the cynical any more than for the naive.

The possibility that the future is open may send interpreters scurrying to the ramparts, fearful for their lives. There is reason for sobriety. The Gospel offers little promise that we have control of our destiny. Interpretation only makes matters worse. The deeper into the narrative we delve, the less control we are promised. If the unresolved ending offers promise, it is surely not because we are encouraged to believe that we can do better than the disciples or the women. We do not "have" Jesus even at the end of the story, and there is no guarantee that we can wrest a promise from him or lock him safely away by hermeneutical tricks. Here Kermode is surely correct. But perhaps that is just where the promise resides. "There you will see him, as he told you." Jesus has promised an encounter with him against which there is no assured defense. God will be put off neither by our failures, or infidelity, nor by our most sophisticated interpretive schemes. And if this "good news about Jesus Christ" is God's work within the intimate realm of human speech, there is reason to hope that our defenses will finally prove insufficient and that we will not have the last word. The history of the Markan ending is perhaps ample testimony that this "gospel" will not be easily dismissed.

One's choice of images by which to open readers to a narrative can be a matter of cunning and violence. A choice is necessary nevertheless, and I believe there are good reasons for choosing an image other than the closed door in Kafka's parable. Given Kermode's fascination with John's Apocalypse, I would suggest this one:

> These are the words of the holy one, the true one,
> who has the key of David,
> who opens and no one will shut,
>   who shuts and no one opens: . . .
> Look, I have set before you an open door, which no one is able to shut.
>   (Rev 3:7-8)

4

Interpretation for Christian Ministry

coauthored with Richard Nysse

This article reflects on how academic study of the Bible has largely failed to help those in Christian ministry—and congregations—come to terms with what the Bible is good for. Attention to what the Bible does, as a means of bearing witness to a living God, drives us to focus on the experience of reading the Scriptures as an experience of encountering God.

————

As the title of this essay suggests, interpretation is always for something; it serves some end.[1] The particular "end" in view here is "Christian ministry." That end presumes certain commitments and prejudgments. We read the Scriptures because they are to serve as "the norm in matters of faith and practice." The rather straightforward statement invites Bible readers into a conversation that begins with a prejudgment: the Scriptures are to be accorded a privileged status in our reflection about God and what it means to be children of God. The prejudgment likewise suggests that the Scriptures are for us; they have to do with our faith and our practice. This is not to deny that biblical works were written at another time and place, for other audiences as well; it does not specify precisely in what sense they will serve as "normative"; and the particular bias does not deny that the Bible may be good for other things, like writing histories of antiquity or providing data for Greek and Hebrew grammarians. Christians read the Bible, however, because we are convinced that in our engagement with it we encounter the living God.

Such convictions help to define what will count as "critical" scholarship and adequate readings. Those who choose to define "critical" as "reading from an alien perspective" begin with different prejudgments. Their vantage point is not necessarily more sophisticated or "critical." It is by no means apparent, further, that those who limit the work of biblical scholarship to historical descriptions of ancient faith communities produce more convincing commentaries than those interested in how God works through gospel narratives in the present to awaken and sustain faith or to shape a Christian imagination. An important aspect of our work as interpreters should be to find ways of discussing those prejudgments and to determine what will count as reasons for or against such commitments.[2] That such conversations rarely occur in public settings, like professional society meetings, only reflects a cultural bias that religious beliefs are essentially private in character.

We suggest that in our present setting, what is required of us is a reconceiving of the vocation of exegete. The questions are not new, and there are many who have found a personal way through the hermeneutical labyrinth, but theological educators have not succeeded in identifying a strategy for shaping interpreters who will in turn engage the Christian community in a reading and hearing of the Scriptures that will renew and sustain the church. It is to the possibility of such a strategy that we devote our attention.

Biblical Authority

When discussions of scriptural authority can still elicit strong emotions, even dividing churches, it is clear that a crisis exists. That such discussions are needed is itself a mark of the problem. The Bible does not exercise much influence in the church. People do not read it. Even students who have been raised within the bosom of the church and who enter theological seminaries to become pastors are largely unfamiliar with biblical stories. That is all the more problematic given the enormous burgeoning of biblical scholarship in the last century. There are thousands of Bible courses offered at colleges and universities around the country taught by people who have devoted their lives to study of the Scriptures. Pastors educated in the last decades, whose education has included study of the biblical languages as well as current methods of interpretation, have not succeeded in bringing the Bible to life in their congregations.

There are reasons why biblical scholarship has not produced more fruit within churches. For much of this century—and particularly in

North America—the exegetes of the church have settled for adapting to one degree or another a methodology generated and shaped by the interests of the secular academy. Objective, value-free, institutionally independent scholarship was the ideal. Much was achieved during this era; we know vastly more about the world in which the Bible emerged. In recent decades, however, many who have no ostensible religious interests have questioned whether secular scholarship has been or could ever be objective, value-free, and institutionally independent. In an effort to avoid being parochial or even sectarian, historical-critical methodologies have contributed, wittingly or not, to a distancing of the Bible from many of its readers.

Such criticism, however, necessitates neither a return to some golden precritical age nor a repudiation of the knowledge accrued through the application of the historical-critical methods in which we have been trained. We must rather reimagine the interpretative task: what do we think we are doing when we interpret Scripture, and what is interpretation good for, particularly in the practice of Christian ministry?

The reimagination of interpretation for Christian ministry requires a return to basic questions, some of which will seem mundane. For example, what do we think the Bible is? As Christians, we accord the Scriptures a privileged status. But how shall that status be conceived? Claims about the Bible ought to respect "the facts." We are obliged to pay attention to the particularities of the Scriptures and to ensure that the claims we make are for the writings actually before us and not for Scriptures or classics in general.

What the Bible Is

What is the Bible? If we understand this question to be a question of genre, obviously Scripture exhibits a wide variety: letters, narratives, songs, proverbs, visions, etc. Interpretation must pay attention to the particular forms in which biblical works are cast. Categories like "story" or "preaching" may be appropriate for some biblical material but certainly not for all.

Taken more broadly, we could answer that Scripture is the testimony of and witness to the faith of ancient Israel and the early Christian community. The category is useful for several reasons. It serves notice that the Bible is "interested" literature. It was produced by people with a case to make and particular views about God and the world—real people who spoke languages different from our own, who wrote out of their own experience in situations where testimony was required. The literature was written for people who were expected to share that vision. But here is where the problem begins. For whom is the testimony? We read the Scriptures because we believe they can speak to us—but they cannot do so at the expense of their particularity. It is clear that already by the second century the particularity of Paul's letters were a problem for those who wanted to read them as Scripture. Are we not simply reading someone else's mail?

It is not difficult to become preoccupied with the historical particularities. Who actually wrote this material and under what circumstances? When and where were these works produced, and how were they used by the first recipients? The questions are fascinating enough to sustain a whole industry. But if interpretation must await answers to such questions, we may never get beyond historical study (in many cases, historical speculation). And if the primary mode of reading the Scriptures is to determine what they meant for another audience at another time and place, it is not difficult to understand why there are problems retrieving the biblical message. We are left with "the spent voice of the text," with the leftovers.

Viewing the Scriptures as "testimony" likewise raises truth questions. In what sense is the witness true and reliable? One approach has been to understand the importance of the testimony as the realities to which it points—the "facts." Did the exodus really take place? Which of Jesus' sayings can we regard as "authentic"? Others have chosen to focus on the character of the biblical writers—demonstrating that if we cannot prove they were "apostolic," we may at least acknowledge their courage and their religious genius, which makes their testimony reliable. It is perhaps worth noting how seldom truth questions are posed within biblical scholarship and how uneasy they make us.

There are still many within Christian churches who are convinced that the only way to protect the authority of the Bible is to hold to a theory of inspiration that sidesteps or minimizes the role of humans in the production of Scripture. Few interpreters will speak of direct dictation by God, but there is no lack of formulations about the divine qualities of Scripture, formulations that leave little room for any meaningful human involvement in its production. Scripture is seen as unique, without parallel in one characteristic or another. Divine production is seen as the guarantor of veracity. Scripture is seen not as Israel's testimony, but as God's.[3]

However tempting such theories may be, they will not solve the problem of the Bible's lack of authority in the culture. The Bible spoken about does not in fact exist; every copy in use reflects textual and/or translational decisions that are under dispute or are even in error. Even the production of the Bible is embodied in human processes. Unless our notion of inspiration includes the work of text critics and translators, it is a theory that has nothing to do with the Bible we read. Greater clarity and truthfulness on the part of biblical scholars and pastors about the realities of textual criticism and translation would be salutary. Many people simply do not know the facts.

What the Bible Does

Beginning with a focus on what the Bible is does not automatically lead to greater appreciation of its authority. More promising, we would suggest, is to begin with a focus on what the Bible does—or ought to do. While not ignoring the particularity of the biblical writings, we propose taking more seriously their linguistic character. Language is important not first of all for what it points to but for what it does.[4] The current fascination with narrative takes its cue from the observation that stories change people. They enliven and inspire; they also frighten. A pastor once observed that he had read the Bible from beginning to end when he was fifteen. "I was terrified," he confessed. "What if God is really like that?" The rest of his education served to domesticate God—to show there is nothing to be frightened of— and to demonstrate, in fact, that the Bible can be read without ever thinking about God. "My education has succeeded in quieting my fears," he observed, "but now I have to work hard just to find the Bible interesting."

We propose that the discipline of biblical studies focus on the experience of reading. Such a view is not antihistorical. It takes seriously, however, the function of psalms and narratives and letters as linguistic events. They were written to be performed; their goal was to move people to praise or to action, to shape the way they understood their place in the world so as to give confidence or offer judgment. Form critics have been interested in such matters for decades. Practitioners of literary approaches, particularly those dealing with narratives, have enriched the experience of reading, narrowing the gulf between biblical stories and contemporary audiences.

We would add that our focus should be explicitly theological: we read the Bible because it has to do with God. Such a statement must be made in the face of scholarly traditions in which God is neither object nor subject. We study Scripture because we are convinced that God was at work in ancient settings, creating and sustaining communities of faith. Scripture witnesses to this generative work of God and is itself a product of that generative work of God. God has continued to create, renew, and sustain communities of faith. These communities have consistently testified that the study of Scripture has been a means for the spirit of God to generate their own existence, renewal, and sustenance. Their own writings were understood to be commentary on Scripture, not a replacement; for, in their experience, Scripture had an effect on them which could only be described as the work of the living God. The Reformation is only one of the more self-conscious moments in that history of interpretation. Locating ourselves within those faith traditions, we ourselves undertake our interpretive work with the confidence that God continues to create, renew, and sustain communities of faith. And we are convinced that Scripture is a fundamental means employed by the spirit of God to accomplish this work.

Historical circumstance and the history of interpretation will have a decisive shaping effect on the present hearing, but the focus of scholarship that serves the mission of the church ought to be on the experience of reading the Bible in the present—and on shaping a community of competent readers who are open to the working of God.

Our conviction that in the engagement with the Scriptures we encounter God is a prejudice that ought to shape our own reading. It will have to be tested in practice. Is it the case that we hear anything but our own voices or experience anything but what is already inside us? We cannot answer such questions in advance; the proof will come in the interpretive conversation. We must recognize, however, how easily we can guarantee that such questions will never be posed. The experience of scholarship suggests that we can define as "critical" and responsible only those studies that insure the "God question" will never be posed or that we can so distance readers as to insure they will hear the message of the Bible as intended only for other people at another time and place. We are suggesting that there are likewise ways to set up the interpretive conversation in such a way as to maximize the possibility that readers will be caught up in the biblical story. Beginning with and returning to the actual experience of reading and hearing the Bible is one aspect of that strategy. And insisting upon asking questions about God is a crucial aspect of that strategy.

What the Bible Is Good For

If we focus on the actual experience of reading and hearing the Bible, we will soon recognize that there are numerous possibilities for what people see and hear. When turned loose on the Bible, "unenlightened" readers come up with amazing suggestions. Those suggestions are not always wrong or wrongheaded. Some of the most liberating and promising interpretive comments have been made by readers whose horizon has not been totally determined by scholarly traditions. Yet there are good reasons to attend critically to the kinds of discussions the Bible engenders; they reveal how expectations have been shaped, what people think of the Bible, and what questions they bring. Preparing an audience of competent hearers means engaging those expectations and reshaping them.

In observing students and the sorts of discussions that occur in congregations, we would suggest the following categories as a way of organizing expectations.

1. Moral Authority

In many Christian congregations today, the Bible is viewed as a source of moral authority. That people even outside the church community should have such a view is hardly surprising. Sunday school materials have for decades taught young children that the Bible is full of stories that tell us what we ought to do, from the very first tales of Adam and Eve to stories about Samson's haircut and Jacob's cheating and King David's adultery. Children learn the Ten Commandments and the Golden Rule.

Little wonder, then, that at a time of great social upheaval people should turn to the Bible in hopes of finding some stability in a moral order. In many congregations these days, talk about biblical authority is directly related to concerns about homosexuality and abortion.

Is the Bible good for moral conversation? Judging from current practice, it does not build a community of moral conversation. Some people use historical arguments to disqualify potential moral examples, while others attack such historical approaches as marks of faithless reading. If the Bible is good for shaping a community of discourse, we will have to learn how that is to occur. A major agenda item for theological educators must be helping pastors learn how to make use of the Scriptures in moral deliberation—which presumes that the learned community is able to come to some agreements about practices that edify.

It is appropriate to ask in what sense God has a place in this process. How is God at work in the building of a community of moral discourse?

2. Pieties or Spirituality

While related to a moral reading of Scriptures, the interest here is not in precise directives as much as in lifestyle. "Lifestyle" might include a rather fully delineated piety or a less clearly defined "spirituality," by which people often mean living with a clearer sense of God's presence.

3. Sound Doctrine

There are still many for whom the Bible is important as a source of doctrine. This is true for academics as well, who still find such categories as "Christology" and "soteriology" useful as a way of organizing biblical teaching. For some believers, doctrine can provide a kind of systematic stability. Some of the great debates within Christian communities have to do with the kinds of doctrinal statements that Scripture authorizes.

4. Ulterior Motives

Bible readers, particularly the educated, have been convinced by particular ideologies of reading that stories are about more than they claim. One might suggest, for example, that biblical works are actually windows into the unconscious. The popularity of *The Last Temptation of Christ* indicates how convincing psychological reductionism still is in our culture. Life has to do largely with the interior, so the argument goes. What is important is that we understand our feelings and those of others. Jesus, in particular, still fascinates those whose interests are psychological. Whole programs of Bible study have been developed with an explicitly therapeutic, psychological agenda.

The Bible is about other things as well. It is enlisted (as well as criticized) by those who insist that the most significant realities in our society are political. The Bible is read to shed light on class struggles, and it is studied as the product of such struggles. Liberation theologians are among those who read the Bible with such interests and expectations. Phrases like "God's preferential option for the poor" serve as thematic summaries for readings of the gospels.

Feminists insist rightly that the Bible is about gender matters. Their questions have opened a whole horizon of study within which interpreters are invited to ask not only what the Bible explicitly teaches about male and female relations but what the various narratives and letters imply about writers, audiences, and their symbolic universes.

5. Encounter with the Living God

Far less common is the experience of reading the Bible and finding oneself confronted by the reality of God. There are reasons why this experience is uncommon. Perhaps the most obvious is the insulation provided by traditions of interpretation, particularly in academic settings. The "God question" is seldom posed even in the sense of asking what texts reveal about the God concept of ancient peoples. Distancing methodologies succeed in protecting interpreters and their audiences from experiences that earlier generations of believers found common.

There are the exceptional cases. The hard words in Mark 4:10-12 about Jesus' reasons for telling parables ("in order that they may not see") strike most readers as scandalous. There is hardly a commentator whose anxiety about the words is not apparent in the attempt to dismiss the verses as "Mark's parable theory" or to insist that they represent a mistranslation of something more palatable. In a class, a student reacted differently. She wrote, through clenched teeth, "I will not believe in a God who conceals reality from some." While not a naive Bible reader, her knowledge could not insulate her from the theological offense that has led to some of the most profound reflection within the history of the Christian community, from Augustine to Luther to Calvin. Where could she be directed for some assistance in her wrestling that was surely a struggle with God? There is hardly a commentator who is any help. Commentaries are to help understand the words by providing a context. The student's problem was that she understood the words perfectly—and could not abide them.

This was a precious moment in class and an important test for professor and students. The question raised the ante in the interpretive game, suggesting that what is at stake is nothing less than life and death. How does one deal with a God who claims the right to conceal—and to reveal? By denying the right? By formulating a more palatable concept of God? By dismissing the verse as a mistake, due to unthinking redaction? At the very least, the question demanded an accounting from the evangelist. Does the story offer any possibility that such a message can be heard as good news? That the words come from Isaiah offers further possibility for discovery. Perhaps this notion of a God who conceals and reveals is more than a Markan aberration; perhaps it is in fact "biblical." If so, the question provides an occasion for doing biblical theology—and perhaps even for speaking a promising word to a very specific someone who is in the present moment wrestling with God.

That student's struggle, which is surely not over, has suggested a strategy for interpreting Isaiah and Mark. Rather than using interpretive method as a way of distancing a group of hearers from an encounter with the text, a teacher may head off any such escape and gently allow for the possibility of an encounter with God. The Bible and the Christian tradition suggest that such an encounter will be life-giving. That is worth testing.

Those familiar with the history of hermeneutics, particularly with hermeneutical theories in the late Middle Ages, will detect many similarities between the sorts of expectations common among Bible readers today and the four-fold structure (literal, allegorical, anagogical, and tropological). Most of the categories we have suggested above would fall under the "tropological"; the Bible is important for what it has to say about how we are to live. The last category—reading the Bible to experience the presence of God—does not fit easily into the ancient categories. Pursuing this experience should lead to a distinctive notion of what the Bible is good for and may engender a distinctive sort of preaching.[5] Such matters must be explored on another occasion, however. Here we want only to suggest that the whole matter of interpretation—understanding what expectations are appropriate and what the Bible is good for—deserves study by biblical scholars as well as systematic theologians. The conversations that occur in each of the areas indicate how much work needs to be done if we privilege the Scriptures, if we focus on the actual experience of reading, and if we insist that God and the work of God be explicit topics in all discussions.

Interpretation for Christian Ministry

What shall we say then? The literature in the biblical field is vast and growing. No one can read more than a portion of it. Reflection on interpretation—the field of hermeneutics—is daunting itself, and much of the literature requires an initiation into another language. And if the actual experience of reading and hearing is to be the focus of scholarship, careful study of what actually occurs at the level of performance in congregations is warranted as well. One cannot do everything. Choices are necessary for seminaries and graduate schools.

There are graduate programs where the Bible will continue to be used to shape a community of interpreters interested in what it meant for someone else, at another time and place. Such study is not without merit. The Scriptures are written in another language; they were composed in particular settings. Jeremiah's oracles were delivered at crucial points in the history of Judah; they were collected by those who witnessed subsequent events and read his prophecies in light of what actually came about. Paul wrote letters to the church at Corinth on at least two occasions. Someone collected Paul's letters after his death and "published" them as a unit. Anyone interested in reading the Bible ought to be interested in all these settings, to the degree they are recoverable.

Yet the major issue still remains: Jews and Christians read the Scriptures because they believe God still speaks through them. The kinds of interpretive questions generated by such convictions will not arise in graduate programs that exclude explicitly theological questions and concentrate on historical work. The intellectual work required of those whose interpretation is in service to the ministry of the church is no less strenuous, but the agenda must be formulated differently. And one of the major tasks facing graduate programs at church institutions is to determine what ought to be on that agenda.

We wish to offer some modest suggestions, mostly by way of summary.

1. More attention must be paid to the actual experience of reading and interpreting the Scriptures as addressed to the present. This would suggest that no clear line ought to separate what occurs at the level of congregational involvement with the Bible and academic study. The task of church scholarship should be to determine what ways of study are most helpful in creating an audience for the Scriptures, with the goal of shaping actual practice at the level of congregations and small groups.

In this regard, we expect that literary approaches to the Bible will take precedence over the more historical—not because they provide a way of avoiding sensitive historical questions but because they facilitate engagement with the literature.

As a corollary, we would suggest that while many students have been convinced that sound method is a way of avoiding mistakes, in most cases the greatest danger is not wrong answers as much as lack of engagement. For fear of fundamentalists who may control the discussions, many pastors seek to determine in advance how studies of the Bible will come out. One cannot—and ought not—control the actual experience of engagement with the Bible. There is no sure way to predict or to control the movements of the Spirit; and where people are encouraged to try out their own ideas in a group, there will always be pleasant surprises. Expectations can be shaped and guidelines developed for what counts as a reasonable interpretation; this is the proper sphere for consideration of method. Success in leading Bible studies will depend upon the ability to develop and free the imagination, which remains crucial for experiencing new ideas and realities beyond one's experience.

2. The agenda must be explicitly theological. A critical question is how we imagine God to be involved in the process of reading and interpreting the Scriptures. The practical atheism of the culture is very much in evidence. Scholars are only now discovering how little attention has been paid in New Testament studies to God as a character (or an implied character), and much of contemporary scholarship rules out consideration of the "living God" whom the Scriptures and the Christian tradition commend to present readers.⁶ Interpreting the Bible for Christian ministry cannot avoid an engagement with the theological tradition of the church. The task cries out for cooperation with colleagues in history, worship, and systematic theology as well as those who focus on pastoral practice at the congregational level.

3. A new assessment of the role of historical study is required. To put the question simply, we must ask, what is history good for? Historical study has provided a means to expand the horizons of interpreters who are bound by their own experience. That was important when dogmaticians threatened to dominate the reading of the Bible and to make of it a task for theologians only. Historical criticism provided a means of critiquing dogma and providing access to another world of meaning. It is still important for readers whose world is limited by their own culture and their own experience.

Yet historical approaches have come to dominate the scholarly imagination. One reason is perhaps that they have provided an effective means of keeping the Bible at a safe distance in sensitive discussions. This is perhaps most obvious in the various ecclesial studies of sexuality, in which the expected move is to locate statements about sexuality in a particular historical and cultural context in the past—only to dismiss them as pre-scientific or as focused on a specific problem unlike our own. Keeping the Bible out of the hands of the "crazies" is on the agenda of most who have had theological training. But such defensive reading has often succeeded in creating chasms between reader and text that cannot easily be bridged. It is for this reason that we grant literary and not historical approaches pride of place.

What, then, should be the role of traditional historical disciplines? They remain indispensable to those who study literature from another time and place. While the function of biblical language cannot be reduced to its referents, the Bible still speaks of particular people and times and places. The more we know of those people, times, and places, the richer will be our hearing of the biblical stories and letters. Our bondage to our own culture, race, and social class requires that our imaginations be expanded, and that will remain an important role for the historian. And not least, because the Bible makes very particular claims about people and times and places, it is appropriate to ask about the truthfulness of those claims. Such study is testimony to the particularity of the Scriptures. And while available evidence may not yield unambiguous answers, we are surely obliged to deal with questions believers will raise about Jesus and Pontius Pilate, about whom the Bible makes very specific claims.

"Where Two or Three Are Gathered"

What we propose as a starting point and focus for interpretation that has its place within the life of the church is the actual experience of reading the Bible as intended for us. The shift in the discipline to literary and rhetorical methodologies should be welcomed. Literary studies will not necessarily yield theological fruit, of course. The setting in which the material is studied will have a crucial bearing on what questions are allowed, which will be followed up, and what will count as "critical" and "responsible" answers to questions. Teachers of literature are as capable as historians of blocking access to theological dimensions of the literature they study. And that is why we are obliged to press the question: What is the Bible good for? In what ways will literary, as well as historical, modes of study open Bible readers to the reality of God? Numerous questions remain. In response to a paper on Mark that suggested the experience of the Gospel's ending was, in fact, an experience of the working of God, a colleague responded, "That was one of the best sermons I've heard in a while." While perhaps sincere, the comment revealed the obvious discomfort of coming out from behind the protective rubrics of the academic setting.

We do not imagine things will change easily. There are some good reasons why biblical interpreters sought to free themselves from ecclesial restraints, and there are reasons to be uncomfortable when questions about God and truth are allowed to intrude into our public conversations. We nevertheless believe that the resulting modes of interpretation that have come to dominate biblical scholarship are at some points deeply flawed, at others genuinely hostile to the theological enterprise. What is required for Christian interpreters is a recasting of the imagination of the exegete— and considerable reflection on the part of seminary faculties about how best to go about reshaping a practice that will turn the Scriptures loose in the church.

What this will involve—and what we commend to colleagues—is not just a different methodology but trust in the promise that God still works in our midst.

5

Hearing Peter's Speech in Acts 3
Meaning and Truth in Interpretation

What does it mean to identify Scripture's statements as "true"? Biblical narratives and academic scrutiny of them cannot adjudicate truth claims. As Juel's reading of Acts 3 shows, determining the "truth" of what the Bible says depends in part on how the Bible moves us to act and how it leads us to greater reliance upon God in our own contexts.

————

It is remarkable how significantly interpretation can be shaped by the sorts of questions asked of the Bible. Consider, for example, the question, "What does Peter's speech in Acts 3 mean?" For ordinary Bible readers, the question may seem perfectly appropriate. The more sophisticated might insist that the first question should be, "What *did* the speech mean?" It was, after all, written to people of a different time and circumstance—people who spoke a "foreign" language. Students of beginning Greek soon sense the distance between themselves and the original audience. A still more sophisticated Bible reader might insist that the question be more precise: "What does the Bible mean to a particular person or audience?" The speech might mean one thing to Peter's audience, something different to Luke's readers, and something else entirely to a modern-day audience. Even "modern-day audience" may be too general, since there are many. Perhaps we can ask only, "What does this passage mean to you?"—a rather different question from, "What does this passage mean?" Who speaks for a "general" audience—and what would such an audience look like? What would be their interests? In what ways would they be addressed by the speech?

The academic community has dealt with such questions by limiting them. Interpreters ask what a passage means to an imagined audience, usually the historical audience for whom Luke wrote (an audience about which we know little and that must thus be "imagined"). We seem to have agreed to speak and write for a contemporary audience that will discuss only how others are addressed by the Scriptures. Public conversation keeps the Bible at a distance, providing a safety zone for personal opinion about what the material "means to me" and making it difficult to imagine how we could speak about what it "means to us."

What then of the question, "Is it true?" Such a question cannot be addressed to Peter or to Luke or even to the church that preserved Luke and Acts in its canonical collection, since none of these can answer. The question can only be addressed to one another, and it makes sense only if it is asked about our interpretations of what the speech means. What public claims do we wish to make in our interpretations of the speech, and what would qualify them as "true"?

Most interpreters, if pressed, would probably feel most comfortable dealing with "truth" questions by restricting them to historical matters, i.e., to matters of "fact." Discussions about whether or not Peter could have given such a speech and, if so, how it would have been preserved and translated, deal with one small dimension of the truth question. "Did it really happen?" is a legitimate question, though a limited one. Those who ask such questions must be prepared to operate within the rules laid down for historical argument, rules of evidence which spell out how a convincing argument can be made about a proposition.

Dealing with such matters of "historical fact" does little to assist interpreters in determining what a passage means, however. For as students of history recognize, history is rhetorical in nature: history is written to make arguments. "Facts" are important within a framework that makes them significant—that renders them meaningful. Luke tells the story of the early Jesus movement because he intends to convince an audience of something—and to change and shape that audience in view of the story he tells. The events reported mean something; they set out to convince readers "of the certainty concerning the things you have been taught" (Luke 1:4).

Most students of Acts are well aware of such matters and are willing to make arguments about the literary form and the rhetoric of the work. Not any interpretation of Luke and Acts can be sustained. We know something about conventions in the ancient world and in our own that make conversation possible. There are good reasons to believe one thing or another about the function of the speeches in Acts, knowing as we do their place in the narrative and conventions among ancient historiographers. We can offer arguments about how scriptural exposition in the speeches is to be understood—arguments that we expect to be convincing—in view of the exegetical rules and the ethos of the Jewish community in the Hellenistic age. While scholars might hesitate to claim that their interpretations are "true," they do expect others to be persuaded.

While historical and literary matters require attention, the real question is how we will hear the claims made in the two-volume work. Luke-Acts makes public claims about God and Jesus that it expects readers to find convincing, claims that promise to enrich and sustain life. The narrative seeks to make a case that "what you have been taught" is reliable—that it is true. As readers, we are challenged to determine if we are included in the "you" who will find the narrative argument convincing. Historical study and literary analysis can assist in the process of becoming a sensitive audience. But until we have asked what the narrative means to "us" in our historical particularity and have heard its claims, we have not finished the task of interpretation.

What follows is an argument about Peter's speech in Acts 3:11-26. It seeks not to determine what the speech meant for its narrative audience in Jerusalem or for Luke's first-century readers, though we may ask about such matters, but what the speech means for us—and how we may understand its claim to be true.

Interpreting Acts 3: What Does It Mean?

To understand Peter's speech is to read it first within its setting in Acts. The speech, the second major address in Acts, is set in the temple precincts. It follows a dramatic healing of a lame man and is addressed to the astonished crowd that has gathered at Solomon's gate ("the whole people," whom Peter addresses as "Israelites" [3:12]). In simplest terms, the speech seeks to explain to the crowd what the healing means. It is not a sign of Peter's own power or piety but a sign of what is possible through "faith in this name" (3:16, a reference back to Peter's previous speech, in which he quotes the passage from Joel: "whoever calls on the name of the Lord will be saved" [Acts 2:21]). The speech calls the crowd to respond ("Repent, therefore, and turn . . ." [3:19]), and it makes promises. God intends that sins be forgiven and that people be turned from their wicked ways (3:19-20, 26). Unlike the previous account of a speech, this one reports no response from the crowd but only from the religious authorities, who immediately have Peter and John arrested (Acts 4:1-3).

The speech offers an interpretation of the healing by tying the event to an account of what God has accomplished in Christ, then spelling out the implications. A major feature of the speech is the interpretation of the Scriptures. Understanding what the speech means requires a sense of that scriptural argument. There is an explicit citation of Deuteronomy 18:19-20, supplemented with words from Leviticus 23:29. God's promise to Abraham, recounted in verse 25, combines features of Genesis 22:18 and 26:4. Verse 13 clearly alludes to Isaiah 52:13 ("my servant shall be exalted and glorified"); the references to "name" in verse 16 allude to Joel 2:32 ("whoever calls on the name of the Lord will be saved"), already quoted in Peter's speech in Acts 2. Behind Jesus' identification as "seed of Abraham," "servant," and "lord" lies an elaborate tradition of scriptural interpretation for which messianic oracles like 2 Samuel 7:10-14 and Psalm 89 are important.[1] Jesus can be identified as the "seed" of Abraham in Genesis because as Messiah he is the "seed" promised David (2 Sam 7:12). In similar manner he may be identified with the mysterious "servant" of Isaiah 52-53, because the king (the coming Messiah-King in particular) is referred to as God's "servant" (Ps 89:50; Zech 6:12). "Lord" is used to speak of the Christ in a passage regarded as a messianic oracle (Ps 110:1; see Acts 2:33-36). Scriptural interpretation is a major feature of the speech and not, as Martin Dibelius argued, a stock feature of sermons in Acts.[2] It presumes an audience familiar with the Scriptures and with the rules of scriptural argument (according to which verbal correspondence provides the primary means of connecting biblical passages).[3]

Certainly the most prominent citation is Deuteronomy 18, an oracle in which Moses speaks of a prophet whom God will raise up, to whom God's people are obliged to listen. The oracle, as we know from Jewish and Samaritan sources, was heard as an eschatological promise before the Christian era and beyond the boundaries of Christian scriptural interpretation. Striking here is the use of the passage to speak about Jesus. Elsewhere Jesus is identified as the Christ from David's line. While the identification of Jesus as "one of the ancient prophets that has arisen" may be a familiar assessment to the crowds who saw and heard Jesus, the disciples (and readers) know that Jesus is "the Christ of God" (Luke 9:18-20).

Understanding the meaning of the identification involves a sense of earlier Christian tradition. One of the developments that occurred in Christian tradition was the transfer of all eschatological titles to Jesus.[4]

We may observe in Luke 4 one of the ways in which confession of Jesus as "Christ" (Anointed) came to incorporate prophetic imagery that had not been part of Jewish messianic tradition. Jesus' citation of Isaiah 61, where the prophet is identified as "anointed" by God's Spirit, provides a means of filling out what it means that Jesus is the crucified and risen "Anointed One": he is "anointed" to preach and heal. The vocation of prophet may be ascribed to him as well.

The point of identifying Jesus as the "prophet like Moses" from Deuteronomy 18 is less christological than "ecclesiological." The passage provides a way of understanding what is at stake in the disagreements within the Jewish family about Jesus. The Scriptures identify the battle over the apostolic preaching of Christ as a crisis within Israel's history. As membership within Israel depended upon allegiance to Moses, so, in the present, membership within the family depends upon heeding the word of the prophet like Moses whom God has raised up. Jesus is that prophet; he is likewise the "seed" promised Abraham in whom all the families of the earth will be blessed.

Crucial here is Jesus' descent from Abraham and David, as well as his relationship to Moses' promise of a new prophet. Jesus belongs within the scriptural heritage of Israel. Those Jews who accept the gift offered in this "Christ," "lord," and "prophet"—who believe in his name—will be saved. Those who do not will be rooted out of the people (Acts 3:23). According to Peter's speech, that is the message of the Scriptures.

The speech offers to interpret a critical feature of what begins here and develops through the story in Acts: the preaching of the gospel results in a division within Israel. Many Jews believe (tens of thousands, Acts 21:20); most do not. Only those Jews who have faith in Jesus can lay claim to their heritage. Only they can rightfully identify themselves as "the people," that is, Israel, children of Abraham. Those who reject Jesus (like the Sadducees who cannot believe in resurrection) forfeit their rights as Jews. Stephen's speech builds on this construct, completing the framework within which conflict in the family of Israel is to be understood. While he and his would-be judges are all children of Abraham ("our father," Acts 7:2), there is now a gulf between them. Those who believe in Jesus are descendants of the prophets whom "your fathers killed" (Acts 7:51-53). Israel's family has always been one marked by conflict, with the majority usually on the wrong side.

It has been customary to refer to the early speeches in Acts as "missionary addresses." The category is too narrow to capture all that the speeches mean. Peter's sermon has a critical function not only in chapter 3 but within the whole narrative. Its rhetorical function is aimed not simply at converting a large group of Jews in Jerusalem but at making an argument for the reader of Acts that gathers up the whole story. This speech and Stephen's speech in Acts 7 are perhaps the critical pieces for understanding an essential aspect of Luke's thesis about the story of the early "church": the gathering of the law-observant Jews who believe in Jesus (among whom Paul is included) represents the continuation of Israel. It is the purified remnant. Those who refuse the apostolic testimony thrust their heritage from themselves.

Nothing has been said yet about Gentiles. There is no suggestion in these early chapters that Gentiles are involved at all. Peter addresses a Jewish audience; Stephen's troubles are internal to the Jewish community. There is no debate in these chapters about replacing Israel by a Gentile religious body. Peter remains determined to keep the law (Acts 10-11). James and the elders in the Jerusalem church never abandon food laws (Acts 11 and 15).[5] The best they can do for Barnabas, Paul, and the Antioch-sponsored mission to Gentiles is to identify those places in the scriptural tradition where provision is made for non-Jews to live among Jews by observing a minimum of dietary laws (Acts 15). The "apostolic decree" imposes on Gentiles those purity laws essential to carry on social interaction with Jews within the community of the faithful; specifically, it permits table fellowship.

What does the speech mean within the context of Acts? It makes a claim about what is occurring (from the perspective of author and reader, about what has already occurred). The speech characterizes the division within Israel regarding Jesus as a decisive purge of God's people, a purge foretold in the Scriptures. As the "prophet like Moses," Jesus is the one chosen by God to speak words by which divisions will be made (cf. Luke 2:34, where Simeon says, "This child is destined for the falling and rising of many in Israel"). There is no suggestion that God has rejected Israel and replaced the old people with a new one. There is the audacious claim, made from within the family of Israel, that only those Jews who believe in Jesus can claim membership in Israel. The case is argued in the speech largely by appeal to the Scriptures, operating according to the rules of the game within the community of the first century. If we are to understand the argument, there are things we must know about the Scriptures, about speeches and forms of argument in the ancient world, and about the movement of Luke-Acts as a unified composition.

Peter's Speech: What Does It Mean for Us?

The speech makes claims about God and the history of which we are a part, claims that are meaningful and that presume to be heard as true. We can understand what is at stake in Luke's argument. The Gospel opens with a litany of God's promises to his people (especially Luke 1:46-55, 67-79; 2:29-32; 4:17-21). The story recounts the "events that have been fulfilled among us" (Luke 1:1). If God keeps promises—if he kept promises even when things looked darkest, raising Jesus from the dead and sending out apostles to preach repentance and forgiveness—there are reasons to be confident that God will not abandon his people in the future and will overcome hostility with mercy. We are invited to "acknowledge the certainty of what you have been taught" (Luke 1:4).

But what have we been taught? For centuries Christians have learned that a Gentile Christian church has taken Israel's place as the people of God. Luke makes no such argument. Peter's sermons do not speak of a new people of God but of a refined Israel. What the story "means" depends upon who hears it, not in the sense that his argument is read differently but that it strikes the hearer differently. It is one thing for a Jew or a Jewish believer in Jesus to hear the story Luke tells. It is another for a non-Jew. One of the tasks of interpretation is to highlight our investment in the story as the "you" for whom it is written—and to acknowledge the difference between ourselves and other audiences.

The story of God's dealing with Israel is meaningful to us as it was to Cornelius the Gentile (Acts 10:1–11:18): in Christ, we have been cleansed and invited to sit at the table with God's people. For Luke, that does not imply a change in the rules. Cornelius is a Gentile who observes the law. The apostolic decree reaffirms the validity of kosher laws for all Gentiles who become members of the family of believers (Acts 15, especially verses 28-29). When were such rules abandoned? And if the law has been abrogated—something Acts never even hints—what are we to make of the Old Testament, of God's election of Israel, of God's fidelity to promises? What right do Gentiles have to Jewish promises?

These are questions Acts does not pose. The story is largely about the fulfillment of God's promises for Israel and the division within the Jewish community that results from Jesus' ministry. As Gentiles, we are invited into that branch of the Jewish family that understands its heritage through the preaching of Jesus the Christ. We are addressed by the story as strangers with no claim to a place at the table. We become part of the "you" for whom Luke writes only by the gracious act of Israel's God through Jesus the Christ.

Meaning and Truth

If the story Acts tells is meaningful—meaningful, that is, in a way that determines how we understand ourselves, our place in the world, our relationship to God, and our tasks—and if it claims to be true—true in a public way that makes a potential claim on everyone—certain questions take on an urgency. In our own setting, perhaps one of the most important questions may be formulated in this way: how does a Gentile hear the story as meaningful and true?

There is space for only a few suggestions.

1. The meaning of the speech has much to do with scriptural interpretation. Peter claims that Jesus is the "prophet like Moses" from Deuteronomy 18, presuming both that his audience understands the eschatological character of the oracle from Deuteronomy and that Jesus' identity as that "prophet" can be convincingly asserted. Understanding the nature of scriptural argumentation in the New Testament is essential for understanding the assertions. Whether or not such arguments are convincing depends upon our own rules of scriptural argument.

2. The meaning of Peter's speech is tied principally to its place in the narrative. The issue in the speech is not Jesus' identity, nor is the speech essentially a "missionary address." In Acts, it functions to provide some framework within which to understand the conflict within the Jewish community over the gospel.[6] It is the identity of believers in Jesus that is at issue—more specifically, it is their identity with respect to Israel's heritage. The speech asserts that only those Jews who believe in Jesus can claim to be real Jews. The speech does not yet deal with the status of non-Jews who believe Jesus to be the Christ.

3. Acts argues that in Christ and in the mission of his followers, God has kept his promises to Abraham and his offspring, as well as his promises to David. The "fallen tent of David has been raised up" (Acts 15:16-17, quoting Amos 9:11-12).[7] Unbelief within the family, always a mark of Israel's history, remains a reality even after the resurrection of Jesus from the dead. That the preaching of the death and resurrection of the Messiah causes family division has precedent, and itself only fulfills "what is written." Because the

Scriptures foretold the story of the apostolic preaching as well as of the Christ, they can be trusted. Thus God can be trusted as one who has kept his word to his people. And in view of God's fidelity to his word in past and present, there is reason to trust God with the future of his people—"trust" being the form of "certainty" appropriate to faith.

4. Such claims can be meaningful even to non-Jews, since in that "offspring of Abraham" all the families of the earth will be blessed (Acts 3:25). Are the claims true? They are to the degree that Jesus was and is actually a blessing to the nations of the earth. While Peter's speech is not simply a missionary sermon, there are missionary implications. If there is power in the name of Jesus, it must be spoken. If those who call on the name of the Lord will be saved, that possibility must be made available through new generations of preachers. If Jesus is the blessing God promises, the gospel must be spoken so that people can repent and be forgiven. The "truth" of the speech depends upon an activity it engenders. Its truth must be confirmed in the mission of Jesus' followers. Luke's testimony makes sense only if it leads to mission.

5. If we are included in the promises made in Peter's speech, we must also acknowledge that our relationship to the story is different from that of Jewish believers in Jesus who observe the law. The "truth" of Acts' assertion about God's faithfulness cannot be demonstrated in historical terms alone. The absence of law-observant Jews from a Gentile Christian church places the claims of Acts in jeopardy. Has God kept his word to Israel? Acts does not anticipate a time when Jewish believers will no longer serve as the theological heart and the foundation of God's people. That is our own situation, however. It is appropriate that the book of Acts ends without a conclusion. The "truth" of Peter's speech cannot be determined solely within the confines of the narrative.

Will God remain faithful? Will promises be kept? Luke-Acts does not envision the problem in the way we must, though it does end with a sense that the future lies with Gentiles. Israel's fate, however, is still uncertain. That Jesus is the promised Christ and the prophet like Moses may be asserted. That Jesus is the seed promised to Abraham in whom all the nations will be blessed may be argued from our own history. That this "seed of Abraham" is a blessing first to Israel remains in question. At least in regard to this matter—central to the narrative argument Luke makes—we may say that the verdict is not yet in. That it is true cannot be determined by a study of the past. Faith lives by God's promise. While there may be good reasons to believe in the certainty of what we have been taught, final confirmation of the "truth" of Peter's speech involves a future of Israel beyond that which Luke envisioned—and thus awaits eschatological confirmation. Here we wait with Peter's audience for the time when God "may send the Messiah appointed for you, that is, Jesus, who must remain in heaven until the time of universal restoration that God announced long ago through his holy prophets" (Acts 3:20-21).

6

Interpreting Israel's Scriptures in the New Testament

This writing, first published in a collection of essays on the history of biblical interpretation, explores how New Testament authors and their theological predecessors drew from Scripture in their discussions about Jesus Christ. What Juel sees happening among first-century interpreters resembles aspects of his own biblical interpretation: interpreters come to Scripture to test their hunches about God and how God has acted in their experience. This manner of interpretation makes Scripture not a voice stuck in the past but something ever "present and alive."

———

Preliminary Considerations

Interpreting the Bible was a major form of theological conversation and formation in early Christian circles. Appreciating the role of interpretation in the development of tradition and its place in the narrative and epistolary literature of the New Testament is an important task of modern biblical scholarship. The enterprise requires discipline, especially because the early Christians among whom the Bible was interpreted were different from most of us who read their work today. The "Bible" for the New Testament community was obviously not the collection of books we regard as the "Old" and "New" Testaments. Followers of Jesus read and interpreted the "Bible" before the New Testament was written; most New Testament authors did not know the works of other New Testament writers and did not regard their own productions as being on the same level as "the Bible."

Less clear to many modern interpreters is that terms like "Hebrew Bible" and "Tanak" are inappropriate in studies of the New Testament, because the New Testament community to which we have access read their Bibles in Greek. "The Bible" means something more like "Israel's Scriptures," read in Greek. While there was surely a period of interpretation during which the text read and heard was in Aramaic and Hebrew, that period lies in the past for the communities out of which and for which the Greek New Testament was written. Even though reconstructing a history of Christian exegetical tradition must attend to such an early stage, the interpretation of Israel's Bible in Greek is more crucial for understanding the Greek New Testament. Greek-speaking Judaism did not descend directly from Aramaic- and Hebrew-speaking circles, nor did its interpretive traditions. The same, we may assume, is true of New Testament communities.

It seems appropriate, therefore, to use the term "Scriptures" and "Israel's Scriptures" to designate those books regarded by New Testament authors as the Bible. Although there are many questions about the particular text forms available to New Testament communities, for convenience we will use the term "the Bible," meaning something approximating what we know as "the Septuagint."

Such a statement immediately raises important questions about the scope of "the Bible." Israel's Scriptures in Greek contain a number of books not included in the Hebrew Bible. Whether to include these "apocryphal" books or not has been a vexing problem, posed most poignantly in the debate between Augustine and Jerome. For his Latin version, Jerome proposed translating the Hebrew Bible as the Christian Old Testament; Augustine favored translating the Septuagint, including the extra books, since this had been the Bible of the early church. Jerome prevailed in his translation, but in the Western tradition the Roman Catholic Bible has included the so-called "apocryphal" books as well. Even when the list of Old Testament books in Christian Bibles corresponds to the Hebrew rather than the Greek canon, the order is closer to that of the Greek than the Hebrew. It is important to note which works New Testament authors cite and draw on as "the Scriptures." As we shall see, there is no agreement about this among biblical scholars.

Finally, we should be clear about our topic. "Interpreting the Scriptures" has popular as well as academic dimensions. From the intense interest in training public readers of the Scripture for worship in the early church,[1] it is clear that interpretation involves "making sense" at the level of public engagement. Biblical works were written to be read aloud, and there is no reading that does not involve interpretation. Knowing where to make breaks and pauses and when to take breaths may make all the difference in making sense of a passage to an audience. Modern scholarship has not taken with sufficient seriousness the oral character of engagement with the Scriptures, both in the past and present. Although the focus of this essay is the more academic question of scriptural interpretation in the New Testament, modern proposals about scriptural "echoes" will require that we pay some attention to the biblical text as experienced in both written and oral form.

The Data

Terminology in the New Testament identifying "the Scriptures" (Matt 21:42, Luke 4:21, John 5:39, Rom 1:2, etc.), particular divisions of the Bible (e.g., "the Law and the Prophets" [Matt 5:17, Luke 16:16, John 1:45, Rom 3:21], "the law of Moses, the Prophets, and the Psalms" [Luke 24:44]), or individual biblical works varies little from contemporary Jewish usage. This is significant because all the New Testament writers presume a relationship to Israel (including their contemporaries in various Jewish groups) very different from the relationship that developed in subsequent centuries. "Christian" is not a term used to distinguish a believer from a "Jew." The term, used only three times in the New Testament, at best identifies a particular group within the Jewish family. For that reason, it would be best to avoid terms like "Christian" and "Old Testament" in our descriptions of first-century works. Understanding "early Christianity" involves knowing as much as possible about the Hellenistic world and Hellenistic culture, but the particular investment in Israel's heritage and Israel's Scriptures suggests that the most helpful analogies for our study will be other Jewish scriptural interpretation, as practiced, of course, in the hellenized world.

The index at the back of the Nestle-Aland editions of the Greek New Testament identifies quotations and allusions to virtually every book in the Hebrew canon, to several works in the Greek (3 and 4 Esd, 1–4 Macc, Tob, Sir, etc.), and even works included in neither canon but belonging to the so-called "Pseudepigrapha" (Enoch, Jubilees, etc.). The Nestle-Aland editors themselves provide an important qualification: "Opinions differ greatly in identifying quotations and allusions. . . ."[2] Those who check the suggested intertextual connections will discover considerable variance in the certainty of the reference. Quotations are least problematic, though false ascriptions raise interesting questions (Mark 1:2), as do references to versions of a text at variance with known Hebrew or Greek text forms. Allusions containing a string of identical words are likewise not problematic. More difficult are connections that may seem possible, but in which there is little evidence of shared wording, or where the words in common are quite ordinary.

Given qualifications, there is evidence that New Testament authors regarded as "scriptural" those books so viewed by the Pharisaic community. We do not need to make a decision about the precise boundaries of such "scriptural" works—a topic that has generated some insightful scholarship but hardly a consensus. Still problematic are the so-called "apocryphal" and "pseudepigraphical" works. Because New Testament authors do not actually quote such material, even evidence of an allusion does not prove that the works were regarded by writer and audience as having the same authority as books of the Bible.[3]

Formal Matters

Significantly, the New Testament is quite different in genre from the literary remains of other Jewish communities. The New Testament contains no commentaries, no retelling of the biblical story as in the *Genesis Apocryphon* or the *Biblical Antiquities* of pseudo-Philo. It is set off from rabbinic midrashic collections or the Qumran *pesharim*, and all such literature of schools. The New Testament contains letters and narratives and an apocalypse. There are passages that explicitly interpret scriptural texts (e.g., Gal 3, Rom 9-11, Heb 1, and the speeches in Acts). Other material presumes interpretation but does not do it overtly. The Apocalypse of John, for example, contains more allusions to scriptural passages than does any other book in the New Testament, but it does not quote a single passage. It uses images and phrases from the Scriptures like stones in a mosaic. It is reasonable to presume a logic to their selection and use, but the "interpretation" must be reconstructed.

That the New Testament is not a collection of school literature does not mean there were not such "schools" or learned interpretation within the circles of Jesus' followers. On the contrary, the New Testament presumes a period of extensive interpretation of Israel's Scriptures. A series of quotations in Matthew, introduced with formulas like "These were done to fulfill what was written in the prophet Isaiah," betray a kind of learned sophistication that has led scholars to speak of a "Matthean School."[4] The Gospel itself is not a product of such a school, but it presupposes and draws on a kind of scriptural interpretation similar to that of the later rabbis or the Essene circles at Qumran. The speeches in Acts likewise give evidence of learned interpretation.

The Use of the Scriptures

Because the New Testament does not contain commentaries or hermeneutical essays, we must begin by observing the use of Scripture in the New Testament writings. The simple phrase "use of Scripture" does not reveal the complexity of the phenomena.

For instance, biblical passages appear in explicit arguments. Paul marshals an impressive constellation of passages to convince the Galatians that faith in Christ, not circumcision, makes one a child of Abraham (Gal 3). Jesus cites Hosea in a dispute with the Pharisees about the company he keeps at meals (Matt 9:13). Peter forges a tight scriptural argument from Psalms 16 and 110 to demonstrate that by raising Jesus from the dead, God "has made him both Lord and Christ, this Jesus whom you crucified" (Acts 2:36). Describing the use of Israel's Scriptures in the New Testament includes attention to such explicit argument.

The "use of Scripture" also includes allusions. In Mark's Passion Narrative, words from Psalm 22 are employed to tell the story of Jesus' death: soldiers cast lots for his garments (Mark 15:24 = Ps 22:19); those who pass by shake their heads (Mark 15:29 = Ps 22:8); and Jesus' last words, "My God, my God . . ." echo the opening verse of the psalm (Mark 15:34 = Ps 22:2). The offer of vinegar may allude to Psalm 69 (Mark 15:36 = Ps 69:22). No formula makes the point that "all this happened to fulfill what was written." Yet there is a kind of argument implied by the use of the terminology, even though it is not explicitly made, and even if, in this and other instances, the respective New Testament authors did not "intend" the argument consciously. Probably from the outset, the language of the Scriptures was used to tell the story of Jesus' death by people who were convinced it was "in accordance with the Scriptures."

Identifying allusions and understanding the kind of scriptural use and argument they imply is less certain than interpreting explicit argument. Where striking similarities in wording suggest an allusion, we may assume there is some reason for using the very words of Israel's Scriptures in telling the story. Understanding why precisely these words are used, however, may involve reconstructing traditions of interpretation that New Testament writers presupposed. Some of the New Testament authors may not even have been aware of the intertextual connections in traditions they inherited; some early readers may well have missed the allusions. The logic of using language from Psalms 22 and 69 to speak of Jesus' death is not apparent in any of the actual Gospel narratives. That the allusions lend a "scriptural" tone to the account is apparent; the reasons for using words from just these psalms is not. The level at which interpreters among the circles of Jesus' followers actually identified and assembled particular biblical passages—the point at which we may appreciate the logic and character of interpretation—is often available to us only as a construct. Understanding the allusions will require, then, a sense of the history of scriptural interpretation, set within the larger context of scriptural use in the wider culture.

Perhaps most difficult are intertextual connections proposed by modern commentators that have to do with large themes and/or patterns in Israel's Bible as much as with identical wording. These "echoes of the Scriptures" would likewise constitute a usage that implies some interpretive approach and even conclusions about the meaning of passages in the Hebrew Bible. Identifying such intertextual connections and drawing inferences about early Christian scriptural interpretation must be still more tentative than in the preceding instances. They presume knowledge of reading practices and usage that is largely unavailable to us.

The Task

Beginning with observations about the use of the Scriptures of Israel, we may proceed in various directions. A first task might be to distinguish the different ways in which the Scriptures are used, including attention to formal issues. Where is the scriptural argument overt and where is it implied? How might we distinguish among the uses of the Scriptures in prayers, hymns, confessions, or visions—formal units that are now included in letters and narratives? What is the difference between actual citation and allusion, or between allusion and an "echo"?[5]

A second task will involve some reconstruction of interpretive traditions that must underlie the usage we encounter in the New Testament. How is it, for example, that certain passages, like Isaiah 53, came to be used to speak of Jesus? Does the usage reveal a logic, or is the process random and haphazard? In unpacking Paul's argument in Galatians 3 or Peter's speech in Acts 2, how are we to account for the particular selection and combination of texts? Much is presumed and left unsaid. What light can be shed on such matters? It remains to be seen if we can observe a logic in such usage, even to the point of offering a reconstruction of early Christian interpretive tradition.[6]

A third task will be to understand the mechanics and logic of all the "premodern" exegesis within the New Testament in light of what we know of the use of texts elsewhere in the ancient world. Although such a general assessment of "New Testament interpretation of Israel's Scriptures" is only an aspect of understanding the various letters and narratives, it is nevertheless useful for readers of letters and Gospels. We need to learn the rules taken for granted in another culture, as it read texts and constructed arguments. These rules in many cases are different from our own.

We will touch lightly on the first, and focus on the second and third tasks in the rest of this essay.

Reading the Scriptures: Rules of the Game

Writing and reading are social enterprises. They depend on shared systems of signs and proceed by largely unspecified "rules" that can be taken for granted. Because social systems differ, interpreting written material from another culture requires knowledge of that culture and its conventions. Basic assumptions about the nature of written texts underlie the whole enterprise of reading and interpretation. That is certainly true for the New Testament and its use of Israel's Scriptures.

Allegory

Allegorical interpretation, while not a respected mode of interpretation among contemporary scholars, was an accepted strategy for dealing with texts up to the time of the Enlightenment. While this strategy is not common in the New Testament, there are some examples. When Paul reads the story of Sarah and Hagar in Genesis 21, he sees in the story something beyond the literal meaning:

> Now this is an allegory: these women are two covenants. Now Hagar is Mount Sinai in Arabia and corresponds to the present Jerusalem, for she is in slavery with her children. But the other woman corresponds to the Jerusalem above; she is free, and she is our mother. (Gal 4:24-26)

The words of the text mean something other than what they appear to mean. Philo of Alexandria, a Jewish contemporary of Paul whose volumes comprise a precious deposit of first-century Greek-speaking Judaism in Egypt, shared such assumptions. His interpretation of the migration of Abraham as the story of reason's journey from the realm of the senses to the realm of pure Mind operates with similar assumptions. While refusing to abandon the literal meaning of the law and adherence to it, Philo believed the most important meaning of words is other than the literal

(*Migr* 89-93, 183-84). God's command that Abraham "Leave your land, your kindred, and your father's house" is actually a command to leave the realm of ordinary sensual life:

> God begins the carrying out of His will to cleanse man's soul by giving it a starting point for full salvation in its removal out of three localities, namely, body, sense-perception, and speech. "Land" or "country" is a symbol of body, "kindred" of sense-perception, "father's house" of speech. (*Migr* 2)[7]

Such reading operates with a particular logic. Philo, for example, frequently engages in wordplay and etymology to make a point. "Land" can be a symbolic term for "body"

> because the body took its substance of our earth (or land) and is again resolved into earth. Moses is a witness to this, when he said, "Earth thou art and into earth shalt thou return" (Gen 3:19); indeed he also says that the body was clay formed into human shape by God's moulding hand, and what suffers solution must needs be resolved into the elements which were united to form it. (*Migr* 3)

Philo's allegorical reading is more elaborate than Paul's, operates from a different philosophical orientation, and comes to different conclusions. Nevertheless, both share common assumptions about reading texts. For allegorists, texts are cryptograms to be deciphered; meaning is located at a level "beneath" the literal. Interpretation of texts is related to the interpretation of dreams, a vocation in which at least two of Israel's heroes, Joseph and Daniel, excelled. To appreciate allegorical interpretation fully, it would be helpful to know as much as possible about the store of symbols on which interpreters drew, some of which appear in actual lists.[8]

If for Philo and later Christian interpreters allegorical method is fundamental, the approach is rarely used in the New Testament.

Midrash

It has become a commonplace among New Testament scholars to refer to early Christian interpretation as "midrash." The term is Hebrew, from the verb "to interpret." While specialists rightly object to the broad and imprecise meaning the term has acquired in recent usage, the designation is helpful as a cross-cultural reminder of the potential distance between our modes of interpretation and those of others.

The identification needs qualification. "Midrash" has a history of usage within Jewish circles of Hebrew Bible interpreters. For the New

Testament, a corresponding Greek term like "exegesis" would be more apt, since the authors read and spoke and wrote in Greek. Unfortunately, there is no corresponding Greek term with the same connotations.

"Midrash" can be used to refer to a body of literature ("the midrashim"), the product of rabbinic schools beginning in the second century, though collections were not edited until the fifth century C.E. and later. The New Testament does not contain this type of midrash, that is, it includes no commentary on a biblical work.

"Midrash" is also used to speak of a specific methodology, identified with lists of rules by Hillel, Ishmael, and Eliezer ben Jose ha-Gelili. The lists of principles (*middoth*) were formulated well after the actual interpreting had taken shape. Although they are interesting, they do not provide the most useful access to the spirit and mechanisms of midrash. Of the various principles, only two are widely practiced within New Testament writings: the principle of analogy (*gezera shawa*) and inference from the light to the weighty (*qal wahomer*)—both strategies of argument that Jewish interpreters shared with other readers of texts in the Greco-Roman world.[9]

The term is employed here in a highly generalized sense to identify an approach to the task of interpretation that was widely used not only by Jews, but also by other heirs of Hellenistic culture. This approach (or these approaches) to reading and interpreting texts are typical of cultures almost until the Enlightenment and the dawning of historical consciousness.

For modern interpreters, the most significant feature of midrash (or exegesis) that sets it apart from contemporary modes of interpretation is perhaps the construal of context. Today, students are taught that the meaning of words and sentences is tied to context, both literary and historical. Commentators writing on the book of Isaiah distinguish between "first" and "second" Isaiah (sometimes even a "third"), arguing that the collections of oracles do not derive from the same period of time and must first of all be located in their respective historical setting to be understood properly. The rabbis make no such distinctions. Their interpretation is ahistorical from the perspective of most contemporary readers. Although they are quite capable of making historical observations about passages, the meaning in which they are usually interested is not bound in any way to the setting in which the words were first spoken or written. It may be, in fact, that the real meaning of a prophetic oracle was not available to the prophet and his contemporaries, as the commentary on Habakkuk from the Dead Sea Scrolls states. Concerning the famous watchtower passage from Habakkuk 2:1-2, the commentator writes, and God told Habakkuk to write down that which would happen to the final generation, but He did not make known to him when time would come to an end. And as for that which He said, "That he who reads may read it speedily," interpreted this concerns the Teacher of Righteousness, to whom God made known all the mysteries of the words of His servants the Prophets. (1QpHab VII)[10]

The words from Paul's letter to the Corinthians make the same point. After a running commentary on Israel's experience in the wilderness, Paul says,

> These things happened to them to serve as an example, and they were written down to instruct us, on whom the ends of the ages have come. (1 Cor 10:11)

The Scriptures are about and for later times. Only later generations—and perhaps only particular inspired individuals—can know the real meaning of the biblical passages.

If historical context is not decisive in determining meaning, neither is the immediate literary context. For those who accepted the Torah, the prophets, and the writings as Scriptures, all were part of the same "mind of God" to which the Scriptures provided access. They were on the same level, even if some passages were more important (and more interesting) than others. Thus the meaning of a word in Deuteronomy could appropriately be determined by the use of the same word in Isaiah, and light could be shed on both from a verse in the Psalms. This is precisely what we find to be the case in the New Testament. Following are two examples of such reading of the Scriptures.

1. Paul's letter to the Galatians includes an extended scriptural argument about the heritage of Abraham. In 3:16 Paul makes what seems an extraordinary claim. In paraphrasing one of the versions of God's promise to Abraham in Genesis (Gen 13:15, 17:8, 24:7), Paul says, "to Abraham were the promises made, and to his offspring." He continues, focusing on the singular form of the noun: "It does not say, 'and to his offsprings,' as of many; but it says, 'and to your offspring,' that is, to one person, who is Christ" (Gal 3:16).

Modern commentators are quick to point out that the singular noun, "offspring" (literally "seed"), is collective. One of the passages to which Paul is referring reads as follows:

> for all the land that you see I will give to you and to your offspring forever. I will make your offspring like the dust of the earth; so that if one can count the dust of the earth, your offspring can also be counted. (Gen 13:15-16)

The context suggests that God is speaking about Abraham's "seed" as a group, a whole people, and the promise is explicitly about possessing the land. Paul speaks of "inheritance" without mentioning the land, however, and he obviously does not read "offspring" (seed) as a collective noun. From the perspective of modern common sense, Paul does violence to the plain meaning of the text.

His interpretation makes good sense, however, if all of Scripture provides the context for understanding the unidentified "seed" in Genesis who will be Abraham's heir. There are other candidates for understanding the specific occurrence of "offspring." One might point to 2 Samuel 7:10-14, God's promise of an eternal dynasty to David through the prophet Nathan:

> I will raise up your *offspring* [singular] after you, who will come forth from your body, and I will establish his kingdom. He will build a house for my name, and I will establish the throne of his kingdom forever. I will be a father to him, and he will be a son to me. (2 Sam 7:12-14)

One might argue that in the literary and historical context of this promise, it refers to Solomon. God did not "establish the throne of his [Solomon's] kingdom forever," however. Later generations came to read this passage as a prophecy of *the* king to come, the "Messiah." Such is the case among the Essenes at Qumran. Of this passage, the Qumran commentator says,

> He is the Branch of David who shall arise with the Interpreter of the Law [to rule] in Zion [at the end] of time. (4QFlor 11-12)[11]

"Branch of David" is an expression borrowed from Jeremiah 23:5, 33:15 and Zechariah 6:12, where it also refers to a future king from the line of David. The Qumran commentary presumes that all these passages refer to the same figure, the Messiah-King who will arise at the end of days.

Paul's interpretation presumes the same reading of 2 Samuel 7:12, now with an additional step: he argues that this royal "seed" promised to David is the specific "seed" to whom God promises Abraham's heritage. Abraham's inheritance, in other words, now flows through the promised Christ. That others held such a view prior to Paul is apparent perhaps even within the Scriptures. In Psalm 2, the Lord's "anointed" (Christ)—whom God calls "my son" (verse 7)—is told, "I will make the nations your heritage, and the ends of the earth your possession" (verse 8). According to the psalmist, it is this one whom God calls "my son" who will inherit not only the land promised to Abraham and his "seed" but also "the ends of the earth." Through this offspring Abraham will become "the father of a multitude of nations."

To understand Paul's argument, one needs to know that "seed" in the singular is used both in Genesis 13:16 and in 2 Samuel 7:12 in promises God makes about Israel's future. The unspecified usage in Genesis is interpreted via 2 Samuel. "Seed" is singular, according to this argument, not because it is a collective noun but because God had in mind the "seed" promised to David that would be Abraham's single heir, through whom all—Jews and Gentiles—would be blessed. The analogy (a form of argument identified as *gezera shawa*) is an accepted form of scriptural interpretation and provides here a way of discovering how God's promise to Abraham could be interpreted "messianically."

The analogies explain other features of Paul's argument here as well. Paul's way of proceeding is completely within the bounds of established Jewish interpretive practice, though he argues for a conclusion with which no rabbi would agree. In making a case that Jesus' coming means the end of the law for all those who have faith, Paul employs the Scriptures once again to make his point:

> Why then the law? It was added because of transgressions, until the off-spring would come to whom the promise had been made. (Gal 3:19)

"Until the offspring would come to whom the promise had been made" paraphrases Genesis 49:10:

> The scepter shall not depart from Judah,
> nor the ruler's staff from between his feet,
> *until tribute comes to him.*

The oracle is about Judah, from whom David was descended and the Messiah was to arise. The phrase translated in the NRSV as "until tribute comes to him" is translated in the Septuagint as "until the one comes to whom the promises belong." It is this reading Paul presumes. That this figure is called the "offspring" in Galatians 3:19 means that Genesis 49:10 is being read in light of 2 Samuel 7:12. The "seed" promised to Abraham is the same as the "seed" promised to David—the king—who is the "one" to whom promises belong, according to Genesis 49. The formation of such constellations of passages through verbal analogies is one of the principal mechanisms by which the Scriptures are interpreted.

Such interpretation violates modern conventions about what makes for a convincing argument. It disregards the specific literary and historical settings of Genesis 13 and 49 and 2 Samuel 7. Within its own setting, however, the New Testament follows procedures for "scientific" interpretation. The constellation of "messianic" texts is not haphazardly formed.

Beginning with royal oracles whose future verbs came to be read as pertaining to the distant (i.e., messianic) future, connections with other scriptural passages were established through verbal analogy.

Such observations do not constitute adequate interpretations of the verses from Galatians. Paul takes most of the christological reading of the Scriptures for granted. He was certainly not the first to associate 2 Samuel 7 and Genesis 49. Beginning with the "assured results" of the developing exegetical tradition within the circles of Jesus' followers, Paul argues for the social implications of his christological reading of the Scriptures. Appreciating the nature of the scriptural argument, however, is essential to a full understanding of Paul's letter and of the tradition to which he belongs. Interpreters will need to know what suggested the links in the first place, how these constellations of biblical interpretations differ from alternatives, and how Paul could use the same methods as those employed by other readers of Israel's Scriptures while arriving at diametrically opposed conclusions.

2. The process of "messianic exegesis" can also help explain New Testament use of other scriptural passages that no one had previously connected with the Messiah. Isaiah 42 and 53, familiar passages in Christian tradition, are used in the New Testament to speak of Jesus. Isaiah 42:1 is quoted in Matthew 12:18-21. The voice from heaven at Jesus' baptism and transfiguration shows traces of the passage ("with you I am well-pleased," Mark 1:11 par.; "the chosen one," Luke 3:22, 9:35, 23:35). Even more prominent is Isaiah 52:13–53:12, with quotations in John 12:38, Matthew 8:17, Acts 8:32-33, an extended comment in 1 Peter 2:22-25, and numerous allusions throughout the New Testament. The unprecedented use of these passages to speak of Jesus the Christ depends on the establishment of intertextual connections. Both Isaiah 42 and 53 speak of an unidentified "servant of God" (42:1, 52:13) and may be read as "messianic" because the Messiah-King is called God's "servant" elsewhere in the Scriptures (Ps. 89:50-51, Zech. 3:8).

Other connections might have been made. "Servant" in Isaiah 52:13–53:12 might be used of Moses, who is called "servant" elsewhere in the Scriptures. Precisely such a move is made in the Babylonian Talmud (*b. Sotah 14a*).[12] References to Isaiah's "servant" could be used of Elijah, since he is spoken of as a servant of God (Sir 48:9-10, alluding to Isa 49:6). Isaiah 42:1, speaking of "my servant," could, in light of analogies, be taken as referring to Israel—as in the Septuagint ("Behold my servant Jacob . . .")— or to any "servant" of God—in light of usage in the psalms and the prophetic writings—as it is when Paul applies the words to himself (Rom 10:16, quoting Isa 53:1).

Appreciating the mechanisms by which intertextual links are established is not the end of interpretation. To understand Paul (and other New Testament writers), we need to know why one association is preferred over another. Where is the catalyst for formation of these constellations of passages? The particular christological readings of the Scriptures make most sense in light of the story of Jesus the crucified Christ—the descendant of David who ended his career on a Roman cross as "the King of the Jews." That this most unlikely messianic candidate was vindicated by God "on the third day" required of his followers a rereading of the Scriptures to understand how the God of Israel could confirm ancient promises in such an unconventional manner. The confession of Jesus as Christ, in other words, is not the result of scriptural interpretation but its presupposition.[13]

Common Convictions

To understand scriptural interpretation among the various New Testament authors, we need to know as much as possible about the interpreters and their argument. We need to study their works within the larger context of ancient Jewish scriptural interpretation, which will involve asking why disagreements arose that were strong enough to divide communities. Regardless of conclusions drawn, however, all of the interpreters of the famous passages in Isaiah, Jeremiah, Zechariah, Genesis, 2 Samuel, and the Psalms share certain common notions about the Bible and the task of interpretation:

1. The words' meaning is not limited to (or even necessarily connected with) their immediate literary or historical setting. When the passages are prophetic oracles, interpreters have argued that the prophet did not know what the passage "really" meant. Similar statements can be made about passages from the Torah. The later rabbis had confidence in reasonable conversation as the way to get at the deeper meanings. Jesus' followers, like the Essenes at Qumran, believed that the meaning is clear only to those "on whom the end of the ages has come" or who have the Spirit of God.

2. The meaning of the Bible is not separated from words and sentences. It is not the disembodied or abstracted ideas that are the locus of meaning, but the words and sentences themselves. For the more schoolish rabbis, the precise order of words and the numerical meaning of letters invited curiosity. Several pages in

the midrashic commentary on Exodus are devoted to the phrase, "And the Lord spoke to Moses and Aaron in the land of Egypt saying . . .," asking if the order of the names "Moses and Aaron" implies a corresponding hierarchy in authority.[14] Is Moses more important than Aaron? Does the opening verse in Genesis 1, "In the beginning God created the heavens and the earth," suggest that the heavens are more important than the earth? The New Testament, like the Qumran scrolls, is less playful—but attention to the particulars of the text is no less apparent (cf. Paul's appeal to the singular form of the noun "seed").

3. The whole scriptural testimony is part of a single fabric. All the biblical books are on the same plane. Any verse can be used to interpret any other. They all disclose the "mind of God." The hymnic passage from the Wisdom of Sirach puts the matter nicely. Wisdom, who proceeded from the mouth of God "in the beginning," has now become embodied in the words of the Scriptures: "All this is the book of the covenant of the Most High God, the law that Moses commanded us as an inheritance for the congregations of Jacob" (Sir 24:23).

4. While it may seem that preconceptions determine what one sees and that exegetical method is simply a way of making the Scriptures say what is already known, that is far too simple an explanation of the data. Some preconception has always been necessary to open the Scriptures, and it still is. Followers of Jesus, like others within the Jewish community, came to the Bible with experiences and questions that determined the shape and direction of interpretation. The Bible likewise exercised an influence on the outcome and on the shape of the developing tradition.

    Several striking examples come to mind. That what happened to Jesus after his death should be discussed, using the language of exaltation and return, has everything to do with the use of passages like Psalm 110:1 and Daniel 7:13. Such biblical passages were not simply proof texts; they provided the means by which Jesus' followers could understand and speak about his—and their—future. Paul's "doctrine" of justification by faith has a great deal to do with the language of the Scriptures, in particular Habakkuk 2:4 and Genesis 15:6. References to "the name" of Jesus in Luke-Acts and Romans are tied to the use of Joel 2:32. What is distinctive is the interplay between events and the Scriptures.

5.   While interpretation could be motivated by simple curiosity and a desire to make the unclear clear,[15] most "midrash" was done with the intent of making sense of the Scriptures for the present life of the faithful. Interpretation was a way of making the Bible present and active.

Echoes

It is far more difficult to assess the mode of interpretation behind what Hays and others have called "echoes of Scripture."[16] Clearly, the followers of Jesus read the Bible, as did others in the ancient world, with particular attention to the words and sentences. But was this the only form in which the Scriptures exercised influence? Is the more "midrashic," word-and-sentence oriented, interpretation even the most common form of scriptural argument? While it is not difficult to detect citations and allusions—the precise wording is the clue—it is far more difficult to detect play on biblical texts in which shared wording is limited or where the alleged associations have to do with larger themes or constructs.

In our own time, for most people, "echoes" of biblical passages appear to be the most common form of interaction with the Scriptures. The Bible exercises most influence in hymns, liturgies, confessions, prayers, and oratorios like Handel's "Messiah." The kind of intertextual play common to a group that shares a canon of stories and images is the most obvious form of scriptural use and interpretation. The question is the degree to which that was also the case in New Testament times, or, more importantly, the degree to which we have sufficient access to the life of those communities to offer an evaluation.

There are numerous proposals. Students of Luke's Gospel, for example, argue that the narrative is a play on major themes in Deuteronomy.[17] Hays proposes that a single allusion to Job in the opening chapter of Philippians suggests that the apostle is drawing a parallel between Job and himself: "Paul the prisoner tacitly assumes the role of the righteous sufferer, as paradigmatically figured by Job."[18] Mark is a variation on major themes from Second Isaiah.[19]

What makes the arguments worth consideration is that many of the proposed echoes are plausible. What makes them plausible, however, may have little to do with ancient modes of scriptural interpretation. Present readers are quite capable of "detecting" intertextual relationships between Old and New Testament passages that no one has seen before—perhaps not even the author of the passage. Learned interpretation, however, has found controls for this in arguments for precedents: Matthew or Paul or John "intended" such an association; their readers would have detected such echoes. Demonstrating this proves difficult, however. In a sophisticated discussion of "tests" for determining the degree of certainty of a proposed intertextual link, Hays proposes seven criteria for "hearing echoes,"[20] including historical criteria (material, historical plausibility, and history of interpretation) and literary criteria ("volume," recurrence, thematic coherence, and "satisfaction"). Literary criteria have to do with the present experience of reading a text; historical criteria have to do with precedent. The argument for precedent requires knowledge of historical context, in particular, familiarity with ancient reading practices.

We know about ancient reading practices in the synagogue, though things become clearer after the second century and beyond. It seems certain that at the major Sabbath service there was a reading from the Torah and from the Prophets. Festival days included reading from the Megilloth (Song of Songs, Ruth, Lamentations, Ecclesiastes, and Esther).[21] Important work has been done on the use of the Scriptures in the life of the synagogue, including attempts to reconstruct a three-year cycle of liturgical readings, correlating readings from the Torah with readings from the Prophets. Scholars have explored the relationship between major festivals and the interpretation of particular Bible stories. One of the most interesting is the work of Le Déaut and others on the place of the "Binding of Isaac" in Passover tradition.[22] Such work has been challenged, however, by other scholars who do not see the proposed links and are unconvinced by the evidence.[23]

The New Testament—Luke-Acts in particular—presumes public reading of the Scriptures in the synagogue (Luke 4:16-20, Acts 17:2, 11). 1 Timothy speaks of "the public reading of Scripture" among believers in Jesus (4:13). Paul assumes that Gentile Christians in the Galatian churches know the Bible and can follow careful scriptural argument. Beyond this, however, we do not know precisely what portions of Israel's Scriptures were read, how they were read, or even in what form they were available. That all churches owned copies of the Scriptures is highly unlikely. Contact with written texts mediated by "testimony books" remains a possibility.[24]

The difficulty in arguing for more broadly and loosely defined intertextual echoes is apparent in Marcus' work on Mark. He interprets the "Old Testament" in terms of "patterns and themes" in the context of which, he argues, Mark and his readers would have heard the story of Jesus.

> A major thesis of our study . . . has been that Mark takes up patterns and themes from the Old Testament and uses them to make clear to his biblically literate readers various aspects of Jesus' identity and his relationship to the community whose existence was inaugurated by his life, death, and resurrection. It makes sense to conclude that these Old Testament motifs have also played a considerable role in shaping Mark's own conception of Jesus.[25]

The problem is anachronism. Marcus employs constructs such as "the Righteous Sufferer" and "the Suffering Servant" that appear to be modern, not ancient, images. To make sense of Mark's use of the phrase "the way" in 1:2 and 10:30-34, he appeals to "the Deutero-Isaian picture of Yahweh's triumphant processional march,"[26] a theme that "in Deutero-Isaiah, how-ever . . . has been fused with that of the holy war of conquest."[27] While references to Deutero-Isaiah may make sense to modern students of the Hebrew Bible, they do not reflect the perspective of first-century read-ers, and there is little evidence that anyone prior to the modern era has detected such "patterns and themes."

Marcus' work may be an extreme example, but it illustrates the dif-ficulty of knowing how to reconstruct a "biblically literate readership." We require knowledge of reading practices and liturgical traditions in the first century, which is largely unavailable. In the case of our closest analo-gies, rabbinic interpretation, there is little obvious relationship between interpretation of texts and their usage. Knowledge that the psalms are songs has apparently little to do with their use as Scripture. The Midrash on Psalms is a (late) collection of commentary in which the form of the psalms as songs to be performed has no appreciable impact on the com-ments. The psalms are read as texts. They disclose meaning as do other texts. Interpreters make sense of them by using techniques appropriate to texts, that is, dealing with words and sentences. Almost half the com-ments in the interpretation of Psalm 22 are devoted to deciphering the cryptic words in the title of the psalm.[28] The case seems much the same in the New Testament. To make sense of the use of Psalms 2, 8, 16, 22, 45, 69, 89, 110, 118, and 132, it is unnecessary to know how they were employed in worship or even that they were performed. They function as scriptural texts whose words and sentences are the focus of attention.

If the proposals of Hays on Philippians and Romans, Moessner and Brawley on Luke, or Marcus on Mark were not plausible, there would be no interest in "echoes of Scripture" and in these more general forms of intertextuality. Their least convincing arguments, however, are gener-ally those that must claim historical precedent. Passages like Galatians 3,

Romans 9-11, the opening chapters of Hebrews and 1 Peter, and the speeches in Acts provide clear evidence of forms of interpretation familiar from sources contemporary with the New Testament authors. Paul's allegorical reading of the Sarah-Hagar story in Genesis is likewise at home in his first-century environment. It is appropriate, perhaps, that an essay about biblical interpretation—in contrast to a topic like "the influence of the Old Testament on the New Testament"—should focus on those phenomena that reveal a form of argumentation that can be documented. That Paul could draw on large blocks of material with which he could assume familiarity and that Luke's anachronistic "biblical" language is a subtle form of argument for people in whose consciousness the Scriptures were deeply embedded remain possibilities. Yet what makes the particular intertextual proposals appealing—and convincing—may have more to do with contemporary reading patterns and less with our ability to demonstrate historical precedent.

Conclusions

In considering interpretation of Israel's Scriptures in the New Testament, it is unnecessary to resolve such matters even if it were possible to do so. Discussions about appropriate forms of scriptural interpretation—including contemporary appreciation and use of intertextual echoes of all sorts in interpretations of the New Testament—can benefit from cross-cultural conversation. Obviously, readers at other times and places have construed texts and engagement with texts differently. Discovering a logic in scriptural interpretation within Jewish circles in the first century of our present era may help to illumine aspects of the New Testament that seem foreign and nonsensical. To what extent these alternative modes of appreciating written texts should shape our own practice is another matter and cannot be answered in advance.

The Trinity and the New Testament

Trinitarianism and the Christian creeds derive from the Bible, but they hardly replace Bible reading. Trinitarian theology prepares us for reading Scripture insofar as it introduces us to a depiction of God we might expect to discover in the Bible. It reminds us that Christian communities read Scripture, not to figure God out, but so they might be shaped by the God to whom Scripture points.

————

A colleague and I took our introductory Bible class to a local synagogue for a Friday evening service. The congregation was accustomed to Christian visitors and had a brief, helpful introduction to the service conducted by one of the lay members. The introductions were usually careful and precise, but one year our host chose to be a bit daring. His introduction began, "In welcoming you to our synagogue, I want to call your attention to some of the differences between us as Jews and Christians. The most basic is that while you believe in three Gods, we believe in one." I smiled at his obvious misunderstanding of the Christian doctrine of the triune God, but I noticed that at least a few of our students nodded their heads in agreement. It was obviously not clear to some of our students—and to many inside and outside the church—what "the Trinity" means and why it is important.

It is likewise clear that the ordinary faith of the church has been shaped by our Trinitarian creeds. When I begin a course on the Gospel of Mark and we deal with the account of Jesus' baptism, more than a few students are troubled by the line, "And he saw the heavens being torn apart and the Spirit coming down, like a dove, into him" (1:10). I explain why I think the Greek preposition *eis* should be translated "into" and not "on" (NRSV). Immediately following the baptism, the Spirit "drives" Jesus out into the desert, as though he is passive. A bit later in the Gospel, we are told that the scribes believe Jesus to be possessed by an unclean spirit— and that their diagnosis is nothing less than blasphemy against the Holy Spirit (3:20-30). Jesus is possessed—by the Holy Spirit. "Isn't that heresy?" students will ask. "Isn't that adoptionism, something the church later condemned? As part of the Trinity, aren't Jesus and the Spirit already one?" The comments are an occasion for discussing the relationship between the Bible and the later doctrine of the church: full-blown Trinitarian faith is a later, creative interpretation of the biblical witness by the church. It is a question, however, what kind of interpretation of the New Testament the Trinitarian creeds offer—and of what use these interpretations are for contemporary Bible readers who may well find the language of the creeds more alien than that of the Scriptures.[1]

In the brief space allotted to me, I would like to pursue two questions: (a) How might we evaluate the later Trinitarian creeds as interpretations of the biblical faith in God? and (b) Of what importance are these creeds for contemporary readers of the Scriptures?

A topic such as this obviously requires the cooperative work of colleagues in various disciplines. The distinction between biblical studies and early church history is highly artificial, since the biblical works were written from within early communities of believers and were influential in shaping the piety and worship life of the groups studied as the "early church." Further, noncanonical literature may provide insight into features of church life that the Bible simply presupposes.[2] Any separation of the creeds and the New Testament is thus artificial even if they are separated from one another by time and situation. Further, to suggest that students of the Bible and church history are not interested in theological matters and must leave such things to their colleagues in another department is another serious mistake. The topic provides a helpful example of how all of our various disciplines are necessarily theological.

God the Father, Jesus the Son

The New Testament contains no doctrine of the Trinity. The "threefold-ness" of God is not the subject of theological reflection. The New Testament writers and the congregations for whom they wrote understood themselves as monotheists—monotheists, that is, as Israel understood God as one. The *Shema*, with its emphatic statement of God's exclusiveness, is actually cited in only one passage in the Synoptic Gospels (Mark 12:30,

33, and parallels); there are allusions, as in 1 Corinthians 8:4 and James 2:19. The phrase "God is one" is used in scarcely more than a dozen passages. The reason, however, is that the confession is something to be taken for granted rather than something extraordinary.

The Trinitarian creeds highlight several noteworthy features of the New Testament. I shall identify one: God is introduced first of all as "Father Almighty." While there are Old Testament passages where God is spoken of as "Father," the term is not common. "Father Almighty" is not biblical phraseology. Nor, one might add, is it typical of Hellenistic religions. "Maker of heaven and earth" is more traditionally Jewish, but in the oldest Western creedal formulations prior to the Apostles' Creed, "maker of heaven and earth" is absent in virtually every case.[3] In thirty-one of thirty-two examples of creedal formulations prior to standardization in the great creeds of the church, *pater pantokrator* appears while "maker of heaven and earth" does not.[4] Identifying the first person of the Trinity as Creator is more typical of creeds in the Eastern church, but in these creeds creation is the work of the Son as well as of the Father (Nicene Creed: "the only-begotten Son of God . . . by whom all things were made").

What it means to speak of God as "Father" is explained only a few clauses later when we are introduced to "Jesus Christ, his only *Son*, our Lord" (who is "seated at the right hand of the Father"). Speaking about "God" requires speaking about a relationship between "Father" and "Son." The appropriateness of these metaphors as disclosing something so crucial to the identity of God as to warrant pride of place in Christian confessions is worthy of some reflection. Do they signal something central to the New Testament witness—and if so, how are they to be understood? The questions touch on issues important not only to historians of antiquity but to all those who worship and pray and preach. They are all the more crucial when it is precisely these metaphors that give offense to many within the church rather than awakening and sustaining faith. Before venturing into deep pastoral waters, it would be helpful to have some sense of how to think about at least this aspect of the church's Trinitarian faith.

Exploring a Metaphor

One way to understand the language of the creeds so as to offer some assessment is to locate them in their environment. Those believers in Jesus who came later to be called "Christians" began as a sect within Judaism. Like other Jews, they had notions about God that set them off from their neighbors. It is not enough to describe them as monotheists, however. While no clear line can be drawn between "Jewish" and "Greek," there was a difference between faith in the one God of Israel and Greek monotheism. Israel's God had a name and a history; the rich tradition of imagery employed to speak of God was tied to that history of interaction with Israel.

Israel's monotheism took various forms. Important for understanding later Trinitarian developments is the rich tradition of speculation about heavenly intermediaries. One of the ways by which various Jewish groups may be identified is in terms of their attitudes toward this heavenly mediation, whether understood in terms of Wisdom or principal angels.[5] In the view of these groups, God's oneness was not compromised by such speculation, but it was surely defined and experienced differently. Those seeking language to speak about Jesus and the relationship of Jesus to God found a helpful tradition at hand. The New Testament is not unique within Jewish literature, in other words, in qualifying faith in the one God in terms of reflection on heavenly intermediaries. What is distinctive is the way in which God's oneness is qualified by statements about Jesus, who is portrayed both as an historical figure and as the heavenly intermediary.

1. The Fourth Gospel

Such statements range across a wide spectrum. The Fourth Gospel is perhaps the clearest example of the use of traditional language about mediation to speak about Jesus. In the prologue, imagery is employed that is explicitly used to speak about Wisdom in such works as the Wisdom of Sirach and the Wisdom of Solomon. In these works, God's Wisdom is depicted as God's agency in creation. Playing on the imagery of Genesis, according to which God's speaking brings about creation, Wisdom is identified with that Word that emerged from God's mouth:

> I came forth from the mouth of the Most High. . . . (Sir 24:3)

> O God of my fathers and Lord of mercy, who have made all things by your word, and by your wisdom have formed humankind. . . . (Wis 9:1-2)

In addition to her role in creation, Wisdom likewise functions as the agent of revelation.

In Sirach, that mediating function of making God's eternal Wisdom known among humankind is tied to the giving of the Torah. It is in the words of the law of Moses that Wisdom has become flesh:

> All this is the book of the covenant of the Most High God, the law that Moses commanded us as an inheritance for the congregations of Jacob. (Sir 24:24)

Following the biblical metaphor, the Fourth Gospel speaks of a personified Word of God that "is" God. The Word is not the totality of God but part of the reality of God. Here the imagery is close not only to wisdom tradition but to those reflections on God's "attributes" in rabbinic writings. The difference is that this "Word" of God became flesh in Jesus. This embodiment of the one "through whom all things were made" becomes a challenge to other views:

> The law indeed was given through Moses; grace and truth came through Jesus Christ. No one has ever seen God; It is God the only Son, who is close to the Father's heart who has made him known. (John 1:18)

Striking here is the use of "Father" for God. It is implied neither by the "Word" metaphor nor by the image of Wisdom. It is obviously related to mention of the Word-become-flesh as "a father's only son" (1:14). And its appearance prepares us for a consistent feature of the Fourth Gospel's theological language: "Father" is used for God even more frequently than the term "God." The few occurrences of the biblical "Lord" for God are almost exclusively restricted to Old Testament quotations. To understand the God to whom we are introduced in the Fourth Gospel is to understand one who is most commonly called "Father."

The data are more particular. With few exceptions, the 118 occurrences of the term "Father" are on the lips of Jesus. He alone refers to God as "Father." One exception is in 8:41, where "the Jews who had believed in him" say, "We are not illegitimate children; we have one Father, even God." But here Jesus explicitly denies the claim: "If God were your Father, you would love me. . . ." (John 8:42). God is spoken of only as Jesus' Father. The term alternates with expressions like "the one who sent me." It is from the Father Jesus has come; to the Father he will return. The metaphor, in other words, is utterly particular, restricted to the relationship between a single Son and Father. If usage is not clear enough, the matter is explicitly stated on several occasions:

> Philip said to him, "Lord, show us the Father, and we will be satisfied." Jesus said to him, "Have I been with you all this time, Philip, and you still do not know me? Whoever has seen me has seen the Father." (John 14:8-9)

The Father and Son metaphor is understood not as typical but as singular, implying a claim that some within the Jewish community regard as blasphemous.

> For this reason the Jews were seeking all the more to kill him, because
> he was not only breaking the sabbath but was also calling God his own
> Father, thereby making himself equal to God. (5:18)

> The Jews answered him, "We have a law, and according to that law he
> ought to die, because he has claimed to be the Son of God." (19:7)

There is some small indication that the metaphor can be extended.
The prologue speaks of "children (*not* "sons") of God."[6] The only occurrence of "Father" as a term appropriate for anyone else is in Jesus' conversation with Mary Magdalene after the resurrection:

> But go to my brothers and say to them, "I am ascending to my Father
> and your Father, to my God and your God." (20:17)

The relationship to God as Father is clearly mediated through the Son:

> As you, Father, are in me and I am in you, may they also be in us, so that
> the world may believe that you have sent me. The glory that you have
> given me I have given them, so that they may be one, as we are one, I in
> them and you in me. . . . (17:21-23)

The Spirit is most significant in John precisely at the point of this relationship. The Spirit (typically, the *parakletos* in John) "the Father" will
send is related intimately to Jesus and the particularities of Jesus' ministry:

> But the Advocate, the Holy Spirit, whom the Father will send in my
> name, will teach you everything, and remind you of all that I have said
> to you. (14:26)

The Spirit is a witness to Jesus:

> When the Advocate comes, whom I will send to you from the Father, the
> Spirit of truth who comes from the Father, he will testify on my behalf.
> You also are to testify, because you have been with me from the begin-
> ning. (15:26)

The functional connection among the three figures is apparent:

> When the Spirit of truth comes, he will guide you into all the truth;
> for he will not speak on his own, but will speak whatever he hears, and
> he will declare to you the things that are to come. He will glorify me,
> because he will take what is mine and declare it to you. All that the
> Father has is mine. For this reason I said that he will take what is mine
> and declare it to you. (16:13-15)

Language about the Spirit is reminiscent of Old Testament usage.
Singular here is the close relationship between the work of the Spirit

whom the Father sends (and in whose sending the Son likewise participates) and the past and future work of Jesus, the Son, whose work reflects the will of the Father. The point of these chapters in the Fourth Gospel is not abstract speculation but clear indications of how God will continue to be experienced for those "who have not seen and yet believe" (John 20:29). The God whom Israel knows as creator and sustainer is known and experienced through the continuing work of the Spirit, whose activity is tied intimately with the career of Jesus—to whom the disciples (and the author of the Fourth Gospel) give testimony.

That God is known in relationship to Jesus is clear throughout as God is identified as Father and Jesus as Son.

2. Mark

The Father and Son metaphor is far less common in Mark than in John.[7] God is explicitly identified as "Father" only four times. As in John, Jesus is the only one to use the term. He addresses God as "Abba" in his prayer in the garden (14:36). The Aramaic term is translated with the Greek *pater* (father), as is customary in Mark. Jesus speaks about the coming of the Son of Man "in the glory of his Father with the holy angels" (8:38). In speaking of the future, he tells his followers, "about that day or hour no one knows, neither the angels in heaven, nor the Son, but only the Father" (13:32). Once, he speaks of God as others' Father ("so that your Father in heaven may also forgive you your trespasses" [11:25]).

More common is the use of "Son of God" for Jesus. Outside the passion story, it is language used only by supernatural powers. The demons know that Jesus is "the Son of God" (3:11) and "the Son of the Most High God" (5:7). Twice God addresses Jesus as "my Son," in language reminiscent of Psalm 2 (1:11, 9:7). Jesus refers to himself once as "the Son" (13:32). Twice in the passion story major figures use the title. In a climactic scene, the chief priest asks Jesus if he is "the Christ, the Son of the Blessed one" (14:61). Jesus responds, "I am; and you will see. . . .," promising vindication in language reminiscent of Psalm 110:1 and Daniel 7:13. Finally, a centurion says at the moment of his death, "Truly this was the (a) Son (son) of God" (15:39).

While not as prominent, the metaphor appears at critical points in the narrative. "Son of God" is important as a christological designation. It is equally significant theologically. The God of whom the narrative speaks is understood from the very first as the one who calls Jesus "Son."[8]

The few mentions of the Holy Spirit are less integrated with christological and theological imagery. The Spirit inspired David in the writing of the Psalms (12:36) and will speak for Jesus' followers when they are brought before courts to testify (13:11). The most suggestive passage is the brief comment in the account of Jesus' baptism that the Spirit comes down "into Jesus" as the heavens are torn apart and God speaks to "my Son," using the language of Psalm 2:7 and Isaiah 42:1 (and perhaps Gen 22). The degree to which Jesus is "inspired" by the Spirit is singular. In Mark, "blasphemy against the Holy Spirit" is restricted to attributing Jesus' mighty works to an unclean spirit. He is the bearer of the Holy Spirit.

3. Paul

The situation is not different in Paul, whose letters represent the earliest writings in the New Testament. Fundamental modifications of traditional Jewish monotheism are present from the earliest stages of tradition to which Paul's letters provide access. Language is used to speak about Jesus that is ordinarily reserved for God. The titles "Lord" and even "God" are used to speak of Jesus. While the lordship of Jesus does not replace the lordship of God, the latter is understood differently in light of such passages as Philippians 2:5-11.

Particularly interesting are statements like these:

> ... yet for us there is one God, the Father, from whom are all things and for whom we exist, and one Lord, Jesus Christ, through whom are all things and through whom we exist. (1 Cor 8:6)

The bold statement of the oneness of God in the context of discussing idols is hardly surprising for a Jew. Surprising is the statement about the "Lord" Jesus Christ that follows. While "the Father" is identified as the Creator ("from whom are all things"), creation is as much an activity of the "Lord Jesus Christ" ("through whom are all things"), identified elsewhere as "the Son." Paul obviously does not sense that the statement about the unique lordship of Jesus violates the oneness of God—yet it qualifies that oneness in important ways.

The Father and Son metaphor is not the only way in which Paul speaks christologically and theologically. He nevertheless makes regular use of the metaphor. God is "the Father" (Rom 6:4, 1 Cor 8:6, Gal 1:1), "the God and Father of our Lord Jesus Christ" (Rom 15:6; 2 Cor 1:3, 11:31). More frequently, Jesus is identified as God's "Son" (Rom 1:3, 4, 9; 5:10; 8:3, 19, 29, 32, etc.).

The metaphor is employed to speak of the relationship of God to believers: God is "our Father." A regular feature of the opening salutation in virtually every letter speaks of God in this way: "Grace to you and peace from God our Father and the Lord Jesus Christ" (Rom 1:7, 1 Cor 1:3, 2 Cor 1:2, Gal 1:3, etc.). In view of this usage, however, it is remarkable how rarely believers are identified as "children of God" (Rom 9:8), "sons of God"[9] (Rom 8:14, 19; 9:26; Gal 3:26), or "sons and daughters of God" (2 Cor 3:18).

That the metaphor can be used of believers is clearly derivative from its use as a designation of Jesus' relationship to "the Father." The elaborate scriptural argument in Galatians 3 draws heavily on messianic testimonies to make the point that only those who are "in Christ" can be regarded as the true children of Abraham. As part of the argument, Paul indicates how it is that believers can understand God as Father:

> But now that faith has come, we are no longer subject to a disciplinarian, for in Christ Jesus you are all children of God [literally "sons of God"] through faith. As many of you as were baptized into Christ have clothed yourself with Christ. There is no longer Jew or Greek, there is no longer slave or free, there is no longer male and female; for all of you are one in Christ Jesus. (Gal 3:25-28)

As in the Fourth Gospel, it is in speaking of this relationship among believers, God the Father, and Jesus the Son that the Spirit appears as an active participant.

> But you are not in the flesh; you are in the Spirit, since the Spirit of God dwells in you. Anyone who does not have the Spirit of Christ does not belong to him. But if Christ is in you, though the body is dead because of sin, the Spirit is life because of righteousness. If the Spirit of him who raised Jesus from the dead dwells in you, he who raised Christ from the dead will give life to your mortal bodies also through his Spirit that dwells in you. . . . For all who are led by the Spirit of God are children of God. For you did not receive a spirit of slavery to fall back into fear, but you have received a spirit of adoption. When we cry, "Abba! Father!" it is that very Spirit bearing witness with our spirit that we are children of God, and if children, then heirs, heirs of God and joint heirs with Christ. . . . (Rom 8:9-17)

The Spirit is variously identified as "the Spirit of God" and "the Spirit of Christ." Its major function here, as in the Fourth Gospel, is to designate the present work of God and Christ in the life of the faithful.

Paul's letters do not attempt a systematization of such varied ways of speaking about God. Statements about Father and Son do not always measure up to the later standards of orthodoxy. In 1 Corinthians, for example, the Son under whose feet God puts all things in subjection is clearly subordinate to the One who subjects all things. At the end, he hands the kingdom over to God the Father (1 Cor 15:24).

> When all things are subjected to him, then the Son himself will also be subjected to the one who put all things in subjection under him, so that God may be all in all. (15:28)

Nevertheless, what is said about God is tied intimately with what is said about "the Lord Jesus Christ." Jesus is the Son whom God did not spare; God is the one who raised Jesus from the dead. God is the Father to whom the Son will hand over the kingdom at the end.

4. Behind the New Testament

The prominence of the Father and Son metaphor in the creeds is an appropriate introduction to the ways the New Testament speaks about God. What it means to call God "Father" is disclosed within the concrete ways the metaphor is employed to speak of Jesus, "the Son." A full appreciation of the language requires not only attention to the particularities of the various New Testament writings. It requires setting the whole New Testament witness within its larger canonical setting. I will make only a few comments here that I hope are suggestive.

While the creeds highlight the Father and Son metaphor, there is other language used to speak of Jesus and God in the New Testament. Perhaps the most common title is "Christ": Jesus is confessed as the promised king anointed by God. The singularity of this claim is becoming more apparent as the various manifestations of postbiblical Judaism are compared and contrasted.[10] The lack of precedent for using messianic (royal) language to speak of one who dies on a cross and is raised from the dead—and the apparent offense created by such use of messianic tradition—makes the particularity of the Gospel narratives more significant.[11] The understanding and experience of God that have found their way through the New Testament into the creeds and into the history of the church are intimately tied to the history and ministry of Jesus of Nazareth, whose ministry included death on a Roman cross as "the King of the Jews." Jesus is confessed as the crucified and risen king—or Christ. God is the one who vindicated the crucified Christ by raising him from the dead.

Important for our purposes are the citations of Old Testament passages in which God addresses the king as "Son." The two most significant are Psalm 2:7 and 2 Samuel 7:14, both of which became part of Israel's visions and dreams of the Messiah-King whom God would raise up at the end of days. Both are cited in the New Testament (Ps 2:7; Acts 13:33; Heb 1:5 and 5:5; see also Mark 1:11 and par., 9:7 and par.; John 1:49; 2 Sam. 7:14; Heb 1:5; 2 Cor 6:18 [where "sons" replaces "son"]; see also John 1:49 and Rev 21:7). Both have had a central role in the development of christology.[12]

The confession of Jesus as "Son" and God as "Father" is one way of hearing what it means to confess Jesus as the crucified and risen Christ. If the God of Israel is now to be identified as the God who raised Jesus from the dead, one appropriate way of speaking about that God is as "Father" of the royal "Son" who is now vindicated and seated at the right hand. The use of such imagery and the related Old Testament passages likewise provide a connection with the Spirit who inspired the prophetic promises about a coming royal Son while at the same time providing confirmation of the promises of God.

This is not to argue that all occurrences of Father and Son imagery can be derived from messianic reading of the Scriptures. Such a theory cannot adequately account for the use of "the Father" and "the Son," particularly in the Fourth Gospel. It is possible, as Joachim Jeremias argued some time ago, that the use of "Father" for God derived in part from Jesus' own singular use of "Abba" as a form of addressing God.[13]

It is not my intention to explain the imagery in the New Testament by speculating about origins. More significant is to observe the range of the metaphors both in terms of their usage in New Testament writings and in terms of previous biblical tradition. The point is again that the language used to speak of God is intimately related to the particulars of Jesus' career. If "Son of God" is a term that could be used of angels and heavenly intermediaries, it only makes the range of the metaphor more impressive.

A Preliminary Assessment

The first question to be asked is if study of the New Testament offers the possibility of assessing later Trinitarian formulations, in particular the Trinitarian creeds. A provisional answer would be yes. The creeds modify biblical monotheism in terms of statements about the concrete historical figure, Jesus, and the experience of the faithful through the Spirit. While the New Testament offers no systematic reflection on these modifications to traditional faith in the one God, it speaks in ways that invite further reflection. In particular, the New Testament speaks of God as the Father of the Son, who became flesh, spoke with authority, healed the sick, died on a Roman cross as "the King of the Jews," and was vindicated by God on the third day. While God is still the Creator of the heavens and the earth, that

God is henceforth to be known first and foremost in relationship to Jesus and the experiences of the Spirit in Jesus' name.

Employing the Metaphor

The second question has to do with the importance of the creeds for those who read the Bible. It is possible to view the creeds as ends in themselves, regarding the Trinitarian formulations as solutions to some theological problem. That would be a serious mistake. The first Trinitarian confessions most likely occurred as part of baptismal services, as Nils Dahl has convincingly demonstrated.[14] They are not complete statements of the faith but seek to make clear in whose name the initiates are baptized and a bit about what that implies. The creeds were and are part of Christian practice, functioning within a liturgical and catechetical setting. It is only in the preaching and the sacraments, the prayers and the hymns of praise, that the Trinitarian confessions come to life. In such activities, God is actually experienced as a saving and liberating presence. The creeds seek to prepare the faithful for an engagement with the God who is known and experienced as God the Father, Jesus the Son, and God the Spirit.

The church's Trinitarian creeds can have an important function for Bible readers. The Trinitarian formulations ought not be viewed as replacing reading of the Scriptures but as an introduction to a fruitful engagement with the Bible. I would propose the following theses:

1. Creeds are helpful introductions to the Bible because people can read the Bible and miss the point. What is "the point"? The creeds suggest that the story be read with God in mind—and that such awareness can prove crucial in appreciating the story.

2. Each of the creeds explicates the faith of the church by speaking about God. The matter is of more than passing interest in a culture where "God" often never crosses people's imagination. To speak about the faith is to say some things about God; to have faith is to experience a kind of engagement with God. Because the Scriptures have to do with the life of faith, reading the Bible ought to be a theological enterprise. That many can read and study the Bible without ever mentioning God is an indication that reading is always done through filters that both screen out and highlight aspects of what we read. Biases and prejudices serve to prepare us for all encounters, literary and otherwise. The important question is what will prove to be fruitful prejudices for our encounter with the Scriptures. The church has proposed a theological bias as

an appropriate introduction to an interpretation of the Scriptures: they have to do with God.

3.   Confessing God requires clarification, since the term "God" can be taken to mean different things. The creeds seek to make clear in what God our faith is invested. The God whose story the Bible tells—whose name was revealed to Moses, who called Israel to be a blessing, and who raised Jesus from the dead—is the God who is the source and focus of Christian faith. That is not necessarily what people understand "God" to mean. We cannot rely on ordinary intuition or common sense, as various critics of Christian tradition have amply demonstrated and as the critical tradition within Christianity makes clear. In this culture in particular, "God" seems to have become captive to the private spheres of life and exorcised from public imagination. The attractiveness and popularity of the song "From a Distance" suggests that for many, the world is a place where God is effectively absent. The nearness of God in the preaching of Christ may well strike people as "foolishness," as Paul suggests in the opening chapters of 1 Corinthians. If so, the creeds are helpful preparation for an engagement with a God who is known not first of all in the imagination but in the life of the church that is shaped by the biblical narrative.

4.   The most important thing to know about the God whom the scriptural narrative discloses is that God is known first in our experiencing Jesus, the Son of God, through the work of the Spirit.

If this is the case, the creeds should serve not to displace Bible reading but to prepare us for it. The creeds introduce us to a God who can be none other than the one disclosed through an engagement with the Bible. It is crucial, then, to keep the Trinitarian metaphors rooted in the biblical witness. The image of God as "Father" does not function as a typical metaphor. That is clearest in John, where God is "Father" only to those who abide in the Son. What it means to be "Father" has little to do with human analogies. It is as clear in Paul, for whom being "in Christ," the Son of God, makes it possible to experience God as Father. Even in Matthew, where God is most frequently depicted as "your heavenly Father," the experience of God is mediated through the ministry of the one whom God calls Son. The teacher and miracle worker is also the one who dies as "King of the Jews" and is raised on the third day. Baptism in the name of the Father, and of the Son, and of the Holy Spirit makes sense only as the followers of Jesus "make disciples of all nations, teaching them to observe all that I have commanded you." God is experienced as loving "Father" only through the Son who is present "until the end of the age" as "God with us."

Trinitarian language can be problematic. It may well contribute to a patriarchalism deeply rooted in Christian tradition. One danger is interpreting the creeds in a woodenly literalistic way, so that "Father" and "Son" are understood solely on the basis of human analogies: God is male. Such reading fails to appreciate how a metaphor both reveals and conceals reality, and it may well underestimate the possibility of expanding Christian imagination rather than limiting it. Trinitarian statements must themselves be interpreted by studying the creeds in their historical contexts and examining their theological and pastoral implications. If hearing Trinitarian language properly is a problem, however, perhaps the most salutary "safeguard" is to view Trinitarian creeds as fruitful prejudices for the reading of the Scriptures.

If the central role of the Scriptures is to shape a Christian imagination and practice, we may dare to hope that regular engagement with the Bible will introduce us to a God who is not generic but particular. The names and activities by which that God is to be known are bound to a particular history and persons—a history and persons that are mediated to us by a particular collection of writings, the tradition of their interpretation, and especially by Christian practice. The God whom we confess is first the "Father"—the Father of the Son, Jesus Christ, who is present to us through the activity of the Spirit. The creeds introduce us to a God whose work encompasses the past, the present, and the future and includes the whole cosmos; who "became flesh" and endured the cross in Jesus of Nazareth; and who works for the liberation and salvation of specific individuals through means of grace through which the Spirit is operative. Christians do not believe in three gods but in a God an encounter with whom requires a new language. To the degree the language of the Trinity serves that end, it is a precious feature of the tradition that deserves attention and use not only by systematic theologians but by those interested in the Bible and Christian practice.

8

Interpreting Mark's Gospel

This material first appeared as the opening chapter in an introductory text-book on the Gospel according to Mark. It offers a basic orientation to Mark and to Juel's embrace of a "rhetorical approach" to the Gospel, an approach that focuses on the narrative's effects on its readers. To understand Mark is to engage the story and see how our reading opens up an understanding of God.

—————

Getting Oriented

Crucial to interpretation is knowing where to begin. Bible reading, of course, has no prerequisites. Anyone can pick up a Bible and start reading. It may be argued, in fact, that anxiety about being fully prepared to interpret the Bible can actually inhibit reading and enjoyment. This volume is written with confidence that there is nevertheless much to learn that can enhance our understanding and appreciation of the Bible.

An important stage in the development of educated readers is learning how much has been written about the Bible. With an almost limitless amount of information available on the text of the New Testament, the history of its translation and interpretation, the historical and cultural context out of which it emerged, and the ways it is currently read by experts of all sorts, a student needs to recognize what is important to know. It is impossible to read everything, even for those who study full time. Further, gathering information does not necessarily result in enlightenment. Information may contribute little to making sense of the

121

Gospel, or it may result in making sense of something uninteresting and unimportant.

As important as knowing *where* to begin is knowing *how* to begin. It has been customary within academic circles to begin engagement with the Gospels in silent, solitary reading. In classes where students can work in original languages, the initial assignment may be to translate the first chapter. This will take a good bit of time for most students and will offer an experience of a particular sort. The exercise will offer a glimpse of only a small portion of the Gospel and is thus more likely to focus on details. Those who know the language at all will immediately recognize Mark's limited vocabulary and rather elementary constructions. They may notice the repetition of simple connecting links ("and immediately") and the episodic character of the narrative. They may be taken by the strangeness of a story told in a language other than their own, captivated perhaps by individual details ("Why this word?"). And they are easily impressed by scholarly arguments that point up the aesthetic shortcomings of the Gospel.

Another initial assignment is to work with a synopsis of the Gospels—an arrangement of Matthew, Mark, and Luke in parallel columns—and to read the opening sections of Mark in comparison to the sections in Matthew or Luke. Such reading calls attention to the very different ways of beginning a story, as well as differences in detail and vocabulary. Some commentaries proceed this way, noting regularly that "while Mark says this, Matthew or Luke say something different." The approach makes clear how differently the same story can be told and how dramatically the differences shape the reader's expectations and experience of the narrative.

More recently I have sent students off from their first class to read Mark from beginning to end in translation (in their own language; the presence of students who do not speak English and whose Bible is in another tongue makes for interesting comparisons from the outset). Their observations and questions are different. They are less likely to be taken by particular words than by scenes or themes or the whole story. Often someone will ask why Jesus silences people he heals; someone else, a more careful reader, will ask also about the exception, where a former demoniac is instructed to go and tell. A retired schoolteacher commented, "I was impressed with the number of imperatives. Jesus is always commanding someone or something." Some will note parallels or duplicate forms of a story, like the feeding of the five thousand and the four thousand. They are less likely to be impressed by arguments that point out the aesthetic shortcomings of the narrative.

When students begin by watching a "performance" of the Gospel by one of several accomplished readers, sometimes live but usually video-taped, they react very differently. Few, if any, are impressed by the alleged literary flaws of the Gospel. It "works" orally. And people are more likely to react emotionally—to laugh, to become irritated, or to experience uneasiness. Deciding that 16:8 is the best choice among alternative end-ings after a lengthy discussion of what is involved in choosing among various possibilities present within manuscript tradition has an impact nothing like that of a two-hour performance of Mark that ends with, "And they said nothing to anyone, for they were afraid." Students are more taken by Jesus' tone of voice, or the elusive roles of characters who appear and disappear.

Finally, when students are asked to study the Gospel in preparation for reading themselves, aloud in the presence of others, another whole series of questions arises that never occur to those who read silently and privately. It matters a great deal if the Bible is interpreted to understand its meaning or if it is read with an eye to actually performing it. Knowing where to begin and what will be relevant to study depend upon the goal of the engagement with the Gospel. How we choose to study, in other words, depends upon what we imagine the Bible is good for.

What Should We Expect? Examining Prejudices

Few people come to the Bible without some expectations. Preparation may be subtle. That the New Testament is read in schools and in churches—and has been read for almost two thousand years—suggests that the various writings are valuable. Those who find the writings like Mark strange or difficult are least encouraged to press on, knowing that others have found them meaningful. Preparation is also more overt. Churches have always introduced people to the Bible. In the Middle Ages, cathedral windows depicting biblical stories provided the lenses through which people looked at the Gospels. Church music, from hymns to oratorios, combined pas-sages from a variety of biblical works and gave to the biblical text a partic-ular feel or mood. For the more scholarly and literate, there are collected opinions about who wrote the Gospels.

People who know anything about church tradition—or who read the paragraphs introducing each biblical book that appear in study Bibles—will have learned that according to an old tradition, the "Gospel according to Mark" was written by a follower of Peter and onetime traveling com-panion of the Apostle Paul, perhaps a Jerusalem believer in whose house the church met (Acts 12). It comes as a surprise to many that the Gospel itself says no such thing. It is utterly mute on the matter of authorship and occasion. We will spend a little time reviewing the history of interpreting Mark, not so as to feel superior to previous generations of readers but to understand where we stand, how our expectations have been shaped, what suggestions will or will not stand up to critical scrutiny, and what hunches are worth following up.

The first person to say anything about the book we know as the Gospel according to Mark is a bishop named Papias, who lived in the early decades of the second century in Hierapolis in Asia Minor, some of whose words have been preserved by the great fourth-century church historian Eusebius. According to Eusebius, this is what Papias "used to say":

> Mark was the interpreter of Peter. He wrote down accurately, but without form [*ou mentoi taxei*] what he remembered of the things said and done by the Lord. For neither did he hear the Lord, nor did he follow him, but later on, as I said, Peter—who fashioned the teachings according to the needs of the moment, but not as though he were drawing up a connected account of the Lord's sayings. Thus Mark made no mistake in so recording some things as he remembered them. For he had one thing in mind, namely to omit nothing of the things he had heard and to falsify nothing among them.[1]

With so little information about Papias and the context in which he writes, scholars have disagreed about how to understand his comments. Those scholars interested in Mark as a possible historical resource for getting back to the real Jesus of history tend to think that Papias was interested in the "order" of Mark's story: "Mark wrote down accurately, but not in order [i.e., chronological]," since disagreements among the Gospel writers about the exact sequence of events in Jesus' ministry pose a problem for historians trying to get at what really happened. More recently, interpreters interested in literary and rhetorical questions have tended to read Papias' words as a comment on the literary form of Mark: Mark wrote accurately, but without the form or "order" one expects of written works.[2] Mark's Gospel, in other words, does not sound like proper literature. I tend to agree with this reading of Papias' comments.

In either case, the first recorded comment on the work that we know as the Gospel according to Mark reflects some embarrassment about it and a need to offer an apology. Mark did what he was supposed to do, says Papias. His goals were modest. He recorded what he heard from his source (Peter), who also had no literary pretensions. His only concern as an author was to be complete and accurate. One ought not therefore expect too much of the work.

The good bishop's sense that Mark is a strange book is reflected in the entire history of the church. Mark's Gospel is virtually ignored. Matthew, then John, are the Gospels that were most widely read and quoted.

A more important reason for the lack of attention paid Mark's Gospel is the work of another bishop, the influential Augustine of Hippo, who lived and worked in the early fifth century. Somewhat embarrassed by the presence of four Gospels instead of one, Augustine sought to give some reason for the abundance. Mark, he argued, was the "epitomizer" of Matthew. That is, Mark abridged Matthew's Gospel. His arguments make some sense, since almost everything in Mark's Gospel can be found in Matthew—except that Matthew includes other material as well (e.g., the Sermon on the Mount, birth stories, accounts of the resurrection). The relationship of Mark to the other Gospels is an important matter and will occupy us later. If it is true that Mark is only a shortened version of Matthew, it is not surprising that church leaders and teachers preferred the "real thing" (Matthew) and ignored Mark.

That Mark is a secondary version of Matthew was held almost without question into the nineteenth century. Griesbach, the German scholar perhaps most responsible for the use of a synopsis of the three "synoptic Gospels" as a study tool (an arrangement of Matthew, Mark, and Luke in parallel columns), was convinced that Matthew wrote first, Luke next, and Mark later ("Matthean priority"). His synopsis, however, provided one of the tools by which students of the New Testament began to look more carefully at the relationship among Matthew, Mark, and Luke, eventually concluding that Mark was most likely the first Gospel narrative to be written. A nineteenth-century scholar named Karl Lachmann is credited with arguing in a convincing way that Mark was the earliest of the Gospels.

The arguments for "Markan priority," as it is known, have convinced most scholars. The patterns of shared wording among Matthew, Mark, and Luke seem to demand a literary solution—that is, one or more of the Gospel writers must have seen the work of the other(s) or all have a common source. Scholars have found it easier to explain Matthew and Luke as expanded rewrites of Mark than the reverse. Augustine's argument that Mark abridges Matthew, for example, cannot explain why in some of the miracle stories Mark's version is far longer and Matthew's sounds like a condensation (e.g., Mark 5:1-20 and Matt 8:28-34). The Greek of Matthew and Luke is in general superior to Mark's and in specific instances can be viewed as conscious improvement. The greatest difference between Matthew and Luke, on the one hand, and Mark on the other, is the considerable body of Jesus' sayings common to Matthew and Luke that are absent in Mark. The standard explanation is that there existed a collection of Jesus' sayings (called "Q," for *Quelle*, the German word for "source") shared by Matthew and Luke. In addition to the two common sources— Mark and "Q"—Matthew and Luke apparently had independent sources as well. The matters are well discussed in standard introductions to the New Testament.

"Markan priority" provided a considerable boost in the popularity of what now came to be known as the earliest Gospel. Ironically, what attracted scholars to Mark in the eighteenth and nineteenth centuries was the same alleged lack of artfulness signaled by Papias centuries earlier. These scholars were principally interested in the Gospels as historical resources. Some were convinced that Christian writings had distorted the facts of history, making an ordinary Jew into the Second Person of the Trinity. A whole variety of scholars took their turn in writing about the "real Jesus" in hopes of rescuing Jesus from the rigid doctrines and tired piety of the church. Mark was important to them as the earliest available source for their reconstructive project. The alleged artlessness, coupled with the remarkable sense of verisimilitude, seemed to make the Gospel invaluable as a source. The author, according to this view, simply collected material but was (fortunately) too unsophisticated to transform it into a coherent narrative. Matthew and Luke, being more creative, were more likely to have altered traditions to make them fit into their literary productions. Well into the twentieth century, a prominent German scholar could say of all the Gospels that their authors were not really "authors" but "collectors, vehicles of tradition, editors."[3]

One great exception to this whole tradition of scholarship was Wilhelm Wrede, whose book on the so-called Messianic Secret, published in 1901, treated Mark's Gospel as a creative piece with a theological agenda.[4] While not claiming too much for the Gospel writer's literary or theological sophistication, Wrede nonetheless appreciated Mark's achievement, which was to produce a new genre of literature. He did this, Wrede argued, by combining the tradition about Jesus that did not view him as Messiah with the tradition that proclaimed Jesus as the crucified and risen Christ, most clearly articulated in Paul's letters (e.g., 1 Cor 15:3-7). Had scholarship found Wrede's work more persuasive, it might have come to focus on the Gospel narrative rather than its sources. That was not to be. Not until the 1950s would a major shift in scholarship occur that would direct attention more to the narrative than to what lay behind it.

What Are We After? Standing and Understanding

Sorting out alternative strategies for reading is itself an interesting topic and can become all-absorbing. We could spend all our time thinking about how to proceed, only to discover that we have no time to read the Bible. That would be unfortunate. A few moments of reflection will prove useful, however. I would like to suggest spatial images by which to understand what we are after and what sorts of questions will prove most helpful. The images—the "World Behind the Text," the "World of the Text," and the "World in Front of the Text"—are borrowed principally from the philosopher Paul Ricoeur. They are both simple and useful in locating ourselves among the various traditions and methods of interpretation.

The World Behind Mark's Gospel: Interpretation Through Dissection

Students of Mark in the nineteenth and most of the twentieth century have been interested in the Gospel principally as a window that affords a glimpse of an earlier period in the history of tradition. As interpreters, our task is to stand before the window and look through it at the various things it allows us to view, which may include the actual recorded events, the "intention" of Jesus or the church or the Gospel writer.[5] Questions have to do mostly with how reliable a window the story provides. Is the glass tinted, or does it distort? The elaborate methods that allow such an assessment all begin with source criticism, that is, trying to break the story down into its various sources. If the narrative were a seamless cloth, source criticism would be far more difficult. The episodic nature of the Gospel, however—whole series of anecdotes with abrupt transition from one to the next—can be studied as evidence for the book's compositional history.

That such dissection of Mark can be done with such ease is indeed impressive. In a famous study,[6] the German Karl Ludwig Schmidt demonstrated that when a handful of summaries are removed from the narrative, the story disintegrates into individual episodes or collections of episodes. The author, he argued, has provided a primitive framework within which to set bits and pieces of prior tradition, like a mosaic. Because Mark's technique is so undeveloped, it is relatively easy to show how the whole was fashioned. If the Gospel can be compared to a mosaic, one may study the Gospel by observing the use of individual stones. One result of this observation has been *form criticism*, a school of interpretation that focuses on the form of individual story units as an indication of their function.

The school of form criticism took as its point of departure the features of written biblical works that seem to betray the marks of oral culture. Borrowing insights from studies of folklore in German and Scandinavian universities, students first of the Old Testament, then of the New Testament, undertook the task of reconstructing the communities who told stories about Jesus and remembered his sayings. Typical of the oral setting in traditional communities are features that make for easy remembering or that facilitate performance. Most easily recognizable are confessions and hymns and liturgical texts that can be isolated in Paul's letters. Paul's summary of "the gospel which I received," for example, has a simple structure that scholars identify as "confessional" (1 Cor 15:3-7). Jesus' words to his disciples at the Last Supper that Paul recalls in 1 Corinthians 11 seem to betray the marks of regular usage in a worship setting (1 Cor 11:23-25). While formal patterns are not so clearly identifiable in narrative material, form critics were convinced that they could identify "controversy stories" and "miracle stories" and "wisdom sayings" for which a regular setting in the life of the community could be identified.

An example of this kind of formal analysis is the case of what some call "controversy stories." In the second and third chapters of Mark's Gospel, Jesus engages in discussion with Pharisees who question his practice:

> And as he sat at dinner in Levi's house, many tax collectors and sinners were also sitting with Jesus and his disciples—for there were many who followed him. When the scribes of the Pharisees saw that he was eating with sinners and tax collectors, they said to his disciples, "Why does he eat with tax collectors and sinners?" When Jesus heard this, he said to them, "Those who are well have no need of a physician, but those who are sick; I have come to call not the righteous but sinners." (2:15-17)

> One sabbath he was going through the grainfields; and as they made their way his disciples began to pluck heads of grain. The Pharisees said to him, "Look, why are they doing what is not lawful on the sabbath?" And he said to them, "Have you never read what David did when he and his companions were hungry and in need of food? He entered the house of God, when Abiathar was high priest, and ate the bread of the Presence, which it is not lawful for any but the priests to eat, and he gave some to his companions." Then he said to them, "The sabbath was made for humankind, and not humankind for the sabbath; so the Son of Man is lord even of the sabbath." (2:23-28)

The anecdotes include regular features. There is a general setting, a question is posed—usually in the form of a challenge or criticism—and Jesus gives a short, pointed response. Those unfamiliar with Jewish ritual matters will have some difficulty following the discussions. We will have occasion to deal with that issue later. Here we should notice the simple formal patterns in which the episodes are cast.

Such patterns can be studied and compared with other story forms. In the recorded writings of the Jewish rabbis, for example, controversies about legal matters are a regular feature of interpretation. The forms are somewhat different. Answers to questions are often structured according to two responses, one from the "house of Shammai," and one from the "house of Hillel" (two prominent first-century rabbis). An opinion is given, sometimes with the argument, followed by an indication that this is the view of the majority. Often a minority opinion is recorded. Such forms are similar to other legal discourse. This is the way lawyers and judges talk—and the way they remember cases. The form of the story reflects something about its function in a regular social setting.

Students of the Bible have argued there also exists such a relationship between New Testament "forms" and a regular social setting they reflect. Controversy stories seem to imply a community that was interested in matters of Sabbath observance and purity laws that settled such matters not by gathering the opinions of respected teachers but by recalling sayings of Jesus.

What scholars hope to learn from such study is something about the setting in which the material was remembered and used. Who were the anonymous people who handed on stories about Jesus and remembered them? What were their interests? Interpretation is understood here as providing the materials with which to reconstruct a history of the early church—or at least to reconstruct the "original" audience of the various traditions that have found their way into the written Gospels. The focus of interpretation is the practices and beliefs that characterized this particular group of people—thus, their "mind." To read the Gospel of Mark is to have insight into the lives of real people in the first century of our era.

"Controversy stories" suggest a group invested in questions having to do with Jewish legal observance. Whether or not the issues in the stories arose from actual controversies in Jesus' ministry, the questions make sense within the later setting of the church. Why are we casual with regard to Sabbath observance? What about fasting? Should we not be more careful about food laws? The criticisms aimed at Jesus identify a matter still important to the faithful. The answers to the questions in the form of pithy sayings of Jesus indicate how the community understands itself and its practices, and they suggest one of the ways in which Jesus serves as an authority.

For such study, the narrative is dissected into its components, whether these are cycles of stories or individual episodes. Such analysis of sources does not yield "history" in the sense of getting back to events in the ministry of Jesus, but history as an earlier stage of tradition, most likely oral and not written. While these traditions can be studied to determine their historical reliability, they can also be examined for what they disclose about the people who remembered such stories and handed them on.

Such dissecting of the narrative can move in two directions. On the one hand, those interested in the "historical Jesus"—the Jesus who can be reconstructed through critical use of sources, including the Gospels—can continue to work behind the alleged oral sources from which Mark drew. Such scholars formulate criteria on the basis of which to test the historical reliability of these oral sources (see below on the historical Jesus). On the other hand, the same information can be examined for what it discloses about the author of the Gospel. If we know Mark's sources, we can study the way he combined them to form the present Gospel. Many scholars are convinced, for example, that Mark was the first to write a whole story of Jesus and that his sources were at best cycles of stories and perhaps a small collection of parables, as well as a longer and more coherent account of Jesus' trial and death. How he chose to tie them together to tell a story is partly revealed in how he does his editing or redacting (thus *redaction criticism*). The focus of interest here is the peculiar views of the author, understood as somehow distinct from those of the tradition that he edited, and thus most visible in overt changes or alterations of sources.

Both form and redaction criticism, as the approaches came to be called, study the Gospel by taking it apart. The disciplines take seriously the form of the story units and the cultural setting in which they developed. They take less seriously the final form of the narrative. Like Papias, they tend to find it aesthetically lacking. The interest of such scholars is not first of all in the narrative as a whole, which they do not find coherent or compelling, but in the personalities it discloses or the historical facts it reveals. That the Gospel is a coherent piece that intends to be performed is something they ignore or reject.

Scholarship in the last twenty-five years has made a decisive break with such approaches, not because the methods of study are invalid but because interpreters choose to focus on a reading of the whole narrative or an experience of it. Dissecting a narrative to make sense of it turns out to be more like an autopsy than an operation. The doctor may learn many interesting things by carving up a human body, but something must die as a result. We will be interested principally in the Gospel as a story that comes to life when read.

The World of Mark's Gospel: Literary Analysis and Gospel Narratives

A crucial shift in scholarship occurred in the midfifties. Scholars trained in source and form criticism whose strategies were to dissect the narratives so as more closely to study the component parts suddenly became interested in the body. Willi Marxsen's *Mark the Evangelist* was one of the first to use the methods of source criticism to speak about the "evangelist" and to ask after the message of the whole.[7]

Methods derived from an earlier era were soon supplemented by approaches more common in the field of literature. The chair of the English department at Indiana University published essays on Mark.[8] Major literary scholars like Frank Kermode began publishing studies of Mark and other Gospels.[9] Within the guild of New Testament scholars, a major force in refocusing scholarship was Norman Perrin, who turned his considerable energies to study the evangelist rather than the historical Jesus. His *What Is Redaction Criticism?* marks an important transition from an era dominated by source criticism to a new era in which literary study in the proper sense began to flourish. While he speaks of redaction criticism, Perrin means something quite different, more akin to the kind of study familiar from literature classes.

> The fundamental premise of redaction criticism, then, is that the pericope can be analyzed from the perspective of a Marcan purpose. The goal of such analysis is to understand the purpose and the theology that is revealed in the purpose. To this end we concern ourselves both with the individual parts of the narrative and with the story as a whole. In other words, we analyze the constituent parts of the narrative . . . to see what they tell us of Mark as one who gathers, modifies, or creates tradition, and we analyze the total narrative in terms of its overall purposes . . . to see what this will tell us about Mark as an evangelist.[10]

For those who were not trained as source critics, it may be difficult to imagine the impact of the shift. A generation of Bible readers had been trained not to read stories, and their training was successful. Those who read Mark with historical interests never imagined the book worked as

a story. Fine scholars never observed the simplest connections within
the story that students pick up almost immediately—provided they look
for such things. In the story of Jesus' trial, for example, Peter's denial of
Jesus "brackets" the actual trial report. The narrator takes Peter as far
as the courtyard of the high priest (14:53-54) before shifting to the proceedings inside (14:55-65), only to shift back to Peter when Jesus' trial is
over (14:66-72). The breaks in the story turn out to be more than signs of
deficient sources. The shifting from the outside to the inside and back is
a simple way of relating the two episodes. Once that becomes apparent,
all sorts of things stand out. Perhaps the most obvious is the relationship between the taunt of those pummeling Jesus at the conclusion of his
trial ("Prophesy!" [14:65]) and the events in the courtyard (14:66-72). The
narrator informs us that after Peter's third denial, the cock crows—for a
second time. The detail is important because Jesus predicted that "before
the cock crows twice, you will deny me three times" (14:72). Careful readers will recall that prophecy (14:28-30). One of Jesus' prophecies is being
fulfilled to the letter—at the moment Jesus is being mocked as a prophet
inside the house. Readers are expected to appreciate the irony in a way no
one in the story can. The relationship between the mockery and Peter's
denial seems obvious—but not a single commentator preoccupied with
Mark's sources ever noted it.[11] Seek, and you will find.

Scholars now speak of Mark's "bracketing" or "intercalating" the
account of Jesus' trial (14:55-65) with the story of Peter's denial (14:54,
66-72) as a feature of style and not simply a mark of connected sources.
The bracketing of the cleansing of the temple with the cursing of the fig
tree works in similar fashion (11:12-26). Once the stylistic feature is identified, patterns begin to appear throughout the narrative. It may be, for
example, that the whole story of Jesus' ministry is "bracketed" by the *tearing* of the heavens at Jesus' baptism (1:10) and the *tearing* of the temple
curtain at his death (15:38).

The host of works on Mark that have appeared in the last twenty years
have assumed that the Gospel is a whole fabric to be appreciated. Robert
Tannehill published a significant essay on the disciples in Mark, asking
about their "narrative role."[12] The theme of discipleship has been treated
systematically in the work of Ernest Best.[13] The trial and death of Jesus
became a particular focus of study.[14] David Rhoads and his colleague in
the English department at Carthage College, Donald Michie, wrote a literary study of Mark,[15] nicely complemented by Rhoads' performance of
Mark's Gospel (at first live, then recorded on video). Mary Ann Tolbert[16]

and John Donahue[17] have read Mark, taking the parables in chapter four as a point of departure.

What is crucial here is not the particular literary methodology chosen or the concept of narrative. The point is more basic. One can read Mark's Gospel as a whole story. Individual pieces are important as they relate to the other parts of the whole. If Mark's Gospel is like a mosaic, one needs to stand far enough away to glimpse the whole picture.

The World in Front of Mark's Gospel

Books are not the same as pictures. While the analogy may be helpful, Mark's Gospel is not a mosaic or a weaving. It is a story that intends to be read. While silent "readers" can dissect the words or even appreciate the whole construct of words and sentences, Mark's Gospel was written to be heard, and hearing requires performance. Attending plays or symphonies is a more apt analogy. Crucial is what happens at the present moment, when the work comes to life. Experiencing a performance is not the same as studying. There is less distance. That is all the more apparent when we are called upon to perform and not just to listen. Analyzing Mark's Gospel should include reflection on what happens "on this side of the text" as well as what is "in" the story or "behind" it.

The Role of the Reader

A school of interpretation has developed that studies literature by focusing attention on the reader. It is for readers (or hearers), after all, that books are written. What they "mean" is at least as much a function of what readers get as what authors intend. This approach, associated with scholars like Stanley Fish, questions whether it is really helpful to speak about "texts" at all, given how much depends upon reception and how differently books can be read by different audiences.[18]

In a monumental work entitled *Let the Reader Understand*, Robert Fowler has helped New Testament studies focus on the role of the reader in the enterprise of reading and interpreting. While virtually all scholarly energies have been focused on the author and the "author's intention," Fowler demonstrated how literature actually works with an audience.

> Literary critics have until recently given slight attention to the reader and the reading experience. To cite one glaring example, Robert Scholes and Robert Kellogg, in *The Nature of Narrative*, describe narrative as "distinguished by two characteristics: the presence of a story and a story-teller. . . . For writing to be narrative no more and no less than a teller and a tale are required." Someone to hear the story or, in the case of

literature, someone to read it was apparently too obvious to mention. Yet why tell a story if no one is there to listen to it? Who writes a story not expecting it to be read?[19]

Seeking to remedy the deficiency, he focuses his attention on the audience of Mark's Gospel—or perhaps more accurately, on the interplay between the narrative and the readership. His work provides an important transition to a more rhetorical approach. His argument is that literature "works" by shaping the experience of an audience. Features of the narrative are not important in themselves but are part of an interaction involving an author and an audience. While we may speak of "intention," it cannot exclude the desire to move an audience, and any such interaction requires attention to the experience of reading as well as writing.

His discussion of irony is particularly helpful. Irony is not a property of narrative, as though it existed in and of itself. "Irony" is the effect on a reader. Following Seymour Chatman, Fowler distinguishes between story and discourse. The story (or "text") is the material itself; "discourse" is how it impacts a particular hearer, on our side of the printed page. Irony works by awakening in the reader a sense of distance from the narrative audience. It becomes clear that the reader hears words as meaning something different from what they mean to characters in the story. As readers, we can understand why the Roman soldiers might think the claim that Jesus is "King of the Jews" worthy of sport (15:16-20). Jesus looks nothing like a king. Dressing him in royal garb and kneeling in mock homage gives them an opportunity to demonstrate the distance that separates pretenders from real power, serving also as a reminder to others of what happens in the real world to those who oppose Caesar. At the same time it is clear to readers that the soldiers are saying more than they know. Their words are true in a way only readers can appreciate, who know that Jesus is the Christ, the Son of God. Distinguishing the material (story) from the way it affects the reader (discourse) is necessary to appreciate what occurs when the story is heard by a real audience.

This emphasis on the reader requires attention to "the world in front of the text"—the realm in which the words on the page take life as they are read and appreciated. It may be useful to speak of what is "behind" Mark's Gospel, since there was a history that led to its writing. It is useful to speak of the "world" of the text in the sense that pieces are part of a larger whole that has a structure and themes and order. Books are written, however, to be read and heard. Interpretation ought to attend first of all to the event of reading, not least because words intend to move an audience as well as to inform. It is on this side of the Gospel we stand, after all, among contemporaries in whose company we read. Summarizing the "point" of a parable in a sentence or two is hardly the same as appreciating what happens when a parable is read to a particular audience. Our strategies of reading and interpretation ought to have as their goal a richer and more sensitive reading and hearing of the Gospel of Mark. To that end I wish to suggest an approach that may be called "rhetorical."

To Teach, to Delight, and to Move: A Rhetorical Approach

There has been a burst of activity in recent years that falls under the general heading of "rhetorical criticism." The strategy arises from an appreciation of the persuasive character of all speech—in particular, the speech-literature of antiquity. The case is perhaps most obvious for Paul, who wrote letters to particular congregations to move them in a variety of ways. Letter writing was something learned in the schools that trained people for public life. Letters were a substitute for personal presence, but even in the absence of the writer, the letters were read aloud by someone. The rules for writing and speaking are thus not as far apart as they might be for us. When the purpose of the letter is to persuade, the "rules" of rhetoric generally apply.

The Gospels are no less persuasive literature. The author of Luke-Acts says explicitly that he is writing "in order that you may recognize the certainty of the things you have been taught" (Luke 1:4, my translation); the author of the Fourth Gospel writes so "that you may believe that Jesus is the Christ, the Son of God, and that believing you may have life in his name" (John 20:30-31, RSV). While the agenda is not stated as explicitly in Mark, we may presume the narrative is written to move an audience. Interpretation that focuses on the rhetorical will want to know more about the desired persuasion and the strategies adopted. "Strategies" here does not necessarily imply conscious reflection or calculation on the part of an author but an appreciation of how an author actually seeks to make a case and to convince.

Traditional biblical scholarship has usually attended to such matters by asking historical questions: Who was the author of Mark's Gospel? What can be known about the original audience and their location? Many within the discipline of biblical studies have understood themselves to be historians, interested in the Bible as something that, to be understood properly, must be located at another time and place for a distant audience. A prominent New Testament scholar put it this way: "The task of the biblical scholar is to understand what the original author intended for the original audience."

One might propose, on the contrary, that the task of biblical scholars is to help a contemporary audience understand the Bible, and that the task of a contemporary audience is to experience the force of the narrative's argument in the present. Historical information may be important for such an enterprise, but it is neither the beginning nor the end of the task. Some biblical scholarship has become an exclusively historical discipline, interested in the Bible as an artifact of the past. That will not be the strategy pursued here. The "rhetorical approach" we will take focuses on the contemporary setting of the Gospel, on "this side of the page."

The task of the interpreter is different if the image used of engagement is drawn from the aesthetic world of drama and music. The student of Euripides' plays will read them differently if the goal is a production at a local theater, whether one participates as director, actor, or audience. Many things will go into such a production, including learning as much as possible about Greek theater and its rules. Of interest, however, is what happens when the narrative comes to life. The language plays here, on us and our contemporaries. The question is, How can we be both faithful and effective in our performance of the play and perceptive and receptive as an audience? Interpretation that stops short of actual engagement and performance is akin to reducing a great play or symphony to a few sentences about its "meaning."

How does Mark's Gospel "work" with an audience? The question need never be asked until it comes time to read. Why are there so few transitions? One may offer explanations of the episodic nature of the Markan narrative based on a hypothesis about sources and how the Gospel was written. But for performers and audiences, more interesting is how the episodes will "play." Do the individual episodes put off an audience, or do they engage readers? The impressiveness of oral presentations suggests the Gospel is effective in such a medium. A rhetorical approach may focus on how it teaches, delights, and moves.

The Three "Characters" in Mark's Gospel

One of the things a rhetorical approach highlights is the relationship among three "characters" in any act of communication. There is the character of the speaker, the character of the speech, and the character of the audience. Interpretation that does not reflect on all three will yield an inadequate account of how literature and speech work. Aristotle's three categories have proved helpful for centuries. They may provide a good place to reflect on the sorts of things that should interest us as we read and interpret.

Who Is Telling the Story?

It is normal in our culture to study a work by asking about the author. We like to know about writers—who they are, when they have lived, how they feel about things. An effective way to market a book is to arrange appearances for the author on talk shows. Perhaps the most important thing to say about the author of Mark's Gospel is that he (presumably a he) chooses to remain anonymous. At no point are we given a direct glimpse of the author, as in the opening verses of Luke's Gospel (Luke 1:1-4). And while the "author" is not necessarily identified with the narrator, in Mark not even the narrator intrudes with an "I heard" or "I saw" or "I think." The only author we can know—apart from the one created by church tradition—is the one "implied" in the Gospel narrative. That author chooses to remain in the shadows or offstage, and the narrative strategy he employs allows no place for evaluating the work in terms of our personal knowledge of the writer—despite the endless curiosity about the "historical" Mark.

This has implications for interpretation. It is quite common to speak of the intentions of an author. Where something is unclear, it would be most helpful to ask the writer, "What did you mean by this?" We have, of course, no such access to the biblical writers. Not only are they long dead, but they are not in any explicit sense available to us. We may learn a few things about Paul from his letters. We know the Gospel writers only through the story they tell and how they choose to tell it. Those interpreters who try to correlate features of the Gospel with the ideas or feelings of "Mark" are engaged in fiction. The creation of the "historical Mark," the alleged author of the Gospel who was a disciple of Peter, is interesting for what it discloses about interpreters throughout history. That "historical Mark," however, is not terribly useful for actual engagement with the Gospel narrative. Few convincing arguments can be made about the particular identity of the author; even less convincing are attempts to read the mind of this hypothetical historical figure.

What we know from reading the Gospel is a narrator. In modern literature narrators can be reliable or unreliable. In the Gospels, the narrators are reliable. That is surely the impression we are given in Mark. The impersonal narrator is never corrected. Judgments about characters turn out to be true. The opening identification of Jesus as "Christ, Son of God," is confirmed by God, who calls Jesus "Son" on two occasions (at Jesus' baptism [1:11] and at the transfiguration [9:7]). Other supernatural beings—unclean spirits—likewise confirm that Jesus is "Son of God" and "Son of the Most High God." With the name Judas Iscariot, the list of the disciples includes the comment that he was the one "who betrayed him" (3:19). Later in the story we are told how Judas goes to the temple authorities to betray Jesus (14:10-11). We have every reason to believe the insights we are given ("they were jealous"; "they were utterly afraid"). Summaries are particularly important in gathering together themes and focusing them (1:32-34; 3:11). In miracle stories we depend on the narrator for appreciating the plight of the ones who come to Jesus for help (5:3-5, 25-26).

The narrator is not limited, as are the characters in the story. His perspective is far more encompassing and penetrating. Perhaps this is what the church has meant by "inspiration." Mark's Gospel does not make explicit claims for itself, but its mode of narration implies an extraordinary claim to authority.

The character of the narrator will be a major feature in constructing the author, whom we call "Mark." That narrator must be given voice in order to come to life, however. If we ask about who is telling the story, the fact is that in public, some particular person is doing the telling for the ancient narrator. How should the narrator be embodied in a reader/performer? Should the reader be a baritone or a tenor, a mezzo or a coloratura? There are no stage directions. Anyone can read. How they embody the narrative, how they give it voice, will differ. Significant differences may require some adjudication. Who is correct? The legitimacy of a performance must take into account the effect of a particular reading as well as the "meaning." What does hearing the passage do to readers? What should it do? Does it instill confidence in the narrator among readers? Does it raise anxieties or challenge long-held conventions? While such questions are more difficult than simple historical or literary queries, they will make for a far more lively and interesting engagement with Mark's Gospel.

Readings disclose the character of the reader. A student attended a performance of Mark's Gospel by a famous actor. During the performance she became uncomfortably aware that she was coming to view the performer as an unbeliever. She had no idea about the actor's personal faith; all she knew was the impression he was giving through his reading. The particular occasion was his portrayal of the disciples as buffoons. His performance elicited no sympathy and offered no hope of their eventual redemption. In her view, that disposition toward the disciples conveyed the impression of someone who had no investment in the story and no sense of its future. The performer might have been surprised by the reaction. He might have indicated it was not at all what he intended. Embodying the story nevertheless has such effects on an audience—and may even reveal an "intention" the performer does not recognize in himself or herself.

Attention to the character of the "implied author" can serve as discipline for our own reading and hearing. That we have no access to the historical author of Mark's Gospel does not mean we are completely at a loss about the author. There are important things we learn about the "implied" author—the sum total of judgments behind the story that we may reconstruct—for whom the narrator presumably speaks:

1. The work is written from the perspective of a believer. From the outset we know that the story is the "good news of Jesus Christ" (1:1). While the story is told anonymously, it is told from the perspective of someone invested in the story.

2. The work is written in simple Greek—not translation Greek, as one might expect of an author whose native language was other than Greek (e.g., Aramaic). The author available to us is not "literate" in the sense of following aesthetic convention and does not expect readers to find that a fatal flaw. Mark's Greek is the ordinary language of the street—not typical of literature of his day, where literature was produced by the upper classes largely for upper-class enjoyment.

3. The author knows the Scriptures of Israel (the Christian Old Testament)—in Greek. The Scriptures are quoted on some occasions, alluded to on others, and perhaps echoed elsewhere. The author apparently expects readers to know the Scriptures. The second line, "As it is written in the prophet Isaiah," presumes that readers know who Isaiah is and will be impressed that Jesus' story has something to do with Isaiah's prophecy.

4. The author is familiar with Jewish customs and beliefs. The religious community is divided into Pharisees, Sadducees, and Herodians; at other times, into scribes, chief priests, and elders. Among the Gospel writers, this author is the most careful to distinguish various groups within the larger Jewish community. Jesus is questioned about ritual matters like Sabbath observance and purity regulations. Apart from one explanation (7:3-5), the author presumes readers understand what is at issue. Even in the extended discussion of ritual purity in chapter 7, which explains

what "the Pharisees, and all the Jews" do, the narrator explains Pharisaic purity rituals in technical terms, presuming familiarity with terminology and issues among readers.

Forming an impression of the "character of the speaker" is an important aspect of interpretation. Our task must also include forming an impression of the audience.

Who Is Listening to the Story?

One way to approach the question of audience is to ask the historical question: Who were the people for whom the work was originally written? As in the case of the author, we are once again on unstable ground. There are no sure markers of the particular occasion and location of composition. One of the crucial events used to date the Gospels is the destruction of the temple in Jerusalem by the Romans in 70 C.E. Do the various Gospels give evidence that they were written after this crucial event? The question is complex, first of all because none of the authors purports to trace the story of Jesus' followers to this date. Even Acts ends the story about a decade before the temple fell. Evidence, therefore, will be indirect. Mark was most likely written after the destruction of the temple. That serious scholars can still argue for a date prior to 70 indicates just how insubstantial the evidence for dating is.

The same is true for locating the composition geographically. Tradition locates Peter in Rome where he was apparently martyred. If "Mark" was a companion of Peter, it is possible that his Gospel was written in Rome. Lacking convincing evidence about the identity of the author and his relationship to Peter, however, the composition can be located almost anywhere Greek was spoken—which, since the time of Alexander the Great, was virtually the whole Mediterranean world. The attempts to locate the composition of Mark in Syria or Rome again indicate a lack of hard evidence.[20]

Another way to address the question is to begin with an actual audience's experience of reading. How are readers to be involved in the story? Readers are addressed directly only two times, both in chapter 13. The first address is an allusion to Daniel: "When you see the desolating sacrilege set up where it ought not to be (let the reader understand) . . ." (13:14, alluding to Dan 9:27). The second comes at the end of Jesus' address to a small group of his disciples: "What I say to you I say to all: Keep awake" (13:37). Readers are "present" at other obvious points, as when the narrator gives translations of Aramaic phrases Jesus uses (5:41; 7:34; 14:36; 15:22; 15:34).

This became obvious as a student "performed" the story of Jesus' raising of Jairus' daughter. To make the story dramatic, the student looked down at an imaginary little girl and said, "Talitha cum." Without looking up, he added, "which means, 'little girl, get up.'" It was immediately clear to the audience that the comment was not for the little girl but for readers who would not understand Jesus' words.

Elsewhere, readers stand apart from the story, benefiting from the narrator's commentary on what is occurring as well as access to events (like the "confessions" of the demons) to which participants in the story are apparently not privy.

Some argue that the "task" of readers is to identify with characters in the story. That seems a limited notion of engagement. First, the Gospel story does not paint characters as "typical," with the exception of those Jesus heals who are rarely named. His disciples are given names. Jesus is not at all typical. He is identified from the outset as singular: "the Christ, the Son of God." Demons testify to his special character: he is the Holy One of God, the Son of God, and the Son of the Most High. The Passion Narrative does not depict Jesus as an exemplary sufferer or martyr but as the mocked and crucified "King of the Jews," "the Christ, the Son of the Blessed One," and "the Christ, the King of Israel," "God's Son." It would seem more likely that the narrative makes it almost impossible for readers to identify with characters in the story. As readers, we are cast in the role of insiders, privy to information we share with the narrator and not the players in the story.

In determining our role as audience, we are once again limited by our historical distance from the story. Yet, as with the author, we can learn about the people for whom the work was written—the "implied audience"—by asking what they are expected to know. While the glimpse of "audience" is limited, the exercise is worth the effort: it may offer to present-day readers a sense of where study is necessary simply to recognize some basic knowledge the author presumes for the audience (like knowledge of the Old Testament). We may note the following:

1. Readers are expected to know a great deal: about geography (where is the Jordan, Capernaum, Tyre and Sidon, the Decapolis, Bethany, not to mention Jerusalem?), about people (John the Baptist, Herod, Caiaphas, and Pilate, about whom little is said), about the Scriptures and their interpretation (see especially Mark 12), Jewish rituals (Sabbath observance, dietary matters, and purity requirements), about specific terminology ("the Holy

One of God," "Son of God," "Son of the Most High God," "the Christ"). Both the content of the story and the lack of explanations presume readers with knowledge and particular interests. It is significant, for example, that the author expects readers to be concerned about Sabbath observance and that Jesus "declared all foods clean" (7:17-19).

2. Readers do not think of themselves as "Christians." The term never appears in the Gospel. There are a few indicators that readers include Gentiles, most notably the extended explanation of washing practices in chapter 7, but there are at least as many that the majority of readers are Jews—most likely Jews, however, who belonged to the "Jesus Movement." We must be careful, therefore, about characterizing the readers of the Gospel in terms of their relationship to Israel.

3. Readers speak Greek and read (or hear) Israel's Scriptures in Greek (the Septuagint).

Readers are not merely taken as they are, however. Any story "constructs" a reader, placing him or her in a particular position and making all sorts of demands. We shall have occasion to return to this feature of the story, but at least a few preliminary observations may be made:

1. Readers must exercise their imaginations if they are to make sense of the story. In the opening scenes, few explicit connections are made. Readers know that John the Baptizer is speaking about Jesus in 1:8—not because John or the narrator says so, but because Jesus is mentioned in 1:1, and because immediately after John's promise about the "stronger one" who will come after him, Jesus appears on the scene.

2. Readers are cast in the role of insiders from the beginning of the Gospel. "Identifying" with any characters in the story is made difficult when we hear what no one else can and receive explanations unavailable to those in the story. The impersonal narrator invites readers to watch the story unfold from a privileged position as people who are told from the outset that the story is "the good news of Jesus Christ, the Son of God" (1:1). As hard as we may try to sympathize with the disciples, we know what they cannot. In the account of Jesus' trial and death, readers are in a position to appreciate the irony of what is occurring as Jesus is invested and acclaimed as "King of the Jews" by people who have no idea that what they are saying is true. If there is some "secret" about Jesus'

identity in the story, readers of the story are related to that secret differently from the characters.

Precisely how are readers to relate to the story? Historical questions about an ancient audience are important and helpful; at least as relevant are observations that have to do with actual readers in the present. Perhaps the question is best deferred until an actual engagement with the narrative. Certainly those who perform the Gospel relate to the narrative very differently from those who silently evaluate its meaning and reliability. One of our tasks will be to determine what would count as a reason for reading (and responding) in a particular way. And that cannot be determined in advance. There is no such thing as a universal audience. Appreciation of the story depends on single hearers. Individual experience is not the end, however. Reading and interpretation are public matters. Personal experience of the Gospel should contribute to a conversation in which it may be critiqued and enriched, so that the community of readers is built up and the hearing and reading of the Gospel become richer. My own reading of Mark is an extraordinary mosaic composed of little insights provided by a host of students. I do not imagine my hearing of the Gospel is any more completed now than it was some decades ago when I began my studies.

What Are We Reading?

If we are to view the Bible as literature, we must recognize its distinctive features. Those accustomed to psychological novels devoted to an exploration of character will recognize the Bible as something different. As for Aristotle, plot is perhaps the most important feature of Mark's narrative. Characters are largely flat. We are given little insight into the psychological profile of any of the characters, even Jesus. We are introduced to him without any glimpse of the forces that brought him to be baptized by John. What was his family life like? Who were the influential people that shaped his decisions? And the disciples—Why were Peter and Andrew, James and John willing to leave their occupations and families to follow? What about the disciples who are only named? What did they think? Why did Judas betray Jesus? The story is uninterested in such questions. The reason may be that the author does not know the answers. More likely, it signals that the story is about other things, social and political realities rather than psychological. Jesus is important as one who changes the face of the world. Crucial in interactions with others is not how he feels but how they respond—not just at the moment, but over the course of the story. Why is it that Jesus must die? Why does he so unsettle and alienate the religious and political leaders that they decide to do away with him? What will their rejection and Jesus' death have to do with his message about the kingdom of God? How will God respond?

Do we have reason to believe such questions are worth asking? As we have noted earlier, many readers have come to Mark with low expectations. Common among scholars from the very first comments about Mark is an uneasiness with its literary form. No less a scholar than Albert Schweitzer could speak of the Gospel as "inherently unintelligible."[21] The dramatic shift in appreciating the earliest of the Gospels in the last twenty-five years requires some sort of explanation.

Making a case for the aesthetic shortcomings of the Gospel has not been difficult. The episodic character of the story, the lack of transitions, lack of motivation for characters are all visible. Equally impressive is how well the narrative works when it is performed. It may be, of course, that the coherence experienced by an audience is due more to the work of the performer than the work—but the mere fact that the Gospel works in an oral setting shifts the discussion.

The presence of "doublettes" is a good example. In Mark, there are two accounts of Jesus' miraculous feeding of people in the desert. In one, he feeds five thousand (6:35-44); in the other, he feeds four thousand (8:1-9). Scholars have tended to view the two stories from the perspective of the tradition "behind" Mark's Gospel and to see them as two versions of the same story. In this view, Mark is too unsophisticated to appreciate the duplication. When the stories are performed, however, the experience is most interesting. When Jesus tells his disciples to feed the crowd in the second account (8:1-3), they seem utterly bewildered: "How can one feed these people with bread here in the desert?" (8:4). Jesus' question, "How many loaves do you have?" (8:5) may be played with a touch of sarcasm and weariness. In the performance of Mark by David Rhoads, audiences actually laugh at this point, at the disciples' expense. This experience of the second feeding story is possible only because a few moments earlier (in terms of narrative performance) the same scene has been enacted: the disciples panic, Jesus takes the few loaves they have and miraculously feeds the thousands. The disciples have apparently learned nothing. Whatever conclusions one may draw about sources, the two stories play off one another well in their present context. How to evaluate them depends entirely on what interpreters deem as important.[22]

Another reason for the increased appreciation of Mark is an awareness of—and even preference for—alternative narrative strategies. Modern readers have a particular sense of what it means to say a story is "realistic." A story that moves smoothly, without mystery and ambiguity, tying up loose ends, may strike readers as having little to do with the world they know. The context in which the story is read is, as we have noted, an important factor in appreciating the Gospel.[23]

In the following chapters we will examine the major players in the story, with a particular focus on the various aspects of Jesus' ministry. We will examine major themes and read closely some important passages. The goal is not to be comprehensive but to suggest ways of approaching the Gospel that will deal with its various features. The strategy emphasizes performance of the Gospel for contemporary audiences, since that is what books are for. While we may speak of historical matters, the Bible intends to shape the imagination of each new generation of readers who will find promise in its pages.

Over the last few decades, engagement with Mark's Gospel has proved to be stimulating and evocative. Mark's Gospel has suddenly become perhaps the most popular. No single reading has come to dominate the world of scholarship and the church, perhaps one reason for its popularity. A rhetorical strategy should be less concerned with arriving at the one correct interpretation than with making possible actual engagement with a story. Only when the narrative comes alive among real audiences can we speak about what it means and how it seeks to move us. The more inclusive the audience, the richer the hearings.

Study is significant. There are things to learn about the language of the Gospel and the world of which it is a part. The story makes particular claims about Israel's God and specific individuals, notably a Galilean Jew named Jesus who lived at the time of Pontius Pilate. Reading Mark's Gospel will involve appreciating its particularity and taking such claims seriously. Greater familiarity with the story, its characteristics and plot, will likewise enhance appreciation. Study ought not make unnecessary a reading of the Gospel, but should facilitate a richer experience for those who read and hear. While there are other strategies that may be valid, I will emphasize those that hold the most promise for enhancing engagement with the story. The analogy to the study of other works of art and music is instructive: we study Shakespeare's plays and Beethoven's symphonies so that the next time we hear them performed we will be a more appreciative audience and the works will come to life in new ways. The same should be true of our study of the Bible.

What Will We Read As "The Gospel According to Mark"?

Before beginning our reading of Mark's Gospel, we ought to spend a few moments thinking about the actual book we will be using. There are several alternatives, and educated readers should know what is involved in deciding among them.

The Text

It may not be obvious to those studying "the Gospel according to Mark" that they must decide which "Gospel of Mark" to read. Those whose Bible has been the Authorized Version of 1611, prepared by translators appointed by King James, will discover that "Mark" in the RSV, NRSV, NIV, NEB, or TLB is different from the one they have known. Sometimes the differences are insignificant. On other occasions they are weighty. King James' Mark reads as the second verse, "As it is written in the prophets, 'Behold . . .'" (1:2); modern translations read, "As it is written in Isaiah the prophet." In 15:28, the KJV reads, "And the scripture was fulfilled, which saith, And he was numbered with the transgressors"; in modern translations there is no 15:28. A footnote at the end of 15:27 reads, "Other ancient authorities add verse 28." Most important, in the KJV, Mark's Gospel continues through verse 20 in chapter 16; in modern translations, Mark's Gospel ends with 16:8 (usually followed by a complex set of footnotes and alternative endings). What people know and experience as "Mark's Gospel" depends entirely on what translation is used.

In the three instances above, the difference between the KJV and all modern translations is that the king's translators had a different Greek text from which to translate. The New Testament writings were written in Greek, not the language of Jesus but of the next generation of believers. Prior to the invention of the printing press, works were written by hand (manu-scripts) on papyrus paper or animal skins, on scrolls or in book form (codex). Since the Bible became an important book, it was copied— by hand—many times. As a result of the work of archaeologists and collectors of ancient libraries, we now have access to thousands of handwritten copies of the Bible or portions of it. All extant manuscripts of the New Testament are from codices and not scrolls.

Not surprisingly, there are differences among the handwritten manuscripts. Some are small variations in spelling; others have to do with whole lines of text. Because there are so many copies of New Testament works, someone must decide what will be printed. The problem is quite familiar to students of literature, who must prepare "critical editions" of novels or dramas that have come down to us in multiple editions. We would prefer to have a play of Shakespeare as he wrote it—and not as it has been "improved" by copyists. Deciding on what is "original" is a complex business, however. Students working with several editions of the same text must develop some principles on the basis of which to decide among alternatives. This enterprise, known as textual criticism, is of particular significance for students of the Bible. Scholars have no access to original authors, nor to original editions of any biblical work. They must sort through all known copies, compare the texts, identify differences, and choose among them. They must do so for the simple reason that publishers must have a single text to publish.

The history of the New Testament text is a fascinating one. Looking at the manuscripts that have been located and deciphered—sometimes only with the help of modern X-ray or photographic techniques—one can only be impressed by the whole enterprise. Behind all modern translations lies a Greek text that has been constructed by text critics from known evidence. Differences among manuscripts have been evaluated, and finally committees have had to vote on what choice to make. Sometimes the choices are relatively easy; on other occasions complete agreement is impossible given conflicting evidence. In any case, "the Gospel according to Mark" to which we have access is translated from a critical edition that is the creation of scholars and still subject to change. The most important reason for using a modern translation rather than the King James Version is that the Greek manuscripts on the basis of which the king's translators did their work were no older than the tenth century. Today, we have manuscripts from the fourth century and fragments from much earlier times.

The differences with which we began—in 1:2, 15:28, and 16:1-8—all depend on decisions made among alternatives. When a group of manuscripts reads "written in the prophets" and another reads "Isaiah the prophet," a text critic must ask which is the more reasonable original reading. Number of manuscripts and their age are relevant but not as important as other factors. Crucial here is an understanding of copyists who transcribed the text. Is it likely that a copyist has changed a correct ascription to an incorrect—or is it more likely that a scribe has "improved" what appears to be an error? The citation in Mark 1:2 is not only from Isaiah, in fact, but also from Malachi, which makes it likely that a scribe has sought to correct the text by changing it to "the prophets." The most reasonable text, therefore, is the more difficult.

While 15:28 is present in a large number of manuscripts, it is absent from a group that has proved to be the most reliable. Is it more likely that a scribe has added the "proof from the Scriptures" or omitted it? Relevant here is the way scriptural material is handled elsewhere in the passion story. Scholars reckon that it is easier to explain the addition of the verse from a pious scribe than an omission. Scribes tend to expand texts rather than abridge; thus the principle "the shorter text is generally to be preferred." Verse 15:28 therefore belongs not in the "Gospel according to Mark" that will be printed but in a footnote indicating what "other ancient authorities include."

The ending of the Gospel is a particularly interesting—and significant—textual problem. We will examine the matter in detail later in the volume. At this point it may be enough to note that on the basis of the two standard principles by which the work of scribes is analyzed (the more difficult and the shorter readings are generally to be preferred), 16:8 should be regarded as the most likely among all the alternative endings the manuscripts offer.

The "Gospel according to Mark" to which we refer, therefore, is the product of scholarly committees who continue to sift available evidence and rethink the arguments for and against particular choices. The latest "critical edition" of Mark, used by the vast majority of scholarly readers, is the twenty-seventh edition of the Nestle-Aland Greek New Testament. A twenty-eighth edition, with some changes, will be forthcoming. Modern readers of the Bible owe an enormous debt of gratitude not only to the anonymous scribes who painstakingly copied biblical works but also to the textual critics who painstakingly sorted through available manuscript evidence to produce the only "Gospel according to Mark" to which we have access.

Translating the Text

Very few people read the Bible in its original languages. Someone, therefore, must assume responsibility for taking the critical edition of the Greek text of Mark and rendering it in ordinary languages people use. The amazing variety of translations indicates there is more than one way to translate. Those who are unable to read Hebrew and Greek should probably consult a variety of translations to get a sense of the possibilities. Readers should know something about the theory behind the particular translation they favor. Introductions to the various Bible translations are often very helpful in making such matters clear.

Translators must make various sorts of decisions. One is how to "voice" the Gospel. The language of the King James Version sounds like Shakespeare, probably because it is the language of the great master of drama from the early decades of seventeenth-century England. That may suggest to contemporary English-speaking readers that Mark should sound like a classic, using a vocabulary that presumes two years of college education. The Greek of Mark is quite different, however. The story is not cast in the language of high literature. Mark's Greek is the language of the street, with a simple vocabulary and sometimes primitive syntax. A comparable language in our contemporary setting would undoubtedly strike people as too colloquial for church.

Decisions by translators shape the experience of reading. In Mark, Jesus regularly uses an unprecedented Greek phrase as a self-reference, variously translated "the Son of Man," "the son of Man," "the human one," or "the Man from heaven." Knowing how to render the phrase is made difficult because the particular expression does not occur outside the Gospels. The use of capital letters (the Son of Man) suggests that the expression is a title, while "the son of man" may point in a different direction. Without more knowledge, readers of the English text will believe what they see. Most modern translation committees regard "the Son of Man" as a title with some implied content. A growing number of scholars doubt that is the case.[24] Because the original Greek manuscripts are written throughout in capital letters, we cannot rely on them for clues to our own practice. Those who must rely on English translations will in such cases benefit from comparing English versions.

In Mark 1:10, the RSV reads, "And when he came up out of the water, immediately he saw the heavens opened." The NRSV reads, "And just as he was coming up out of the water, he saw the heavens torn apart. . . ." Neither quite captures the sense of the Greek term *schizomenous*, which suggests an ongoing action ("being torn apart"). The NRSV is far closer to the sense of the Greek word, however. It is difficult to imagine how a translator could render the verb *schizo* as "open"—except that Matthew and Luke both use the same Greek verb, different from Mark's, which is best translated "open." The translation in the RSV probably reflects the ancient tendency of reading Mark through the eyes of Matthew.

One of the differences between "opened" and "torn" is the impact of the term. Though there is a core meaning both share, one term ("opened") suggests something natural, perhaps even peaceful; the second ("torn") is a far more violent image, perhaps dangerous. Another result of the translation in the NRSV is that readers who know only English may discover a relationship between the initial image in Jesus' ministry ("the heavens were being torn apart") and the concluding image ("the curtain of the temple was torn in two" [15:38]). The same Greek verb is employed in both passages, the only two occurrences in the whole Gospel. Their relationship is obvious and suggestive, as we shall see. Without sensitive translating, however, English readers cannot appreciate the parallel and a whole dimension of potential meaning is lost.

The NRSV will be cited regularly throughout this work, except in places where an alternative translation seems required. Those who have no access to the Greek are dependent upon translators. While that may have an unsettling effect on serious students of the New Testament, it is an important reminder that reading the Gospel according to Mark is a cross-cultural exercise. There are differences among languages and language systems, as those who have studied a language other than their own are aware. Not recognizing the differences is to risk captivity to a kind of imperialism that assumes everyone thinks as we do and experiences the world as we do. Awareness that translations are interpretations and that serious readers should consult more than one is a mark of humility proper to those who seek to engage the Scriptures. It likewise serves as a reminder that we owe a debt of gratitude to those translators who struggle to make the Bible accessible to people in every language under the heavens.

Voicing the Text

Biblical literature was written to be heard. The majority of people in the New Testament world could not read.[25] Their access to literature was through an oral medium. Even those who read for themselves made sounds when they read. The sound of the words is an aspect of their reality that many never experience in our contemporary culture that has developed a very different view of language.

Because the Gospel of Mark is still part of an oral culture in contemporary churches, the question about bringing the text to life orally remains an issue. It may even be the case that people who read to themselves supply a voice. The question is what the voice sounds like. Most "performances" of the Gospel in churches are uninspired. People have even been taught not to inflect their voices lest they interpret the sacred text. The result has been boring readings. There are alternatives.

Those who have watched the performance of Mark by someone like Alec McGowan or David Rhoads understand how different the same words can be made to sound. Actual speakers can, of course, accomplish a great deal by body language and gestures. Even simple alterations in voice can make a difference, however. One particularly dramatic example is in determining how to "play" the role of Pilate in Mark's story of the passion. A prominent feature of the story is Pilate's interchange with the crowds.

> So the crowd came and began to ask Pilate to do for them according to his custom. Then he answered them, "Do you want me to release for you the King of the Jews?" For he realized that it was out of jealousy that the chief priests had handed him over. But the chief priests stirred up the crowd to have him release Barabbas for them instead. Pilate spoke to them again, "Then what do you wish me to do with the man you call the King of the Jews?" They shouted back, "Crucify him!" Pilate asked them, "Why, what evil has he done?" But they shouted all the more, "Crucify him!" (15:8-14)

When Pilate addresses the crowd, is he sincere or mocking? "What shall I do with the one you call the King of the Jews?" Perhaps he is asking a sincere question. Or perhaps it is a taunt. "The one *you call*" can be ironic; Jesus is on trial as king only because the Jewish leaders have brought him to Pilate. They have said it all. The point is explicitly made in the Fourth Gospel, where the priests ask Pilate to change what he has written from "This is the King of the Jews" to "He said he was the King of the Jews." "I have written what I have written," says Pilate (played with a wry smile) (John 19:21-22). Perhaps Pilate's exchange with the priests and the crowd is a taunt from the Roman official who is enjoying the irony that his subjects have turned on one of their own at Passover when they are commemorating deliverance from bondage to Pharaoh. That they are requesting the aid of Caesar's governor in disposing of their "King" is too good an opportunity to pass up. If this is how we are to experience the story, reading the verses in public will require a note of sarcasm in Pilate's voice. Such a tone will surely change dramatically the way people experience the story. The additional irony that Pilate is speaking the truth indicates how rich the passage is and how much thought can be invested in determining how it is to be played.

A refusal to make such decisions and to take responsibility for voicing the text in a particular way is itself a decision about how to bring the words to life—or more accurately, how not to bring them to life. Readings are always embodied. How to think about the particular embodiment is an important aspect of biblical interpretation, even if it has not been a regular feature of biblical scholarship.

The Historical Jesus

The strategy I am commending is one that understands the narrative as a whole and respects its ability as language to move and to shape imagination. The story is important not simply because it has "meaning" but because it has power.

"But is it true?" The question will be asked no matter how prominently literary and rhetorical questions are highlighted. When they ask, people usually mean, "Did that really happen? Was there someone named Jesus? Was he baptized by John in the Jordan River? Did he cast out demons? Was he crucified under Pontius Pilate? Was he raised from the dead?" While often betraying a limited notion of language that understands words primarily as pointers to something more "real," outside language, the questions also reflect a proper appreciation of the Gospel story. It is particular. The parables—the figurative language—are clearly marked: "the Kingdom of God is like. . . ." The rest of the narrative refers to particular people and places and times. Such narrative may still be fictional, but it at least demands a different sort of evaluation. Mark's Gospel makes claims about a specific historical figure named Jesus. Its truthfulness, if not exhausted by questions of historical reliability, surely includes them.

Here clarity is important. Even raising historical questions suggests there are reasons for doubt. Some faithful Bible readers refuse to grant the legitimacy of doubt. They understand the truthfulness of the Scriptures to be a matter of faith. That is to misunderstand the nature of "historical argument." Historical studies are a realm of human intellectual endeavor. Claims to truthfulness within the historical realm must be made according to rules of argument and use of evidence. Without good reasons, the assertion that Mark's Gospel is historically reliable is only an assertion, and the "game" of historical inquiry operates according to good reasons. Pronouncements of the faithful may be personally satisfying, but they do not change the community of inquiry. They do not convince the neighbor. Christians have engaged in historical study with their neighbors because they have recognized the legitimacy of the questions and the need to test convictions.

The rules for historical argument are not peculiar to faith traditions. They are worked out within a community of inquiry. What we expect of historical deliberation is not certainty but probability. "True" in this case has to do with what reasonable people can be expected to give their assent to after a case has been argued.

It matters what case is being argued. The group known as the Jesus Seminar has stirred up controversy by publishing its own version of the Gospels, offering an appraisal of the reliability of Jesus' sayings. The most certain are in red, probable in pink, improbable in gray, and highly unlikely in black. People must understand what the published volume intends. The seminar has asked itself the question, "About which of Jesus' sayings can we offer a convincing argument?" Their criteria are stringent because they want to identify an "assured minimum," excluding material about which anyone might have a doubt. The volume suggests there are few of Jesus' sayings we can prove he said beyond a doubt, given available evidence and rules of historical argument. That is hardly surprising.

The study might be done differently. Someone might publish a volume that asks which sayings we can prove Jesus did not say. The results would be the reverse: virtually every passage would be in red, since there is always the possibility that Jesus said or did such a thing even if we cannot prove it. The volume might appeal to troubled believers but would hold little interest for the general public. The interesting historical arguments will be in the pink and gray areas. What might be said historically about the Jesus tradition with some degree of confidence?

This volume is not a contribution to the study of the historical Jesus. There are many fine volumes devoted to the topic, with Albert Schweitzer's *The Quest of the Historical Jesus* perhaps the most important, though written nearly a century ago. This study is devoted to a reading of Mark's Gospel that will enhance the ability of the work to delight and to move. Nevertheless, because the Gospel makes historical claims, students of Mark can be expected to take historical questions seriously—and they may thus expect the same of this volume. I tend to find the work of the Jesus Seminar less convincing than the work of other less "radical" scholars. I think it quite possible to sketch a profile of Jesus from the Gospel accounts that credibly locates him in a particular historical environment. My personal opinions, however, are less important than arguments. I have included a discussion of the reliability of Mark's narrative in the chapter on the death of Jesus, since this is the central feature of the story. The discussion will necessarily include reflection on how we make historical arguments and what should be convincing. For the moment, it is to the literary and rhetorical tasks that we turn.

Sermons

SERMON 1 (SEPTEMBER 25, 1992)

John 14:25-27 and John 16:13

It is necessary for communities of faith to engage in the difficult and uncertain task of interpreting the Bible together in the present rather than clinging to some imagined past in which truth and meaning were fixed and unchanging. But this warning against a retreat into the past is accompanied by hope and promise, for in this contemporary engagement with the Bible believers will encounter afresh the living word of God.

———

A student in a Doctor of Ministry course was a Mennonite. He had undertaken his educational venture, he said, to explore ways to counteract the corrosive effect of seminary education on Mennonite pastors. Mennonites, he explained, believe that God's most important work, the work of the Spirit, occurs within the life of the community of faith. Mennonites encourage to be pastors those who are sensitive to the movements of the Spirit within the life of the community. Communities cultivate people in whom they discern those gifts until they're old enough to be pastors. The problem, he explained, was that Mennonites have been impressed by the professionalism of other people's clergy, and they've decided that their clergy ought to be as well educated and accredited. Yet what young Mennonites discover when they come to most seminaries is that the curriculum is not terribly interested in the present work of the Spirit. They study the Bible and history, the History of Pastoral Care, the History of Liturgy, the History of the Mennonites—and they come to the conclusion that God's most important work was located somewhere in the past. The

157

result has been an increasing number of Mennonite pastors who know about biblical times and about ancient liturgies and historic creeds, but aren't very much use at sensing the movements of the Spirit in the present.

> "These things I've spoken to you while I'm still with you, but the advocate, the Holy Spirit, whom the Father will send in my name, He will teach you all things and bring to your remembrance all that I have said to you."

> "When the Spirit of truth comes, he will guide you into all the truth . . ."

People in the early church found those words disquieting—they still do. The movements of the Spirit are difficult to discern, and many who presume to speak for the Spirit are discovered to be untrustworthy. You may well have been convinced that there is little sign of the Spirit's work in the present where empty promises and shallow conversations are the norm, and so you may be tempted to flee to the past, hoping for some foundation in the Scriptures or in the confessions or in ancient liturgies.

But you'll discover—if you haven't already—that there is no refuge in the past, no firm foundation. We, after all, have to interpret the Bible, and there are disagreements. Scholars do battle over every jot and tittle in the writing of great thinkers. It's quite possible that the more you seek some foundation in the past the more insubstantial it will become and the less helpful in shaping the present. What's more frightening is that some of you may be captivated by your studies and may disappear into the mists of antiquity. In some respects, the Mennonite pastor was right.

Be sure that you will not leave this place without some confrontation with the extraordinary richness of our past: the Bible, the thoughts of theological giants, the extraordinary breadth of Christian experience. What you must learn—what all of us must learn—is what the past is good for: it opens us to possibilities in the present and the future that we would never have imagined. It is to our time that the Bible is addressed. It is the future of our religious past that drives our study. Please note the use of "our" and "us." Jesus speaks to you in the plural. He does not promise that the Spirit will lead "you," singular, into the truth, but that he will lead "you all." Jesus is present wherever two or three are gathered in his name.

Studying the Scriptures, testing the spirits, finding a word for the present is something we do together. I will learn something new about the Bible if you challenge my interpretation. My experience will be enriched by yours. It's what conversation is about. The most important work of God is what occurs now, as text critics argue about what will be included in the Bible, and as translators struggle to find just the right voice for the Psalms, and as those engaged in the debate about abortion try to understand how God works through law and gospel to sustain the human family. If the Bible does not cultivate evangelical imaginations, if the confessions do not open us to a world we have not glimpsed, if the wealth of Christian experience does not assist us in making difficult moral decisions and living with differences of opinion, the whole educational enterprise is a waste of time and a cruel distraction.

Recall Jesus' promise: while you may yearn for something more substantial than the Spirit that blows where it will, only that breath of God will infuse life into our tired piety. However overwhelmed you may be by the power of evil and ignorance, you need not be suffocated by cynicism. God has promised that when we study together the Spirit will blow in our midst, leading us to Christ, mediating his presence, sustaining us till our Lord comes again.

Luke 23:34

Don Juel thought that preachers were prone to cheating in their Good Friday sermons. He accused them of shying away from the dark and terrible implications of Jesus hanging on the cross and instead choosing to jump ahead in the Gospel story to the triumph of Easter morning. Juel argues forcefully, however, that the promises and grace of God manifested in the resurrection are able to be appreciated fully only in an unflinching acknowledgment of the horror of the executed Messiah. An important subtheme of the sermon is the tragically misguided tendency to pin the blame for Jesus' crucifixion on the scheming of the Jewish leaders.

————

I expect that many of you have been here before, at a service that takes us as far as Jesus' death. Some of you know the Bible story well enough to recognize this statement of Jesus as one of his "seven last words." You ought to know that there is no story in the Bible that tells of Jesus' seven last words. Each of the four Gospel writers tells the story somewhat differently. In Luke's version that we heard read today, there are three words: "Father forgive them. . . "; "Truly I tell you, today you will be with me in Paradise"; and "Father, into your hands I commit my spirit." You get seven words only by creating a different story from all the Gospels together. From earliest times the church resisted collapsing the four Gospels into one. Today we will listen to Luke's testimony.

It's a brutal story he tells, one that occupies a large portion of his account of Jesus' ministry. To understand Jesus apparently requires understanding

his rejection, trial, and death. The account is detailed. Times are important: "The feast of Unleavened bread . . . which is called the Passover."
Places are significant: "the Garden of Gethsemane," "the high priest's
house," "the place called 'The Skull.'" There is a rich cast of characters:
"the chief priests, the scribes, and the elders"; Judas, Peter, John, and "the
Twelve"; "the slave of the high priest"; Pilate, Herod, Barabbas, Simon of
Cyrene, two criminals, an unnamed centurion, "all his acquaintances and
the women who had followed him from Galilee," "Joseph from the Jewish
town of Arimathea." Even a lone rooster has a role to play. The story is
important in every detail, including the charge against Jesus that he is a
pretender to Kingship.

What's striking about the list of characters is that it includes not just
ordinary people but the most important. Jesus' birth, you recall, took
place in obscurity. While Caesar's decision to have a census forced Jesus'
parents to travel to Bethlehem, where the child was born, no one really
paid attention to the event that occurred in an animal stall—except for
a few shepherds. The great people—the Caesars, the Pilates, the Herods,
and the leaders of the Jewish community—were completely unaware of
what was taking place. Now, however, they are very much at the center
of the action. Jesus has become the sort of person who can't be ignored.
He's powerful and insistent and popular. Those who are responsible for
the well-being of society—the religious and political leaders—must now
take notice of Jesus and make a decision about him. It's their job. They are
responsible for law and order, and someone like Jesus could easily cause
riots that would tear to shreds the delicate fabric of society in Jerusalem.
They had to decide what to do with him—and they did. The whole lot
of them decided their world could not coexist with Jesus, and so they
executed him.

What are we to make of the story? "Father, forgive them, for they don't
know what they're doing," Jesus says. On the one hand, it's a lovely saying,
appropriate to Jesus who tells his followers that they are to forgive their
enemies—seventy times seven, if necessary. But the second part of the saying is harder: "for they don't know what they're doing." The story makes
that point, but it can easily be missed—and the account is far more comfortable if we do miss the point. "They don't know what they're doing."
Jesus asks not that they be forgiven for their meanness or pettiness or jeal-
ousy, but because they have no idea what they are doing.

What makes the story serious is that the religious and political leaders
are not petty people but the world's best. They are the ones charged by God

with the task of deciding how the law of Moses and the law of Caesar will be interpreted. In a world filled with irresponsible, thoughtless people, Judaism was a shining light, offering not only testimony to the One God who created the heavens and earth but a way of life that promised order, stability, and the well-being of the neighbor in whom God was invested. In a world threatened by anarchy and barbarians, the Roman legal system provided the most extraordinary means of unifying and organizing the human family yet known to civilization. The people who finally decided against Jesus were not the worst of society but the best. They were doing what they were appointed to do. Jesus does not argue with their motives. He does not chide Pilate for giving in to the persistent mob or attack the Jewish leaders for their motives. "Forgive them, Father, for they don't know what they're doing." The problem is not a lack of effort but blindness. They can't see. Some power has them in its grasp and they can't escape. Satan gets the whole business going when he enters Judas' heart and apparently still has influence at the proceedings. They're all possessed, and they can't exorcise themselves.

What if that's true? What if the cross is not some sad mistake caused by inept leadership but a necessary event in the history of our dealings with God? That's exactly what the Gospel argues. "It is necessary that the Christ must suffer." Why? Because God somehow needs Jesus' death in order to be gracious? Or is it rather the case that the confrontation is the only possible conclusion to God's incursion into our territory? What if the cross is the best we can do? What if the argument of the story is that the result of our greatest religious and political achievements is an encounter with God's own being in which the only alternative is to kill him?

We could spend time trying to understand what they might mean. You have at least a clue. You know how dangerous it was that Jesus ate with rascals who deserved punishment and shunning; you have some sense of the offense felt by the older brother and the workers in the vineyard who discover that newcomers get paid as much as they do. You ought to have some understanding of how rare and precious justice is in a world that seems on the verge of chaos—how much the poor and the powerless and the vulnerable have at stake in a system that punishes those who harm their neighbors. And that means you ought to recognize how much Jesus' eagerness to forgive and his careless graciousness threaten such a system. If God does justify the ungodly, it could ruin everything.

Today is not a time to be arguing causes, however. We see only the results. Those who should have known best, on whose expertise the world relies, knew nothing. They had no idea that Jesus really was the King, God's own Son. They could not experience his gifts as anything but threatening. They were blind. They had no alternative but to do him in.

Of course that may make you even more uncomfortable, and you may well be tempted to protest. Do you remember the character Judas in *Jesus Christ Superstar*? He somehow recognizes that he has been "selected" to play the role of villain—even though he isn't a bad fellow. He complains to God about it. It's not fair. I'm "damned for all time," he laments. And why me? If this has somehow already been scripted, if God has willed it, then how can it be anyone's fault? It's God's fault! God is to blame!

If that sounds reasonable to you, I can only say the story has once again demonstrated its truthfulness. The more you think about the story, the more it may offend you that things couldn't have been different. In that case, telling the story of Jesus only hardens your heart. And if you should imagine that you can think your way out of this problem—that you can bring God to heel through some sort of mental gymnastics—I want to assure you that you can't. Your theologizing will just make it worse, until you are prepared to join the leaders in doing away with a God who would act in such fashion.

"Father, forgive them, for they don't know what they're doing." It's true. They didn't. Neither do we. The world is far more comfortable with a God who watches from a safe distance. But when God comes close—as close as the words I speak—there will inevitably have to be some defense. The possibility that we can't see, that we are possessed, that we can't think our way out or exert more effort to generate love of God, is something that is finally too much to endure. Someone's mouth must be stopped; someone must die.

There is no good news here at the cross—no sense of satisfaction that God has somehow been bought off or placated and we can get about our ordinary business without having to worry about God. Jesus prays for you: Father, forgive them, for they don't know what they're doing. This is as far as we can go. Our hopes and aspirations and plans come to this—to a confrontation with a God who wills only to be gracious that ends with Jesus dead. There is no decision for you to make, no effort you can expend. This is the end—unless God refuses to let things end here, unless God hears Jesus' prayer and is able to forgive. But for that we will have to wait. The only one who can touch you and make you whole is dead, shut up in a tomb. We can only hope that God won't leave him there.

Luke 14:15-24

This sermon is an updated retelling of the parable of the Banquet in Luke. It demonstrates Juel's assertion that believers are unsettled by biblical images of God at loose in the world actively seeking them out. Rather than assuring his listeners that God is not really like this, Juel challenges them to find a word of comfort and hope in response to their persistent and inviting God.

————

In the face of the apocalyptic scenes—the sun being turned to darkness by the smoke from fires rising in major cities, fires set by raging mobs— ordinary religious talk sounds particularly innocuous. There's something overly cultivated and cautious about the way we speak of God. Perhaps it grows out of fear of offending others. Perhaps it arises from an attempt to preserve the appearance of respectability and control in our religious lives. In any case, the talk is innocuous. God is confined to the realm of feelings. Religion helps you feel good about yourself and your neighbor. If only we invited more people to church, perhaps there wouldn't be such hatred and anger. Such religious talk seems impotent to deal with things as they are.

The imagery of the Scriptures is far more bold. God is a ruler whose realm is like a great household. "Blessed is the one who eats bread in the kingdom of God," says someone. "You want to know about eating bread in the kingdom?" says Jesus. "Let me tell you a story." It's about a great house-holder who prepared a feast. He sent off his driver to pick up the guests in the limousine, but in each case when he got to the house there was a note. It appears they had other commitments. When the driver returns, the host is angry. "Perhaps we can put up signs for a free meal," says the driver. "It's too late, you nit, the dinner's already in the oven. There isn't time. Take the limousine and bring people back here so that there can be someone to eat— better yet, take the bus. I wouldn't bother with people with ties or skirts, they'll probably have commitments. Go look for people who seem like they haven't had anything good to eat in a while." The driver does as he is told, but there are still places to be filled. "I spent a lot of money and time on this banquet," the householder fumes. "I won't waste good food. Scour the city for anything on two legs. Look under bridges and in old drain pipes and drag them here if you have to. I intend this hall to be filled."

The image of compelling people to come to the supper is quite discomforting. It's quite different from putting an ad in the paper or even sending an engraved invitation. No provision is made for choice. People aren't given the opportunity to ask what's being served or what other guests have been invited. The idea that God's emissaries are prowling around the city in the Sunday school bus searching for people to haul off to a banquet will surely make folks uncomfortable. It's too aggressive. There's probably not a driver in the world we'd trust, even in a blue First Baptist Church Sunday school bus. So we satisfy ourselves with more palatable images. We speak of God as an option. We think of religion as a project that could make healthier, trimmer people of us. We tell people that if they've the appetite, they can come with us for a little taste of bread and a sip of wine— but only if they want to, and, of course, they'll have to provide their own transportation.

Now think of the story the Gospels tell: the Easter story, about an emissary who does not wait to be invited into the world. Jesus did not get an invitation. He wasn't asked to be invited into the lives of those who were possessed by demons. He intruded into enemy territory and set people free. His imagery is as bold as his mission. When a fully armed strong man guards his own palace, his goods are at peace, but when one stronger than he assails him and overcomes him, he takes away his armor in which he trusted and divides his spoils.

God is no less aggressive about the good than are others for evil. Jesus turns a potential disaster in the desert into a banquet in which there are baskets full of food left over. He makes inroads into the community of the unwashed by inviting people to his table and turns mealtimes into parties. When the pious, the careful, the fearful, the resentful try to shut the parties down by hanging Jesus on a cross and shutting him up in a hole, God intervenes by throwing open the door of the tomb and sending out fleets of buses to haul people off to a place where they can be delivered from themselves and their impoverished imaginations.

Jesus has come to set captives free—not because we have chosen it, not even in response to our prayers. He enters a world that cannot imagine anything beyond its own anger and misery. The truth has sought us out, and it tells of a banquet that has been in preparation since God placed a firmament in the midst of the waters. There's more than enough for everyone, and God intends the hall to be filled. So take heart. I've been invited to fetch you. It's not too late. You should know there are other buses around the city gathering people for the party. I can't tell you what's going to be served, and I can't promise who you'll get to sit with—but it may well be that at the party you'll discover that you can enjoy those who are sitting around you. And it may even be that if you have the nerves for it, you'll be asked to drive one of the buses.

SERMON 4 (SEPTEMBER 7, 1984)

2 Corinthians 10:1-6

An early example of Juel's defense of the importance of speech in Christian life and faith, for, as he asserts, "words are one of the principal means through which God encounters us and works salvation." Words in themselves are neither good nor bad; they can be used to proclaim the gospel or to attack it. Because words are capable of being vehicles of divine grace and promise, their skillful use should be cultivated in the community of faith.

————

In an era when military uniforms are no longer fashionable, Paul's imagery is somewhat discomforting. He speaks of himself as a warrior for the Lord, engaged in combat. That language should have gone out with the Crusades. It sounds healthier to speak of pastors as servants or healers or helpers or even facilitators. Being a peacemaker sounds better than being a member of a Salvation Army.

One reason, of course, is that battle imagery is dangerous. The heroic portrait of the warrior for Christ encourages a kind of aggressive zeal that has left too many scars on human society. The specter of unrestrained religious zealots imposing their will on others is a powerful deterrent for allowing religious views out into the public arena. It may seem wiser—safer—to protect ourselves with laws against would-be demigods and religious propagandists so that we can secure our peace and quiet behind locked doors and devote ourselves to less divisive pursuits, like discussing Trivial Pursuit, the imminent collapse of the Twins, or even walleyes.

Or perhaps you don't agree. Perhaps Paul's call to battle stirs something deep inside you, starts your juices flowing. Maybe you're just itching for a fight, dying to find someone to blame. It can be invigorating to snuff out an enemy—whether among Republicans or Democrats, bureaucrats or the laity, historical critics or fundamentalists—to strike a blow on behalf of truth. Some of you may in fact be precisely the kind of people against whom society wants protection: stubborn, unable to imagine opinions other than your own, aggressive, preferring passion to argument.

It was such types, in fact, against whom Paul was defending himself in the verses we just read from 2 Corinthians. There were leaders in the Corinthian church, probably outsiders, who had their own notions of what Christians ought to look like, and they had agreed that Paul was an ill-chosen leader. He lacked charm. Paul admitted that himself; he'd been thrown out of virtually every major city in the empire. He was not particularly impressive in debate. Paul admits that he was not overwhelming physically and that he was untrained in speech.

What bothered Paul about the attack was not simply the threat to his leadership, but the conceptions from which it arose. His detractors preached a strong Christ, and they spoke of successful Christians. They seemed to be making of the crucified Christ a symbol for power that was little more than an excuse for the strong to lord it over the weak, and such views threatened the truth of the gospel. So Paul, the meek and gentle one, had to fight. He was unwilling to withdraw into his private world and to leave the Corinthian church to think what it wanted. That's because he was a preacher of the gospel. The views of his opponents were obstacles to the truth, and so he attacked them. He sought to expose misconceptions and destroy their arguments so that the cross of Christ might remain clearly in view. His weapons were words; he appealed to his own experience; he made use of his opponents' arguments against them; he drew from the tradition—all to gain a hearing for the gospel.

Our culture places little value on words and ideas and argument, but they are all vitally important to the mission of the church. Part of your education here will be to learn, as my English teacher used to say, that words can be your friends—and that they can be enemies as well. Words can lie, manipulate, and make false promises until people believe nothing they hear. That's a desperate plight: not to be able to share the deepest truths, because language is bankrupt and arguments unreliable. In such a world, people can have little in common but trivialities. Evangelism or political persuasion becomes little more than charming an audience or, failing that, coercing agreement.

We have to fight against the bankrupting of language, because words are one of the principal means through which God encounters us and works salvation. We have to fight destructive ideas. Myths, false myths, can isolate us from one another and insulate us from the truth. Many people are convinced that religious truth is purely personal, arising from within. There's little point in discussing it with others, because you have to discover that spark of the divine or truth within yourself and nourish it. Such an idea is both the expression of our bondage to ourselves—sin—and the means by which we are enslaved. Deliverance can come only from a word outside, a word that touches us with the unexpected and inexhaustible love of God that alone can make us whole. If the gospel is to do its work, the word must find its way through defenses formed by mistaken conceptions. One of your tasks as preachers will be to find ways of exposing untruths, dismantling defenses, and opening just a crack so that the light can shine through.

There are other ways of speaking about ministry. Though the imagery may be risky, Paul's description of his task, as demolishing obstacles to the knowledge of God and taking thought captive to obey Christ, isn't a bad way to begin thinking about your own call. Terms like "demolishing" and "taking captive" need to be balanced by terms like "the meekness and gentleness of Christ." But we ought not miss the sense of purpose and even aggressiveness that characterizes Paul's ministry. The love of God is not an excuse for bludgeoning others into submission, but neither is it mere toleration that leaves people in peace to believe what they like. God's love does not leave things as they are, but makes all things new.

For the next weeks and months your task will be to learn about words and ideas—about their dangers as well as their power to redeem. You can learn to make a case for the truth, or to expose a falsehood, or simply to awaken curiosity. You'll never have to save anyone. God does that. But perhaps you can help gain a hearing for a word that's worth listening to, and if you can, your time here will have been well spent.

Mark 14:53-65

Early on, this sermon highlights the role of irony in Mark's account of the trial and crucifixion of Jesus, a literary feature that Juel will go on to develop in rich theological ways in his career. But the latter half of the sermon sketches another frequent theme in Juel's thinking—the resistance of the cross to any attempt to domesticate, rationalize, or manage it.

————

During our first session, I asked a class on Mark what members made of a book that spent one-sixth of the story narrating the death of the main character. One perceptive member suggested that it sounded like the author was a person who had not come to terms with the death of someone close. We spent a long time on that response. Who ever comes to terms with death, particularly the death of someone close? The pain never really goes away. Questions are never quite answered. Jesus, of course, didn't stay dead, but his followers couldn't quite settle with that death. The cross didn't go away. It remained, not simply as a sign of God's graciousness, but as a reality against which whole worlds of thought shattered. That unsettling reality had power for those first believers, power that drove them to change the world. If the cross has less power for us, it is perhaps because we are capable of so little art that we're adept at making the profound seem banal.

Mark was an artist. His story of Jesus' trial and death is art. This morning I'd like to focus on one feature—the irony. In Mark, Jesus' career ends in what appears to be total collapse: his ministry is in shambles; he's sold out by one of his close associates, deserted by the rest except for Peter, who denies him; he's arraigned before the religious authorities, tried, and found guilty; he's brought before Pilate, where he's tried, found guilty, mocked, and executed by the political officials. His only words, "My God, my God, why have you forsaken me?" are misunderstood by the crowd, and with that he dies.

For those with eyes to see, however, the story has another dimension. The long-awaited enthronement and investiture of Jesus the Messiah occurs. Yet it is Jesus' enemies who play the role of subjects. It's the high priest who finally puts the titles together with which the Gospel begins, in his question, "Are you the Christ, the son of the blessed?" (that is, the Son of God). Pilate formulates the inscription "the King of the Jews." His soldiers—unaware that they speak the truth—salute Jesus as King, kneeling in mock homage. The correct words are all spoken, testimony to the truth is offered. The witnesses, however, are would-be judges who have no notion that what they speak is true. The messiahship of Jesus to which they testify is for them blasphemous or absurd or seditious. But they speak the right words. That is, of course, the irony.

Even the mockery of Jesus as prophet that concludes our assigned text for today highlights another of the many ironies. At that very moment that Jesus is being taunted with "prophesy," in the courtyard outside one of his prophecies is being fulfilled to the letter as Peter denies him three times before the cock crows twice. Far from being in control, Jesus' enemies seal their own fate by condemning him to death. Even their worst intentions serve only to fulfill what has been written of the Son of Man, as Jesus says.

There are two ways in which that message may be taken. It is, first of all, good news for people who have drunk deeply from the cup Jesus invites his followers to share. For us, drinking from that cup will probably involve few heroic acts. The challenges we face as children of God are small but persistent. The major temptation is to avoid disillusionment. The most savvy, mature young people, aglow with the Spirit, are still shocked to discover that seminary walls are no protection against the outside world, that people inside the church can be as petty as people outside, that students can compete fiercely, cheat, hold grudges, and hate here as well as elsewhere. Part of the rhythm of the Christian life seems to be discovering how few people there are you can trust. If you've never been betrayed by someone, you will be. If you've never awakened at night in a cold sweat recognizing that your fate lies in the hands of people who probably don't know you, some of whom you don't know, some of whom may be incompetent—you will. If you have never witnessed the strange change that comes over rational individuals when they gather in groups, you'll probably have the opportunity. It's the persistence of the little disappointments and the little betrayals that eventually wears you down.

That's precisely what Jesus told his followers back in Mark 13. "Expect troubles," he warned them. "When they come, don't be surprised; I've told you beforehand." His own experience provided vivid testimony to the truth of his warnings. The world is not a safe place. That's what the cross means. The most intelligent, trusted members of the religious community, responsible for safeguarding the tradition, condemned Jesus as a blasphemer. Roman officials, administrators of the greatest legal system known in human history, condemned Jesus to death as a lawbreaker. Yet—and this is the good news—they didn't have the last word. God's will was done in spite of the defenders of religion and of law and order. Even at the darkest moments, God was there. He raised Jesus from the dead with the promise that one day the Son of Man would return to gather his elect from the four winds. However much life may seem to rest in the hands of the evil and the petty, God's will *will* be done! The faithful will be vindicated.

The message can be heard in another way, however. In the foreseeable future, most of you will not find yourselves among persecuted minorities in our society. After graduation most of you will probably be affluent, relatively affluent, and leaders in a venerated institution. There are probably several bishops, perhaps even a future church president in our midst. Most of you will get along well with leaders in other major institutions responsible for making decisions that determine how life in this country will be lived.

For us—as for Mark—the cross ought to be a sober reminder how easily the most noble motives can be perverted. It points up how quickly an institution can become an end in itself, stifling legitimate concerns of those outside that may seem to threaten stability. It illustrates how frequently insidious forces we scarcely notice can transform the best-educated, best-intentioned among us into insensitive leaders, desperately out of touch with what's real. There's something frighteningly predictable about the way Gentiles operate, eager to impose their authority on others, struggling for position.

The warning that the cross poses is all the more serious when we can't opt out, when we are called to be the leaders and teachers within the establishment. Fortunately for us, the cross does not go away. We will spend our lives probing its depths. It will continue to resist our best efforts to explain it away or to reduce it to something manageable. It stands as eternal testimony to a truth against which other truths are measured, to a truth which exposes falsehood and security, to a truth—the only truth— that can promise life.

Psalm 139

A deceptively straightforward sermon in which Juel asserts that the God who is near to us is not a threat but a giver and keeper of promises who has at all times worked to bring about our salvation. Even our service to this God who searches us and knows us is something for which we have been created and prepared.

————

Spring has finally come. The planting season is at last upon us. It's time to crank up the machines and begin the seeding. Some of you have been itching for this moment all winter. Others of you may be more apprehensive. You've come to enjoy living in the barn, fiddling endlessly with the equipment. Well, it's time for work. Time of preparation is over. Jesus is out of the tomb, and there is much to be done.

The fields in which you will be called to work, to continue the metaphor, are scattered over the whole earth. There are some of you who will undoubtedly feel you are being sent to the end of the earth. One of the things you need to know is that there is no place God has not already been, no place where God is not presently at work, no spot on earth beyond God's reach. The psalmist knew that and sang of it. But there is a disquieting note in the song. "Where shall I go from your spirit? Where shall I flee from your presence?" Flee? Is God's presence something from which people ought to run? Apparently so. That's the story the Bible tells.

One of my favorite pastors has just written a book on Lutheran spirituality. His first chapter is entitled "Hiding in the Tall Weeds." The first human beings we meet in the Bible are not God-seekers: they're afraid. The Bible story is far more about people seeking to escape God than to search God out. Women even fled from the empty tomb at Easter. From the beginning, the story is about God the seeker, rather than God the sought. "Where are you?" God says to that first couple, cowering in the bushes. "What are you afraid of?" They were of course afraid of being known. They had secrets and good reasons to hide. Laying the ground- work for their children, and their children's children, and their children's children's children, by their disobedience, they planted seeds of their own destruction. They sowed the winds, the Bible said; and their children have been reaping the whirlwind.

Such things are not unknown to God. God watches, and not from a safe distance. "You know when I sit down and when I rise up . . . even before a word is on my tongue, O Lord, you know it completely." Does it not make you uneasy to think there is someone who knows all about you? Knows your deceits? Can see behind all the masks into that black hole of a self—that's busy sucking in every spark of light to satisfy its insatiable needs? Isn't it unsettling to know there's no place to escape, to survey those vast, treeless plains like barren giants of the earth and recognize there's nothing to hide behind? There will be times when the words of the psalm will make you shudder. I hope so. For in that shudder, there's an acknowl- edgment of God's real presence and also a sign that faith is still alive.

The one from whom there is no escape and who knows you better than you know yourself is intent not on your destruction, but on your libera- tion and your salvation. In fact, God has been busy with nothing else. He called Abraham and Sarah to a strange new land for you. The reluctant Moses was drawn into bitter conflict with Pharaoh so that slaves could be freed and the promise continue. Jesus came that you might have life. God refused to abandon the reluctant and the frightened to their own desires and imaginings, even though it meant Jesus' death. God was not put off on Easter morning even by women who fled from the tomb. God will not abandon you to your secret fears and desires, and there will be moments when you'll know that—when you'll be able to stand out on the plains with not a tree in sight and simply admire the vastness of the heavens. As for the other times, when you're fearful or openly seeking to hide, know that God is present and God knows. God's is a love that will not let you go.

So go in peace and serve the Lord. The task to which you are called to speak the word, in season and out, is one for which God has been pre- paring you since you were knit together in your mother's womb. If you have the opportunity to plant, be as careless and as lavish with the seed as Jesus was. And if, during that planting, songs rise within you, for goodness sake, don't stifle them. Sing new songs for the Lord. Allow others the opportunity to join in. Invest yourself and all your art in that task, because you'll discover it's worth it and that no matter how intricate your invention, there's something about the familiar tune you can count on, to keep sounding through. The promises—which will sustain you, which you are called to speak, and which will inspire your music—are trustworthy, and they're finally not even complicated. In fact, they are delightfully, remarkably, simple.

Mark 16:9-20

*A provocative and delightful treatment of the so-called "longer ending"
of Mark—the twelve verses that were tacked on to the abrupt ending of
the Gospel sometime in the second century C.E. Juel forcefully rejects the
impoverished vision of Christian life that one finds in the longer ending.
He instead urges his listeners to grapple with the original ending in which
Jesus is absent and the women flee in silent terror from the empty tomb, for
in this unsettling scene one in fact finds the promises of God to and for us.*

————

I will confess that I have never before heard those words, which are identified in the New RSV as the "longer ending," read in church. And I hope I
never will again. Yet, throughout most of the history of the church, that's
the way Mark's Gospel was concluded. One of God's great gifts to modern
folks, at least to those of us living in the last century and a half, was the
discovery of ancient manuscripts that conclude Mark's Gospel with verse
8, a verse that's now become familiar. "And when they came out, they fled
from the tomb, for trembling and astonishment held them fast; and they
said nothing to anyone, for they were afraid."

The problem is that only initiated readers with knowledge of critical signs know that the verses read today don't belong in the Bible and
wouldn't be there except for editors too cowardly to bury them in the
footnotes. Even initiated readers have difficulty leaving the ending alone.
One artless scribe couldn't, and his ending has perhaps been as responsible as anything for the silence of Mark's Gospel in the history of the

church. After all, who wants to commend the reading of a book that ends with verses 9-20? After the long dark period of Lent, believers come to church hopeful for a word of promise . . . and what do they get? Whoever believes and is baptized shall be saved; whoever does not believe will be condemned—good news! The vision of the future stretches us no farther than handling snakes and drinking poison.

Some former students went to visit a little village in the Appalachians where, among some snake-handling Christians, a man had been bitten and had died. The news, of course, made national headlines. They spoke with one sweet, simple man who ran the gas station in town, who told them that his fondest hope in life was sometime to drink a whole jar of battery acid. Who wants such a book?

Of course the worst thing about the ending is not the details, but the effort to control the story. People can't leave the ending alone: it's too unsettling. What terrified the women who went to the tomb, loaded down with spices to do their duty to the corpse, was that Jesus wasn't there. There is comfort in being able to rely on something—death, at least—but with Jesus' resurrection not even the grave turns out to be a solid foundation on which to build. As the Gospel ends, Jesus isn't there. He's nowhere to be seen. There's not even the hem of a garment to touch.

If we're to extract the blessing from this story, some drastic measures will have to be taken. So the project begins. It starts with editors—if not by writing alternative endings, then at least by finding excuses to include them. When editors are unconvincing, theologians take up the challenge: spinning theories about why Jesus had to die, transforming the historical Jesus into the theoretical Christ, providing intellectual satisfaction for people invited to believe in a Jesus who has saved everyone in principle but never gets close enough to unsettle anyone in particular. It isn't a nourishing fare, and if that's what the church is up to, I'm willing to see the hand of God even in the work of the Jesus Seminar—people who, according to one member, see their task as rescuing Jesus from the theological spin doctors.

When you reach the end of the story, Jesus isn't there. There's no way to lay hold of him. If you think courses in theology and Bible will give you some handles, you're in for a terrible disappointment—even members of the Jesus Seminar discovered that. Hoping to establish reliable contact with the real Jesus, they ended up with a few whispers, an echo or two, and long silences.

It's a good thing. If we could get our hands on Jesus, we would surely throttle the life out of him as did his contemporaries. But we can't. Jesus is free, out of the tomb, beyond our control, and beyond death. That's why the story is good news. He's free so that he can make his way into our lives and actually liberate as God had planned since before the foundation of the world. He comes through the medium of ordinary speech to those who might prefer not to listen, as well as to those who dare not hope for a word. Though the words come from human mouths, they are Jesus' words in which he is present and by which he grants promises.

In case you attended a church on Sunday in which there was a dearth of promises, listen. For those of you who are convinced you have done something for which you'll never be forgiven, the risen Christ says to you, "Your sins are forgiven." For those of you who've been badly crippled by the cruelty of others, the risen Jesus says to you, "Stand up, take up your bed and walk." For those of you convinced that life has no prospects, the words of the holy one, the true one who has the key of David, who opens and no one shall shut, who shuts and no one shall open: "Behold, I have set before you an open door which no one is able to shut." Are you someone who needs control and requires endings? There are even words for you: "The end is not yet. There you will see him as he told you."

You want something more; I suspect you'll have to wait. There may be a time for snakes and battery acid, but for now all you have is a promise. You can't hold on to it; you can't build anything on it. All you can do is listen for it. You can live on the promise, and God has removed all the obstacles so that the word of Jesus can be spoken into your ears, by which he will take captive your life and sustain you to the close of the age. My advice to you is, forget the longer ending with its premature "amen." The Gospel that ends with frightened women is far more real and holds considerably greater promise.

Galatians 4:9-11

Juel here warns his listeners about the dangers of making theology or liturgy a means for satisfying our desire for order and control. These tools of the church, properly conceived and practiced, should rather serve to bring us into God's presence.

———

I knew a student once with a mind like a steel trap. He was eternally lying in wait for ideas. When one would happen by, he'd snatch it from the air like some great frog capturing a hapless fly and proceed to digest it. He was good at processing things, making ideas fit into systems. Theology provided him with an algebra, a set of formulas for making sense of life. He was remarkably inventive—could even diagram his theology if you asked him.

It's rare to encounter a student with such love for theology. He did love it, but there was something about that enjoyment that made me uneasy. A good theological discussion produced in him the same satisfaction I've seen in colleagues who've finished a ten-mile run. I decided it was my calling to confront him with a fact he couldn't process. It didn't seem fair that he was so at peace with life, with God. The closest I ever came to cracking him was when I made him read a few Flannery O'Connor stories. He didn't understand them, he said, though he knew enough to dislike them intensely. After we had read a few, he politely suggested we move on to something more positive and uplifting.

I understand something of Paul's frustration with those Christians in Galatia. See, Paul's battle wasn't over whether salvation is to be earned. His so-called "opponents" were Christians who were into circumcision and the liturgical year because they wanted security. Paul's declaration about how they'd been freed from the law filled them with a sense of dread. The Torah was for them a manifestation of some great, cosmic order. It provided structures for life, distinguishing between clean and unclean, between the elect and the nonelect, Jew, Greek, slave, free, male, female. With Jewish sages down through the centuries, they could argue that the law represented the incarnation of God's eternal wisdom by which he had fashioned the heavens and the earth. So the law and the orderly movement of the stars were all of a piece. If everyone obeyed the law for even one moment, creation would discover the cosmic harmony God had intended from the beginning.

Does that seem farfetched? Have you ever yearned for a sense of order? When you finally manage to slay your parents and break free from those authority figures in your past, when you've been liberated from the gender stereotypes you've found so suffocating, when you've managed to poke holes in those traditional images of the pastor that you find so oppressive—you may well yearn for simpler times when it was clear what it meant to be a pastor or a woman or a member of your clan. If you manage to get beyond your distaste for conservative Christians and to get beyond your irritation at their aggressive assurance that they know how things are, and if you ever come face to face with the void, the great nothingness that stands at the boundary of our experience, you will be tempted to grasp for something—anything—that promises order. You may seek comfort from scientific proof that there's life after death. You may be driven to some political position that promises answers. You may even be tempted with millions of enlightened Americans to consult your horoscope in the morning, just in case there is some order reflected in the movement of the stars. Worst of all, you may be tempted to become religious, finding refuge in theology and the regular unfolding of the liturgical year. You can suspect there's something wrong when the greatest satisfaction you've felt is when you've completed your set of stoles.

When such temptation comes—and it will—open to Paul's letter to the Galatians and read these words: "But now having known God, or rather having been known by God, how can you return again to the weak and beggarly elements whose slaves you want to become again? You observe days and months and seasons and years. I think my work among you has been a waste of time." The elemental spirits, of which Paul speaks, are largely the creations of your own imagination, the projection of your fears and hopes on a cosmic screen. Your need for order and for certainty can be a powerful stimulus to that imagination.

You see, the allure of all those imaginative constructs is that they promise control—learning the right techniques to manage people, creating a universe which promises a place for us and keeps God within reasonable bounds. There's no salvation in that, only a quiet desperation that will end with defiance or disappointment. But you know that. You've heard it before. The promise is that God has claimed you. The promise is that you are justified by faith in the God who sent his Son for you. The promise is that he has set you free. Yet, like everyone else, you need to hear those words again. You need to be brought again and again into the presence of the one who is beyond our control, who alone holds the promise of life, and who has set us free from bondage to sin and death.

If theology does its proper work, it will remind us of that, to bring us over and again into the presence of that one. If you are one who is tempted to bring reality to heel by digesting it into your system, by feeding it into your processors, and if answers and order and stability and certainty are the goal of your religious quest, then prepare to experience the God we encounter in the Bible and in our tradition as a threat. But you can also rejoice in that. For that threat may turn out simply to be the other side of the promise—a painful but joyful reminder that we are justified by faith in a God who alone can set us free.

Donald Juel and the Practice of Reading the Bible in the Church's Everyday Life

Shane Berg

Don Juel's tragic illness and death deprived us of a masterful scholar and educator who still had much to teach all of us. At the onset of his medical problems, he was at the height of his scholarly career and was an engaging and delightful writer, teacher, and speaker. As Matt Skinner and I first began talking about this volume of Don's writings on biblical interpretation, it struck me that it would be fitting to include a final reflection on the sorts of work in which he was engaged near the end of his life. What issues captured his imagination and occupied his attention? What theological challenges was he tackling?

Pieces that he wrote in the mid- to late 1990s are useful for assessing his scholarly passions late in his life, but an even more helpful resource was given to me a couple of years ago by Don's wife, Lynda. In response to my request to look through some of his physical files and papers, she also graciously provided me with a copy of his computer files. In these files I was able to find not only electronic copies of some of his published work, but also a number of unpublished talks and lectures and even some unfinished essays. By looking at these files, in addition to his later published works, I was able to get a good feel for what animated Don's scholarship in the last stages of his life.

Much of what Don was writing in his last years demonstrates his conviction that it is fruitless to approach biblical interpretation without attending to its proper goal—to nurture and sustain faith in believing communities. He recognized that the Bible could only be read fruitfully in the church if the practical dimensions of reading the Bible in community are taken seriously. Juel also recognized that it is precisely the practical side of reading and interpreting the Bible that is most often neglected in churches and in the seminaries that train their pastors. Juel believed that the corporate reading of Scripture is a powerful means by which God works within the community of faith, and over the course of his career he became increasingly convinced of the importance of attending to the nuts-and-bolts aspects of biblical interpretation, that is, the structures, habits, and practices that shape and inform it. In particular, he was deeply interested in assessing and revising how the curricula of theological schools treat the Bible, in reflecting upon how exegetical decisions get made in the church, and in finding strategies for a fruitful reading of the Bible that could be clearly and simply communicated to laypeople.

The Bible in Theological Education

Don Juel spent much of the last decade of his life forging new ways for teachers of biblical studies in seminaries and divinity schools to conceive and carry out their task. In concert with a group of like-minded scholars, especially his Luther Seminary colleague and dear friend Patrick Keifert, he initiated and played a lead role in several collaborative projects that sought to rethink the way the Bible is taught in theological schools and to provide new models, methods, and strategies for teaching it more effectively for the benefit of the church. The most important collaborations were a 1991–1994 project entitled "A Rhetorical Approach to Theological Education," funded by a Lilly Grant, and a larger-scale follow-up project, also funded by Lilly but administered by the Center of Theological Inquiry (Princeton, N.J.) and the Church Innovations Institute (St. Paul, Minn.), called "The Bible and Theological Education" (1994–2001).

These projects at their heart attempt to put institutional flesh and bones on Juel's insistence on the importance of rhetoric as a tool for conceiving of the entire task of reading, interpreting, and deliberating upon the Bible in community.[1] If theological education could adopt a rhetorical model, Juel was convinced that a significant step forward would be taken toward a renewal of biblical interpretation in the church at large. A number of files on Juel's hard drive contain sections of the final report of the "Bible and Theological Education" project that he was responsible for drafting. In one such file, entitled simply "Rhetoric," he reflects on the strange contradiction between the general popularity of the Bible in American culture and the stunning lack of knowledge of the Bible on the part of most students whom he has encountered in major seminaries. Juel draws the following conclusion from this unsettling observation:

Pastors have apparently not been able to persuade parents to read the Bible to their children; church school teachers have not been able to ignite the imaginations of young people with Bible stories even to get them to wonder what else might be in the Bible. Moral conversations in congregations, my colleagues discovered, take place most success-fully when the Bible is excluded from consideration. It often increases conflict and does not seem to help. Seniors, a theology colleague told us, are more prepared to make use of almost any other resources in constructing their theology than the Bible—because they have learned how difficult it is to do exegesis, how easily one might go astray, how much one needs to know before venturing into the deep waters. So they look elsewhere for their resources. Exploring this strange divide seems a worthy effort.

For Juel the way to address this "strange divide" was to advocate for a rhe-torical model for theological education. At its simplest, a rhetorical model takes seriously that reading and interpreting the Bible entails much more than studying texts. Biblical interpretation, rather, comprises an entire communicative process that involves an author, the text, and an audience who receives it. In reflecting on the helpfulness of approaching biblical interpretation through rhetorical analysis, Juel writes,

The most basic insight of rhetorical analysis is that every speech or performance or book discloses three characters: the character of the speaker, the character of the speech, and the character of the audi-ence. Through much of my education, I focused on the "text"—attend-ing to the particulars of its language and structure, convinced that meaning was somehow inherent there. An important moment in my education was consideration of authors, however—those who sought to accomplish something with their writings. I remember a professo-rial address in which interpretation of the scriptures was described as conversation—with great minds of the past. Perhaps the most dramatic surprises in my education came with the discovery of audience—how differently people can hear the same text and how essential they are to the discovery of (or production of?) meaning. That all three characters are necessarily part of the rhetorical act comes to many as a surprise.

The rhetorical model has proven useful not simply as a way of analyz-ing ancient texts but as a way of opening up reflection on our own use of texts—our own "performance." We are part of the audience who can appreciate Mark's Gospel. Pastors also function as the speakers who bring the text to life—who form an audience that can listen to it. Learning how to interpret the Bible must include learning how to perform it—learning what is involved in shaping an audience that has

appropriate expectations, sufficient knowledge, and freedom to participate in the task of discovering meaning.

Juel expended copious amounts of time and creative energies into working groups, projects, and consultations with scholars and pastors in the
attempt to secure a role for rhetorical analysis in theological education.
Participating in these kinds of ventures requires considerable administra-
tive work above and beyond one's normal academic duties. But it was not
enough for Don Juel to embrace rhetorical analysis in his own published
work and to embody the idea of "performing the Scriptures" in his own
teaching. His deep and abiding concern for the revitalization of the church
through the reading of the Bible compelled him in the last ten or so years
of his life to pursue wide-ranging changes to the curricula of seminaries
and divinity schools in order to ensure that the promise of a rhetorical
model of biblical interpretation might find a permanent and influential
home in theological education.[2]

Exegetical Deliberation in the Church

One of the results that Juel hoped would follow from a rhetorical model
of biblical interpretation in theological education is that pastors would
draw on the Bible with greater competence and confidence in every facet
of their ministries. Juel worried that the traditional historical-critical
methods typically employed by biblical scholars left future pastors with
limited resources for helping their congregations read the Bible faithfully.
While scholars are free in their work to emphasize the ambiguity and
complexity of exegetical matters and to refrain from coming to concrete
judgments about them, pastors are frequently expected to make exegetical decisions about complicated and possibly controversial biblical texts.
Juel sums up the matter with characteristic brevity in an essay he cowrote
with Patrick Keifert: "While pastors must have the courage to make decisions and act based on limited evidence, scholarship of the sort practiced
among faculty operates under no such constraints."[3] Juel thought that a
way of teaching the Bible that took into account not only the text (as is
the case with historical criticism) but also its reception in the believing
community (as a rhetorical model would) was necessary to equip pastors
to read the Bible effectively in the leadership of their congregations.

In an unfinished draft of an essay for a *Festschrift* for Wallace Alston,
former director of the Center of Theological Inquiry, Juel discusses the
need to "develop a form of pastoral deliberation that is more than simply 'practical' but something different than 'scholarly.'"[4] Juel wanted

theological education to produce pastors who could both read the Bible with great creativity and insight and integrate this effective reading with their pastoral ministries. In the Alston *Festschrift* piece, Juel sets out to demonstrate the importance of this sort of practical scriptural reasoning by discussing a case study of a congregation that wrestled with the perennially contentious issue of whether an American flag should occupy a space on the chancel at the front of the sanctuary. Quite unfortunately, the essay cuts off quite abruptly as Juel is describing competing appeals to the Bible in the debate and before any discussion of how a rhetorical approach might serve as a resource in such a delicate matter.

So how might Juel have gone on to address the flag issue? Surely not by providing any pat answers or exegetical sleight of hand. A clue to his approach is perhaps found in a file on his hard drive entitled "What Have We Learned About Teaching the Bible?" which is another draft of a section of the final report for the Bible and Theological Education project. In discussing the various challenges in teaching contemporary seminary students, he notes that very few read the Bible with a sense of the corporate dimensions of interpretation:

> Few read the Bible ecclesially—with a sense that they read it together with others, that they read it as a "we." And if they do, they have little sense of what it will take to form and sustain a community that can read not necessarily for consensus but with a common awareness of having been called by God and with some common mission. For many, questions of meaning and meaningfulness form barriers to guard against questions that press more deeply and make claims that will surely lead to disagreement. Conflict is something to avoid, since disagreement is as likely to lead to the use of cunning and violence as to genuine growth and change.

So rather than proposing a "solution" to the flag issue, Juel presumably would have gone on to discuss the need to nurture in congregational life the habits and practices necessary for reading the Bible together, even when such engagement with others leads to conflict and contention. For Juel, the first step toward transforming congregational assumptions, attitudes, and practices with respect to scriptural interpretation was for the church to produce pastors who could effectively demonstrate exegetical skill and courage in their ministries. Any approach to teaching the Bible worthy of the church must be able to cultivate in pastors practical reading competencies that prove effective in messy day-to-day life of a local parish.

Reading the Bible with Good Suspicions

A final persistent theme of Don Juel's final years of work is the role of "suspicions" in biblical interpretation. As with his concern for the role of the Bible in theological education and for pastors who are skilled in exegetical deliberation, here Juel demonstrates his commitment to the practical measures necessary for the Bible to be read profitably in the church. In setting forth his understanding of how good suspicions relate to biblical interpretation, Juel is going beyond the realm of theological education and professional clergy and appealing to a lay audience. The reading assumptions and habits that he has in mind would be helpful for every reader of the Bible.

Juel provides a sustained and engaging treatment of suspicions in a lecture delivered at a 1998 Augsburg College Symposium devoted to the theme of the "Faithful Skeptic." The title of the lecture is "The Importance of a Good Suspicion: Some Reflections on the Vocation of a Christian Thinker," and in the initial sections he deals with the importance of being suspicious of claims to absolute truth in exegetical and theological debates. Juel claims that our flawed human natures continually lead us to seek safety in epistemological certainty:

> What's the problem? The Bible suggests we're the problem—limited creatures who chafe at our limitations and are eternally vulnerable to the various offers that promise certainty and security. The more life mercilessly hammers away at our pretense and exposes our errors, the more we're driven to find the secret elixir that will allow us to know for certain. Education promises salvation—or at least security. Knowledge becomes a narcotic. One can get hooked. If we can only learn enough, we will finally get to the point where someone can say, "Let's not argue. I know."

But in classic Juel fashion, he quickly preempts any temptation to valorize suspicion for its own sake by pointing out that unchecked suspicion leads to a resistance to any form of trust in institutions or in individuals and to a dismissal of the very possibility of truth. But trust and truthfulness lie at the heart of Christian identity and proclamation, Juel argues, and so the Christian skeptic is one who embraces the necessity of trust and the possibility of truth and who at the same time asserts the essential role of suspicions. Juel addresses this tension poignantly:

> There are reasons for caution and suspicion. Words can be used to enslave and destroy. The great villains of our century—Hitler and Stalin—were powerful speakers. They spoke lies. We must speak the

truth with the same compelling force. How will we know that we are speaking the truth? I must rely on the Scriptures and the tradition of the church to discipline my speech. Even more important, I must listen to all those who are different from me—like you. I must take account of your experience, your hearing of the biblical story. If the Bible is one thing that shapes our view of life—if that is a common bond—it is possible that the result of our mutual hearing and study of it will result in the creation of a reality that is something greater than any of us has imagined. That, of course, remains to be seen.

For Juel, good suspicions keep Christian thinkers from falling into the polar opposites of fundamentalism, with its dogmatic and uncritical assertion of absolute certainty, and relativism, which categorically denies that truth exists. But Juel is careful to point out that for Christians truth takes the form of the incarnate Jesus, and since we cannot, like Thomas, poke our fingers in his side, we must instead in faith rely on "words that make promises on behalf of one who has the power to keep those promises." Our healthy suspicions are kept in their proper perspective in Christian life and faith by the truth who is Jesus Christ and by the trustworthiness of the promises that he is made present to us in word and sacrament.

So in Don Juel's late career writings one finds all the themes and concerns that are characteristic of the whole length and breadth of his scholarship, teaching, and preaching. What becomes more prominent later in his life, however, is the emphasis on the expression of these core ideas and insights in the church's institutions and habits. He wanted to find ways to make sure that good ideas become good practices when it comes to reading the Bible in the community of faith. This commitment was fitting for one in whom so many penetrating insights and so great a store of wisdom were embodied with such grace, eloquence, and faithfulness.

Notes

Introduction

1   Introduction to *The Gospel According to Mark: Authorised King James Version* (Edinburgh: Canongate, 1998), xi.

Chapter 1

1   Meir Sternberg, in his magisterial *The Poetics of Biblical Narrative* (Bloomington: Indiana University Press, 1987), offers a contemporary version of this confidence in the biblical text. Narrative of the Hebrew Bible, he argues, particularly in contrast to the New Testament, is characterized by "foolproof composition, whereby the discourse strives to open and bring home its essentials to all readers so as to establish a common ground, a bond instead of a barrier of understanding. . . . By foolproof composition I mean that the Bible is difficult to read, easy to underread and overread and even misread, but virtually impossible to, so to speak, counterread" (50). He must immediately add qualifications, however: "Here as elsewhere, of course, ignorance, willfulness, preconception, tendentiousness . . . may perform wonders of distortion. . . . In a hermeneutic and moral as well as a theological sense, interpretation may always be performed in bad faith" (50). One may ask what this means in practice. Sternberg's own violent reaction to disagreement with his reading of the rape of Dinah in Genesis 34 indicates that "foolproof composition" is a helpful category only when there is agreement about interpretation. The only recourse in the case of disagreement is to characterize one's opponent as a fool.

2   The words are those of Albert Schweitzer, *The Quest of the Historical Jesus: A Critical Study of Its Progress from Reimarus to Wrede* (New York: Macmillan, 1968), 399.

3   See the helpful discussion of Spinoza's contribution to historical criticism in Roy Harrisville and Walter Sundberg, *The Bible in Modern Culture: Theology and Historical-Critical Method from Spinoza to Käsemann* (Grand Rapids: Eerdmans, 1995), esp. 32–48.

4   Richard J. Bernstein characterizes the need to find some clear and distinct idea
      on which to establish the self and the world—some "Archimedean point"—as the
      "Cartesian Anxiety." It is, he insists, one of the driving forces of Western culture, the
      response to which is either objectivism or relativism. See *Beyond Objectivism and
      Relativism: Science, Hermeneutics, and Praxis* (Philadelphia: University of Penn-
      sylvania Press, 1983).

5   Wayne Booth, *Modern Dogma and the Rhetoric of Assent* (Notre Dame: University of
      Notre Dame Press, 1974).

6   Frank Kermode, *The Genesis of Secrecy: On the Interpretation of Narrative* (Cam-
      bridge, Mass.: Harvard University Press, 1979).

7   An example of such an argument is Nils A. Dahl's "The Crucified Messiah," in *Jesus
      the Christ: The Historical Origins of Christological Doctrine* (Minneapolis: Fortress,
      1991), 27–47. I have pursued this argument in my *Messianic Exegesis: Christological
      Interpretation of the Old Testament in Early Christianity* (Philadelphia: Fortress,
      1988).

8   A student from Ukraine, now a citizen of Canada, spoke of the "fluidity of the past"
      in the former Soviet Union, where government-ordered changes in history books
      were a regular feature of life. He said students spoke of the Soviet Union as "a coun-
      try with an unpredictable past."

9   Patrick Keifert, "Mind Reader and Maestro: Models for Understanding Biblical
      Interpreters," *Word and World* 1 (1981): 153–68.

10   Wayne Booth makes use of this personalized notion of literature in his *The Company
      We Keep: An Ethics of Fiction* (Berkeley: University of California Press, 1988).

11   For a thorough discussion of this "paradigm shift" that has been extraordinarily help-
      ful for me, see Patrick Keifert's unpublished dissertation, "Meaning and Reference:
      The Interpretation of Verisimilitude in the Gospel according to Mark" (University
      of Chicago, 1982).

12   Peter Berger and Thomas Luckmann, *The Social Construction of Reality: A Treatise
      in the Sociology of Knowledge* (New York: Anchor Press, 1967). See also Peter
      Berger, *The Sacred Canopy: Elements of a Sociological Theory of Religion* (New York:
      Doubleday, 1967).

13   Robert Gundry's commentary on Mark has as one of its stated goals refuting ironic
      interpretation of Mark's Gospel. "The Gospel of Mark contains no ciphers, no hidden
      meanings, no sleight of hand. . . . No Christology of irony that means the reverse of
      what it says. Mark's meaning lies on the surface. He writes a straightforward apology
      for the cross" (*Mark: A Commentary on His Apology for the Cross* [Grand Rapids:
      Eerdmans, 1993], 1). Gundry is well aware of the danger that irony poses for the inter-
      preter who wishes to pin the Gospel narrative down or capture it within an interpre-
      tation. He invests over one thousand pages in an effort to get hold of the Gospel that
      seems so successfully to resist capture—unsuccessfully, I would add.

14   Based on his experience as a university administrator and teacher in the late 1960s,
      Wayne Booth, in *Modern Dogma and the Rhetoric of Assent*, notes the absence of
      such trust and goodwill as characteristic of contemporary American culture. He
      calls for a "rhetoric of assent" as opposed to the hermeneutic of suspicion that char-
      acterizes the "modern dogma."

15   I do not wish to skirt the very real need for a hermeneutic of suspicion. Not only
      interpretations of the Bible but the Bible itself is enmeshed in a world in bondage to
      sin, manifested in racism, sexism, classism, and other forms of discrimination. The

Christian tradition itself operates with deep suspicions about the human enterprise that would suggest there is no place where humans and their words and actions are free from sin. There is no pure form of speech attainable through any means of interpretation. If God works through the medium of human language, it will have to be through the imperfect words of sinful creatures. If the church's statements about the Bible and its truthfulness are to be taken seriously, however, it must be the case that the word of God, as it comes to life among us, actually works to free and sustain people of all sorts and conditions. This is a matter that cannot be determined apart from Christian practice.

16 "Giving you up" and "handing you over" have genuine emotional power here because of their metaphorical setting, which is the experience of Hosea as a husband. That is why, I would argue, the Hebrew should be translated, "For I am God and not a man." The explicit disclaimer finds in human experience a glimpse of God's wrath and compassion, while insisting on distance. The metaphor of God as husband both is and is not analogous—as is the case with all metaphors. The force of the hopeful language is blunted, however, when the image is generalized (as in the NRSV: "For I am God and no mortal").

Chapter 2

1 James D. Smart, *The Strange Silence of the Bible in the Church: A Study in Hermeneutics* (Philadelphia: Westminster, 1970).
2 Leander E. Keck, "The Premodern Bible in the Postmodern World," *Interpretation* 50 (1996): 138.
3 Booth, *The Company We Keep.*
4 On this topic, see Keifert, "Mind Reader and Maestro."
5 One of the texts used for the course is prepared by a professor of speech: G. Robert Jacks, *Getting the Word Across: Speech Communication for Pastors and Lay Leaders* (Grand Rapids: Eerdmans, 1995).
6 W. Kelber, *The Oral and the Written Gospel: The Hermeneutics of Speaking and Writing in the Synoptic Tradition, Mark, Paul, and Q* (Philadelphia: Fortress, 1983).
7 On the matter of referentiality in biblical scholarship, see the dissertation by Keifert, "Meaning and Reference."
8 Jane Tompkins, "The Reader in History: The Changing Shape of Literary Response," in *Reader-Response Criticism: From Formalism to Post-Structuralism*, ed. Jane Tompkins (Baltimore: Johns Hopkins University Press, 1980), 203.
9 Note the very different interpretations of the disciples' role in David Rhoads and Donald Michie, *Mark as Story* (Philadelphia: Fortress, 1982); Mary Ann Tolbert, *Sowing the Gospel: Mark's World in Literary-Historical Perspective* (Minneapolis: Fortress, 1989); and Donald Juel, *Master of Surprise* (Minneapolis: Fortress, 1994), esp. 52–62.
10 Helmut Thielicke, *The Waiting Father: Sermons on the Parables of Jesus* (New York: Harper & Row, 1959), 17–40.
11 In the lectionary, in fact, the lesson reader is given the option of omitting the verses in which the older brother appears.
12 The offense of the story is the most striking feature of a musical rendition of the parable prepared by Garrison Keillor and Roy Blount Jr. on *A Prairie Home Companion*. The father's favoritism is absolutely infuriating.

13   Kenneth Bailey, *Poet and Peasant, and Through Peasant Eyes: A Literary-Cultural Approach to the Parables in Luke* (Grand Rapids: Eerdmans, 1983).

14   The work of scholars from George Foot Moore and W. D. Davies to Jacob Neusner and Ed Sanders would have to be included in the list of significant studies that have changed our reading of the New Testament.

15   Garrison Keillor, an accomplished storyteller and astute reader of the Bible, held a workshop not long ago in which participants tried various ways of performing this parable.

16   This was one of the major arguments of my dissertation, *Messiah and Temple: The Trial of Jesus in the Gospel of Mark*, SBLDS 31 (Missoula, Mont.: Scholars Press, 1977); see also "The Death of the King," in *A Master of Surprise*, 93–99.

17   I am grateful to Robert Fowler (*Let the Reader Understand: Reader-Response Criticism and the Gospel of Mark* [Minneapolis: Fortress, 1991], esp. 22–24) for helping me to understand what I meant by "irony." It is not a property of the narrative as much as an impact on the reader. I have found his volume to be a most helpful clarification of the relationship between scholarship and reading.

18   See David Cunningham, *Faithful Persuasion: In Aid of a Rhetoric of Christian Theology* (Notre Dame: Notre Dame University Press, 1991); Donald Juel and Patrick Keifert, "I Believe in God: A Johannine Perspective," *Horizons in Biblical Theology* 12 (1990): 39–60.

19   Smart, *Strange Silence*, 23. Emphasis in original.

Chapter 3

1   David Rhoads' presentation of Mark's Gospel has been prepared on videocassette by the LITE continuing education center at Trinity Lutheran Seminary in Columbus, Ohio. Because Rhoads works from modern editions of Mark, his performance differs from the more famous presentation of Mark by Alec McGowan, who works from the KJV and ends with 16:20 ("Amen"). See Rhoads and Michie, *Mark as Story*.

2   Andrew Lincoln, "The Promise and the Failure—Mark 16:7,8," *Journal of Biblical Literature* 108 (1989): 283–300.

3   Frank Kermode, *The Sense of an Ending: Studies in the Theory of Fiction* (London: Oxford University Press, 1966).

4   *The New Oxford Annotated Bible* (New York: Oxford University Press, 1977), 1238.

5   For a careful analysis of the logic of text-critical arguments, see Humphrey Palmer, *The Logic of Gospel Criticism* (New York: St. Martin's Press, 1968), 55–111.

6   Brevard Childs, *The New Testament as Canon: An Introduction* (Philadelphia: Fortress, 1985), 94–95. It will be of interest later that, according to Childs, the canonical reading of Mark in verses 9–20 clearly rules out a positive interpretation of the terror and amazement of the women at the tomb.

7   Kermode, *Sense of an Ending* and *Genesis of Secrecy*.

8   Elisabeth Schüssler Fiorenza, *In Memory of Her: A Feminist Theological Reconstruction of Christian Origins* (New York: Crossroad, 1983), 316–23.

9   See the brief discussion by Lincoln, "Promise and Failure," 286. More compelling than most are the comments of John Donahue in his *The Gospel in Parable* (Philadelphia: Fortress, 1988), 196–97:

> Mark's theology of fear and wonder emerges especially in the resurrection account (16:5, 8) and in the jarring ending of the Gospel, "They were afraid"

(16:8). This motif, which throughout the Gospel establishes rapport with the readers and dictates how they should respond to Jesus, now becomes a symbolic reaction to the gospel as a whole. Mark's readers are left not even with the assurance of a resurrection vision but simply with numinous fear in the face of a divine promise.

These reactions of wonder and surprise accompany the revelation of God in Jesus, and they signify the power of this revelation to unsettle and challenge human existence. At the same time, this wonder is fascinating and attracting; it invites people to confront mystery. Such motifs call for a parabolic reading of Mark: for an approach to Mark's Jesus with a sense of wonder, awe, and holy fear. Yet even here, "fear" is understood not as incapacitating and blinding but as opening and inviting. This too easily resolves the tension on which the Gospel plays.

10   Kermode, *Genesis of Secrecy*, chap. 2.
11   Lincoln, "Promise and Failure," 290–92.
12   Erich Auerbach, *Mimesis*, trans. Willard Trask (Princeton: Princeton University Press, 1953), 24–49. Borrowing a term from Harnack, Auerbach refers to the "pendulation" in such characters.
13   Kermode, *Sense of an Ending*, 43–44.
14   Kermode, *Genesis of Secrecy*, 68.
15   Austin Farrer, *A Study in St. Mark* (Westminster: Dacre Press, 1951).
16   Kermode, *Genesis of Secrecy*, 71–72 (among many examples).
17   Kermode, *Genesis of Secrecy*, 27–28.
18   Kermode, *Genesis of Secrecy*, 145.

Chapter 4

1   As professors, respectively, of Old and New Testament, Richard Nysse and Donald Juel have frequently worked together as leaders of the Th.D. Scripture Seminar at Luther Northwestern Seminary. The authors wish to thank the members of the Th.D. seminar in Scripture at Luther Northwestern Seminary during the last several years for their participation and interest in the matters pursued in this article. Other colleagues, particularly Patrick Keifert and Gerhard Forde, have also helped us shape and examine the questions we raise here. This article, preliminary as it may be, is an outgrowth of these ongoing discussions.
2   This is the topic of a thoughtful essay by Patrick Keifert, "An Ecumenical Horizon for 'Canon within a Canon?'" *Currents in Theology and Mission* 14 (1987): 185–93.
3   There exists a secular version of this doctrine that has the same effect. Treating the Bible as a classic of Western culture, a kind of icon, can also lead to a reading that does not take the particularity of the Bible seriously, including the role of culturally particular human beings in its production.
4   The "rhetorical" character of language and of literature in antiquity is nicely described in an article by Jane Tomkins, "The Reader in History."
5   See especially Gerhard Forde, *Theology Is for Proclamation* (Minneapolis: Fortress, 1990).
6   The point was made in a now-famous article by Nils Dahl, "The Neglected Factor in New Testament Theology," in *Jesus the Christ*, 153–64.

Chapter 5

1   All the speeches in Acts presume a complex history of Old Testament interpretation within the church. See my *Messianic Exegesis*, chap. 3, esp. 82–84.

2   Martin Dibelius, "The Speeches in Acts and Ancient Historiography," in *Studies in the Acts of the Apostles* (New York: Scribner's, 1956), 138–85.

3   See chapter 2 of my *Messianic Exegesis*.

4   Dahl, *Jesus the Christ*, 27–64, 117–23; Juel, *Messianic Exegesis*, 80–88.

5   Jacob Jervell, *Luke and the People of God* (Minneapolis: Augsburg, 1972), 188–91; Juel, *Luke-Acts: The Promise of History* (Atlanta: John Knox, 1983), esp. 105–7.

6   This is essentially the argument of Jervell's essay "The Divided People of God: The Restoration of Israel and Salvation for the Gentiles," in his *Luke and the People of God*, 41–74.

7   Jervell, *Luke and the People of God*, 51–52; Nils A. Dahl, "A People for His Name," *New Testament Studies* 4 (1957–58): 319–27; Juel, *Luke-Acts*, 103–12.

Chapter 6

1   Harry Gamble Jr., *Books and Readers in the Early Church: A History of Early Christian Texts* (New Haven: Yale University Press, 1995), 203–41 and literature cited.

2   Erwin Nestle and Kurt Aland, *Novum Testamentum Graece*, 26th ed. (Stuttgart: Deutsche Bibelstiftung, 1979), 72.

3   Brevard Childs, *Biblical Theology of the Old and New Testaments* (Minneapolis: Fortress, 1993), 65.

4   Krister Stendahl, *The School of St. Matthew* (Philadelphia: Fortress, 1954).

5   Richard B. Hays, *Echoes of Scripture in the Letters of Paul* (New Haven: Yale University Press, 1989); Robert L. Brawley, *Text to Text Pours Forth Speech: Voices of Scripture in Luke-Acts* (Bloomington: Indiana University Press, 1995).

6   C. H. Dodd, *According to the Scriptures: The Sub-Structure of New Testament Theology* (London: Nisbit, 1952); Barnabas Lindars, *New Testament Apologetic* (London: SCM Press, 1961); Juel, *Messianic Exegesis*.

7   Philo, *On the Migration of Abraham*, trans. F. H. Colson and G. H. Whitaker, Loeb Classical Library IV (Cambridge, Mass.: Harvard University Press, 1932), 133.

8   Karlfried Froehlich, *Biblical Interpretation in the Early Church* (Minneapolis: Fortress, 1984), 19.

9   Froehlich, *Biblical Interpretation*, 4–7.

10   Geza Vermes, *The Dead Sea Scrolls in English*, 4th ed. (Sheffield: Sheffield Academic Press, 1995), 343.

11   Vermes, *Dead Sea Scrolls*, 354.

12   Juel, *Messianic Exegesis*, 123.

13   Dahl, *Jesus the Christ*.

14   Jacob Z. Lauterbach, ed., *Mekilta de Rabbi Ishmael* (Philadelphia: Jewish Publication Society of America, 1949), 1–3; tractate *Pisga*.

15   Geza Vermes, *Post-Biblical Jewish Studies* (Leiden: Brill, 1975), 63–80.

16   Hays, *Echoes of Scripture in the Letters of Paul*.

17   David P. Moessner, *Lord of the Banquet: The Literary and Theological Significance of the Lukan Travel Narrative* (Minneapolis: Fortress, 1989); James A. Sanders and Craig A. Evans, eds., *The Gospels and the Scriptures of Israel* (Sheffield: Sheffield Academic Press, 1994).

18   Hays, *Echoes of Scripture in the Letters of Paul*, 22.
19   Joel Marcus, *The Way of the Lord: Christological Exegesis of the Old Testament in the Gospel of Mark* (Louisville: Westminster/John Knox, 1992), 26–47.
20   Hays, *Echoes of Scripture in the Letters of Paul*, 29–32.
21   Gamble, *Books and Readers in the Early Church*, 208–10 and cited literature.
22   See R. Le Déaut, "La présentation targumique du sacrifice d'Isaac et la sotériologie paulinienne," in *Studiorum Paulinorum Congressus Catholicus 1961*. Analecta Biblica 17–18 (Rome: Pontifical Biblical Institute, 1963).
23   Bruce Chilton, "The Aqedah: A Revised Tradition History," *Catholic Biblical Quarterly* 40 (1978): 514–46; Philip R. Davies, "Passover and the Dating of the Akedah," *Journal of Jewish Studies* 30 (1979): 59–67.
24   Gamble, *Books and Readers in the Early Church*, 24–28.
25   Marcus, *The Way of the Lord*, 202.
26   Marcus, *The Way of the Lord*, 35.
27   Marcus, *The Way of the Lord*, 36.
28   William G. Braude, trans., *The Midrash on Psalms* (New Haven: Yale University Press, 1959), 297–326.

Chapter 7

1   I have chosen to restrict my comments to the creeds and not the whole tradition of their interpretation among the great theologians of the church.
2   This is one of the important points made in Nils Dahl's "Trinitarian Baptismal Creeds and New Testament Christology," in *Jesus the Christ*, 165–86.
3   The point is made by J. N. D. Kelly, *Early Christian Creeds* (London: Longmans & Green, 1950), 372–74.
4   I have discussed this issue in an article coauthored with a colleague: Juel and Keifert, "I Believe in God," 39–60.
5   The complex issue is discussed in an important work by Alan Segal, *Two Powers in Heaven: Early Rabbinic Reports about Christianity and Gnosticism* (Leiden: Brill, 1977).
6   The prologue (1:12-13) implies a parental relationship ("he gave power to become children of God") while without using "Father" and explicitly rejecting male imagery ("who were born, not of blood or of the will of the flesh or of the will of man [*andros*], but of God").
7   On the use of the Father-Son metaphor in Matthew and Luke, see Donald H. Juel, "The Lord's Prayer in Matthew and Luke," *Princeton Seminary Bulletin*, Suppl. Issue 2 (1992): 56–70.
8   This is particularly true if "Son of God" appears in the opening line of the Gospel. The textual evidence here, however, is uncertain.
9   In one instance, "sons" appears as part of a scriptural citation (Rom 8:26), reflecting the Hebrew idiom. In the few other instances (Rom 8 and Gal 3), the image of "son" is required by the language of inheritance.
10   Among the most important works in this regard are Dahl, *Jesus the Christ*, and *The Messiah: Developments in Earliest Judaism and Christianity*, ed. James H. Charlesworth (Minneapolis: Fortress, 1992).
11   See especially Donald H. Juel, "The Origins of Mark's Christology," in *The Messiah*, ed. Charlesworth.

12   Juel, *Messianic Exegesis*, esp. 59–88.

13   Joachim Jeremias, *Abba: Studien zur neutestamentlichen Theologie und Zeitgeschichte* (Göttingen: Vandenhoeck & Ruprecht, 1966).

14   Dahl, "Trinitarian Baptismal Creeds."

Chapter 8

1   My translation. Alternative translations can be found in almost any introductory text or commentary on Mark. The "Testimony of Papias" is found in Eusebius, *Hist. eccl.* III, 39, 1-7.14-17.

2   The suggestion was made in an important and little-read article by Joseph Kuerzinger published in a collection of essays honoring Rudolf Bultmann in the 1950s, the latest version of which is "Die Aussage des Papias von Hierapolis zur literarischen Form des Markusevangeliums" ["The statement of Papias of Hierapolis on the literary form of Mark's Gospel"], *Biblische Zeitschrift* 21 (1977): 245–64; for a discussion of his proposal, see my *Master of Surprise*, 12–13.

3   Martin Dibelius, *From Tradition to Gospel*, trans. B. L. Woolf (New York: Scribners, 1956), 3.

4   W. Wrede, *The Messianic Secret*, trans. J. C. G. Grieg (Cambridge: James Clarke, 1971).

5   For a helpful discussion of the alternatives, see the article by Keifert, "Mind-Reader and Maestro."

6   K. L. Schmidt, *Der Rahmen der Geschichte Jesu* [The Framework of the Story of Jesus] (Berlin: Trowitzsch & Sohn, 1919; reprinted by the Wissenschaftliche Buchgesellschaft, 1969).

7   Willi Marxsen, *Mark the Evangelist: Studies on the Redaction History of the Gospel*, trans. James Boyce, Donald Juel, and William Poehlmann with Roy A. Harrisville (Nashville: Abingdon, 1969).

8   Kenneth R. R. Gros-Louis, ed., *Literary Interpretation of Biblical Narratives* (Nashville: Abingdon, 1974).

9   Kermode, *Genesis of Secrecy*; Robert Alter and Kermode, *The Literary Guide to the Bible* (Cambridge, Mass.: Harvard University Press, 1987).

10   Norman Perrin, *What Is Redaction Criticism?* (Philadelphia: Fortress, 1969), 42.

11   For a critique of the source-critical preoccupation, see Juel, *Messiah and Temple*, 25–29.

12   Robert Tannehill, "The Disciples in Mark: The Function of a Narrative Role," *Journal of Religion* 57 (1977): 386–405. See also his two-volume *The Narrative Unity of Luke-Acts* (Minneapolis: Fortress, 1986–1990), an experiment with the form of commentary appropriate to narrative.

13   Ernest Best, *Following Jesus: Discipleship in the Gospel of Mark* (Sheffield: JSOT Press, 1981).

14   Juel, *Messiah and Temple*; John Donahue, *Are You the Christ? The Trial Narrative in the Gospel of Mark*, SBLDS 10 (Missoula, Mont.: Scholars Press, 1973); and Frank Matera, *The Kingship of Jesus*, SBLDS 66 (Chico, Calif.: Scholars Press, 1982).

15   Rhoads and Michie, *Mark as Story*.

16   Tolbert, *Sowing the Gospel*.

17   Donahue, *Gospel in Parable*.

18   Stanley Fish, *Is There a Text in This Class?* (Cambridge, Mass.: Harvard University Press, 1980).
19   Fowler, *Let the Reader Understand*, 9.
20   See, e.g., Howard Clark Kee, *Community of the New Age: Studies in Mark's Gospel* (Philadelphia: Westminster, 1977).
21   Albert Schweitzer, *The Quest of the Historical Jesus*, trans. W. Montgomery (New York: Macmillan, 1961), 360.
22   See the comments in Fowler, *Let the Reader Understand*, 10–11.
23   See Auerbach, *Mimesis*.
24   See Barnabas Lindars, *Jesus Son of Man: A Fresh Examination of the Son of Man Sayings in the Gospels in the Light of Recent Research* (Grand Rapids: Eerdmans; London: SPCK, 1983); Douglas Hare, *The Son of Man Tradition* (Minneapolis: Fortress, 1990); and Juel, *Messianic Exegesis*, chap. 7.
25   Gamble, *Books and Readers in the Early Church*.

Conclusion

1   For a full description and discussion of a rhetorical model for biblical interpretation, see in this volume the essay entitled "Interpretation for Christian Ministry" and the section on rhetoric in the essay "Interpreting Mark's Gospel."
2   The work that Juel and his colleague Patrick Keifert carried out in developing a rhetorical model of theological education bore fruit in the wide-ranging curricular revision carried out by Luther Seminary in the 1990s.
3   "A Rhetorical Approach to Theological Education: Assessing an Attempt to Re-Vision a Curriculum," in *To Teach, to Delight, and to Move: Theological Education in a Post-Christian World*, ed. David S. Cunningham (Eugene, Ore.: Cascade Books, 2004), 281–97.
4   Juel's failing health prevented him from finishing and submitting this piece for inclusion in the Alston *Festschrift*, which is entitled *Loving God With Our Minds: The Pastor as Theologian* (ed. Michael Welker and Cynthia A. Jarvis [Grand Rapids: Eerdmans, 2004]).

Index of Scripture and Ancient Sources

7:17-19	142	14:65	132
7:34	140	14:66-72	132
8:1-9	144	14:70	42
8:1-3	144	14:72	55, 132
8:4	37, 144	15:8-14	151
8:5	37, 144	15:17	146
8:31	55–56	15:22	140
8:38	113	15:24	91
9:7	113, 117, 138	15:28	146–48
9:9	56–57	15:29	91
9:11	56	15:34	91, 140
9:31	55	15:36	91
10:30-34	104	15:38	132, 149
10:33	56	15:39	26, 41, 113
10:39	56	16	16, 43, 54, 56
11:12-26	132	16:1-8	147
11:25	113	16:5	200n9
12	141	16:7	54–56, 61, 200n2
12:10	56	16:8	7, 49–52, 54, 56, 123, 146,
12:30	108		148, 181, 200–201n9
12:33	109	16:9-20	6, 7, 50, 52, 181–83
12:36	114	16:20	16, 52, 146, 200n1
13	140, 175		
13:7	61	*Luke*	
13:8	56	1:1	83
13:10	56	1:4	15, 78, 83, 135
13:11	114	1:46-55	83
13:14	57, 140	1:67-79	83
13:32	113	2:29-32	83
13:37	140	2:34	82
14:10-11	138	3:22	99
14:21	56	4	81
14:28-30	55, 132	4:16-20	103
14:28	55	4:17-21	83
14:36	113, 140	4:21	89
14:49	56	9:18-20	80
14:50	57	9:35	99
14:51-52	9	14:15-24	3, 165–67
14:52	57	15:1-2	40
14:53-65	4, 173–76	15:11-32	38
14:53-54	132	16:16	89
14:54	132	23:34	3, 8, 161–64
14:55-65	132	23:35	99
14:61	8, 113	24:44	89

Index of Authors

Subject Index

Abraham, 80–81, 84–85, 91, 93–94, 96–98, 115, 178, 202n7

Augustine of Hippo, 71, 88, 125

baptism (of Jesus), 2, 10, 24–25, 30, 42–43, 56, 61, 99, 107–8, 114, 132, 138, 152

Caesar, 42, 134, 151, 162–63

Christology, 70, 117, 198n13, 203n2, 203n11

cross, 43, 100, 116–17, 120, 161, 163–64, 166, 170, 173, 175, 198n13

David, 62, 69, 80–81, 84, 97–98, 100, 113, 128, 183

death, 2, 14, 24, 26, 29, 41–43, 55, 60, 62, 71–72, 84, 91–92, 101, 104, 113, 116, 130, 132, 142, 144, 153, 161–63, 173–75, 178, 182–83, 186–87, 189, 200

doctrine, 6, 17, 46, 70, 101, 107, 108, 126, 198n7, 201n3

Easter, 25, 161, 166, 178

Enlightenment, 17, 23, 93, 95

form criticism, 128, 130–31

form critics, 50, 67, 128

gospel, 4, 19, 26, 49, 58–59, 62, 64, 70, 81, 84–85, 128, 159, 169–71, 201n9

Greek New Testament, 15, 51, 88–89, 148,

Hagar, 93, 105

Hebrew Bible, 88, 92, 94, 104, 197n1

hermeneutic of suspicion, 43, 198n14, 198n15

historical criticism, 30, 74, 192, 197

historical Jesus, 130–31, 151, 153, 182, 197n2, 205n21

irony, 4, 8, 16, 26, 27, 41–43, 53, 57, 132, 134, 142, 151, 173–74, 198n13, 200n17

Israel, 27, 29, 42, 47–48, 65–66, 79, 81–103, 105, 108, 110, 113, 116–17, 119, 139, 141–42, 145, 202n6, 202n17

Jesus Seminar, 15, 20, 152–53, 182

John (the Baptist), 57, 141, 142, 152

Judaism, 27, 88, 93, 109, 116, 163, 203n10

CPSIA information can be obtained at www.ICGtesting.com
Printed in the USA
BVOW061759260312

286101BV00001B/8/P